W9-ANN-116

The State and Capitalist
Development in Africa

THE STATE AND CAPITALIST DEVELOPMENT IN AFRICA
Declining Political Economies

Julius E. Nyang'oro

PRAEGER

New York
Westport, Connecticut
London

HC
800
N83
1989

Library of Congress Cataloging-in-Publication Data

Nyang'oro, Julius Edo.
    The state and capitalist development : declining political economies
    / Julius E. Nyang'oro.
       p.   cm.
    Bibliography: p.
    Includes index.
    ISBN 0-275-93120-X (alk. paper)
    1. Africa, Sub-Saharan—Economic conditions. 2. Africa, Sub-
Saharan—Economic policy. 3. Africa, Sub-Saharan—Dependency on
foreign countries. 4. Economic development. I. Title.
HC800.N83   1989
338.967—dc19   88-34030

Copyright © 1989 by Julius E. Nyang'oro

All rights reserved. No portion of this book may be
reproduced, by any process or technique, without the
express written consent of the publisher.

Library of Congress Catalog Card Number: 88-34030
ISBN: 0-275-93120-X

First published in 1989

Praeger Publishers, One Madison Avenue, New York, NY 10010
A division of Greenwood Press, Inc.

Printed in the United States of America

The paper used in this book complies with the Permanent
Paper Standard issued by the National Information Standards
Organization (Z39.48–1984).

10 9 8 7 6 5 4 3 2 1

ROBERT MANNING
STROZIER LIBRARY

SEP 21 1989

Tallahassee, Florida

Contents

Acknowledgments

This work was conceived and completed when I was a postdoctoral fellow in African Studies at the University of North Carolina at Chapel Hill. Special thanks go to the graduate school office for providing funds for the fellowship and for other support services. I would like to thank Tim Shaw of Dalhousie University for reading various drafts of the manuscript and for suggesting ways to improve it. Among the many others who gave time to criticize ideas presented here are Herman Bennett, Ann Dunbar, Catherine Newbury, Burly Page, and Karen Shelley. Thanks also go to Agnetta Kamugisha and Debby Crowder for providing moral support. I owe a special debt to Colin Palmer for providing support and encouragement at critical times when this work was underway. I have tremendously appreciated his friendship over the years. Janet Hendrix helped me enormously in the final preparation of the manuscript. I would like to specially thank her for the invaluable assistance with the production of the book.

Introduction

This study is a culmination of three years of studying and reflecting on the current status of sub-Saharan Africa's political economy. It was initially conceived as a continuation and update of my doctoral dissertation—"Development and Dependency: A Theoretical Critique and an African Case Study"—which was completed in the summer of 1983. However, as I reread the dissertation and examined the research being reported about African development, I quickly decided that the dissertation should be permanently shelved and a new study initiated. My dissertation was concerned with the testing of *dependency theory* and its application to Africa. Anyone familiar with data on African economic development can appreciate the difficulty of undertaking such an exercise. Because of the uncertainties involved with data and the demise of the dependency paradigm, it became obvious that any serious study about Africa's political economy had to go beyond the dependency paradigm. This work is my modest attempt in that direction.

Both modernization theory and the dependency framework have been used in this study as a background to understanding current theorization about African development. This approach has been deliberate on my part because of past experience in paradigm change: from modernization to dependency. The 1970s saw the predominance of dependency as a framework of analysis of African (under)development and the successor to modernization. It could be argued that the publication of Walter Rodney's *How Europe Underdeveloped Africa* in 1972 legitimized the dependency approach to Africa. The problem, however, was that emerging dependency scholarship and analyses about development totally ignored some of the relevant concepts employed by modernization theory. As a consequence, the paradigm shift was not accompanied by a deepening of knowledge based on what was already known, but rather a total denial of the relevance of modernization—throwing out the baby with the bathwater, so to speak—a clear violation of the principle of theory building in the tradition of Thomas Kuhn's *The Structure of Scientific Revolutions* (1970). The consequence of this experience has been that with the demise of dependency as a framework of analysis, first, there has been an attempt to fall back on earlier concepts of modernization in spite of their limited utility; and second, there has been an emergence of a theoretical vacuum, especially among scholars who had placed all their eggs in the dependency basket. As the economic crisis that has engulfed Africa in this decade continues to threaten basic human survival, adequate and relevant theory to explain the crisis has largely been conspicuous by its absence. This study is intended to contribute to the filling of this vacuum.

The present study is eclectic in its approach. It acknowledges that social differentiation is a function of differentiation and complexity in the economy, as would be argued by modernization proponents. But it also acknowledges the importance of the international economy in determining the nature of Africa's economic development as would be argued by dependency theorists. This study also recognizes, however, internal socioeconomic and political transitions in Africa that provide the continent with its uniqueness. Our attempt at integrating a *mode of production* analysis to the study of Africa's political economy is a move toward deepening our knowledge both theoretically and empirically in light of what we know from modernization and dependency. We believe that theoretical rigidity does not enhance the process of knowledge acquisition.

Chapter 1 is a presentation, description, and preliminary analysis of data that show the African condition as a crisis. The cut-off point for the data is 1985–1986. Most of the data, however, are complete only up to 1984, because of the difficulties involved in collecting African data. Chapter 1 also looks at the various dimensions of the crisis: agricultural, environmental, industrial, population, etc. To talk about a crisis in aggregated form may not have the same impact as to present it in a disaggregated form. The question of methodology is also discussed in the chapter.

Chapter 2 closely examines African development experience since independence. It addresses the question of the political imperative underlying the choice of comparative advantage as a development strategy in Africa. It also juxtaposes the experience of African development with examples from nineteenth-century Europe as contained in the work of the German political economist Frederick List and others. The question of ideological preference regarding the international economy by African leaders is discussed in light of their objective and subjective interests.

Chapter 3 further extrapolates the issue of development choice with a discussion of the evolution of development theory and its application to Africa. Modernization theory, dependency, and the theses of internationalization of capital are closely examined in relation to how they have (or have not) worked in Africa and in other Third World countries, especially in Latin America. Chapter 3 lays the ground for what we believe is a postdependency imperative.

Chapter 4 takes the discussion of development theory one step forward. It discusses the mode of production approach and its application to the study of Africa's political economy. This chapter argues that the best way to accomplish that task would be to disaggregate capitalism in Africa. Disaggregating capitalism, it is argued, would help to determine whether indeed Africa is predominantly capitalist. If it is not, then serious questions regarding the theory of capitalist development must be confronted. The discussion in chapter 4 suggests that part of the problem in Africa is that the political economy of the continent is fragmented and only marginally capitalist.

Chapter 5 continues the arguments developed in chapter 4 and specifically applies them to the state. Chapter 5 argues that a fragmented political economy necessarily breeds a fragmented and weak state. Given the enormity of Africa's economic problems, it is not possible for a weak and fragmented state to take charge and effect economic development. The inability of the state to take charge in the economic sphere is demonstrated by the existence and growth of a large informal sector. As the state sees its domain in the economy slipping, it attempts a corporatist solution in the political sphere. The limited success of various corporatist projects in Africa suggests a fundamental weakness of the state that contributes to the ongoing crisis.

Chapter 6 is a general assessment of the development options available to Africa given the continuing crisis in its political economy. Chapter 6 concludes that unless a fundamental restructuring of Africa's political economy is undertaken, no amount of foreign aid or political and economic tinkering will be able to save Africa from declining as a modern society.

The African Condition: A Continuing Crisis

To speak of development in most sub-Saharan African economies today is to speak of the past, not the present nor the currently foreseeable future. The world's poorest region is rapidly becoming poorer—in a number of these economies, real resource availability measured in physical gross domestic product adjusted for terms of trade is lower than 1970. In extreme cases, such as Ghana, Uganda and Zaire, it is probably lower than in the early 1960s. The current outlook in many cases is for "more of the same."
—Reginald H. Green, "From Deepening Economic Malaise Towards Renewed Development: An Overview"

INTRODUCTION

There is little doubt that as we approach the end of the 1980s, Africa is still suffering from an acute crisis in its political economy. Since the mid-1970s— but more so in the post-1973–1974 and 1979–1980 oil crises which sent African political economies into a sharp downward spiral—development economists, political leaders, and everyone concerned with the political and economic welfare of the African continent have sounded alarm bells at the deteriorating economic and political conditions on the continent. Indeed, "continent in crisis" has become the code word for describing what has been happening in Africa in the past two decades, as a casual look at recent books on Africa demonstrates. (See, for example, Shaw, 1985; Shaw and Aluko, 1985; Brown and Wolf, 1985; Luke and Shaw, 1984; and Unger, 1985.) Newspapers usually unconcerned with African affairs have also gotten into the act highlighting the crisis in Africa—a prime example being a series in July 1985 by the *Wall Street Journal* entitled "Africa: Imperiled Continent." In the *Wall Street Journal* series, Africa was shown to be suffering from all kinds of crises ranging from overpopulation and lack of food to sheer laziness.

More important, however, has been the acknowledgment by African governments that deteriorating economic conditions on the continent have reached crisis proportions. This acknowledgment (and realization) prompted the Organization of African Unity (OAU) to designate its 1985 summit meeting in Addis Ababa, Ethiopia, an "economic summit." In the meantime, former President Julius K. Nyerere of Tanzania, in his capacity as the 1984-1985 OAU chairman, traveled to Europe and North America to plead the African case for better understanding of the African plight.

Perhaps the most telling action in terms of the acknowledgment of the crisis by African governments came in 1980 when an increase in oil prices in the aftermath of the Iranian crisis of 1978-1979, coupled with stagflation in the industrialized countries that resulted in higher prices of imports considered necessary for survival, made it necessary for African finance ministers to seek help from the World Bank. Thus, in their capacities as governors of the World Bank, African finance ministers submitted a request to the bank asking it to prepare "a special paper on the economic development problems of these countries" (Brown and Cummings, 1984: 21). The Bank's response to this request was the now celebrated (and infamous) report, *Accelerated Development in Sub-Saharan Africa: An Agenda for Action* (1981)—more commonly known as the Berg report, named after Elliot Berg, the American economist who headed the World Bank team that prepared the report.[1]

The World Bank has since prepared several follow-up studies specifically related to the African crisis.[2] The tone of the reports has remained essentially the same—internal political and economic considerations in Africa have played a significant and predominant role in precipitating the crisis. The reports have proceeded to give advice on how to escape and reverse the deteriorating conditions of the economy. The consequences of the policy prescriptions of the World Bank, and its close affiliate the International Monetary Fund (IMF), form part of the second chapter of this study. The serious reservations expressed by many African governments regarding the Berg report are significant enough reasons for a study such as ours, which seeks to cut through the ideological morass created by the implications of the Berg report and to examine critically the issues raised by the contending sides in the debate. Expressing reservations about the report and actually implementing its prescriptions, however, are two different issues. Chapter 2 will also deal with the reservation-implementation distinction and assess the implication of the distinction both historically and theoretically, to Africa's development profile.

Following the above discussion, it should be abundantly clear that Africa's development experience in the last two decades has not been a happy one. This conclusion is a far cry from the jubilant atmosphere that surrounded decolonization in the 1950s and early 1960s. For example, 1960 was designated the "Year of Africa" by the United Nations because 17 African countries became independent. On a single day, September 20, 1960, 16 African countries were admitted to the United Nations. In the meantime, the United Nations Economic Commission for Africa (ECA) had been established in 1958, with its headquarters in Addis Ababa, the capital of Ethiopia—a country symbolizing Africa's independence, since Ethiopia had not experienced colonial rule except for a short period during World War II when it was temporarily annexed by Mussolini's Italy.

Similar to that of other UN economic commissions (for Asia and Latin America), the ECA's task was to address the problems of training, the programming and organization of technical assistance, the study of the flow of international aid to Africa, the improvement of development planning techniques, and the survey of trade and commodity agriculture, statistics, industrial transport, and social problems (Henry, 1962: 94). The ECA's ability to perform these tasks was seen as a matter of routine, requiring no more than following established rules and putting to work the international bureaucracy to diffuse Western-type capitalist development in Africa. But that was not to be. By 1977, the executive secretary of the ECA, Adebayo Adedeji, was lamenting the sad and deplorable economic conditions in Africa, warning of the impending catastrophe.

Africa more than the other world regions, is . . . faced with a development crisis of great portent. . . . If past trends persist and if there are no fundamental changes in the mix of economic policies that African governments have pursued during the last decade and a half and if the current efforts to fundamentally change the international economic system and relations fail to yield concrete positive results, the African region as a whole will be worse off compared with the rest of the world at the end of this century than it was in 1960. (Quoted in Shaw, 1985: 2)

Six years after the above statement was made, the ECA in 1983 released a more pessimistic document: *ECA and Africa's Development 1983–2008*. The document was prepared to commemorate ECA's 25 years of what it considered "service to the African region." Besides being an assessment of its successes and failures of the past (or more to the point, Africa's failure to develop), the study was undertaken as a preliminary prospective view of the future of the African region (ECA, 1983: 1). The ECA's horrifying projections of the African economic crisis, based on trend analysis and other factors, and the relative reliability of the ECA data, more or less dictate that we use ECA data extensively in our own study. And we have done just that. In addition, we have used data from the World Bank and its affiliates, and the United Nations, in presenting the following description of African economies, which helps us to highlight the current crisis in Africa's political economy.[3]

JUSTIFYING A CONTINENTAL APPROACH: PROBLEMS OF METHODOLOGY

Sub-Saharan Africa, comprising 39 countries, is a diverse region. Countries found in this region vary in terms of size, natural resource endowments, physical characteristics (including weather and climate), population, and geographic location. Geographic location influences both physical characteristics and the relative importance of a country in political and economic international relations. For example, in the calculus of superpower relations, countries close to highly contested areas of influence, for example, the Middle East, receive more attention than countries in the heart of the African continent. Similarly, countries endowed with strategic minerals enjoy a higher-priority status, as far as the superpowers are concerned, than countries that have no minerals at all. Any analysis of the sub-Saharan region, therefore, has to recognize the vast variety of circumstances in individual countries and subregions—whether they are in East, Central, Southern, Northern, or West Africa. As the Organization of African Unity recognized:

The member countries of the Organization of African Unity (OAU) of course realise that they belong to the same geopolitical space and aspire to solidarity for their common development; but they know how different they are from each other in geographical situation, natural resources, population, and history both ancient and recent. Four of five of those countries [for example] contain half of the total population of Africa; others are sparsely populated and/or very small and/or very poor. Of the 31 countries designated by the United Nations as the Least Developed Countries (LDCs), 21—two out of every five African countries—are in Africa. (OAU, 1982: iii)

Thus, for example, it is possible, valid, and even desirable to make an analysis of the political economy of a single country (such as Nigeria) by studying trends in its economy since independence, and the nature of class formation and class relations. Furthermore, an analysis of the role of the oil industry in influencing and determining economic planning and political conflict in Nigeria would be a legitimate subject of study. The same can be said of the validity of studying Zambia's political economy or Kenya's political economy in their own right. And indeed such studies have been conducted as a glance at the literature would readily show: Bienen and Diejomaoh, 1981; Onimode, 1982; Woldring et al.; 1984; Turok, 1979; Leys, 1975; and Swainson, 1980. Studies of individual political economies are also important because they provide detailed information about different aspects of countries being studied that may be lost in broader analyses covering several countries.

However, broader analytical and comparative studies like the one attempted here are also important for several reasons. The most important reason, in our judgment, is that this kind of study provides an opportunity to synthesize materials relating to different political economies (in this case, on a continental basis). The opportunity to synthesize such materials also allows the investigator to conduct trend analyses that would be beneficial for economic planning purposes encompassing the whole sub-Saharan region. Broader analytical and comparative studies also enable the investigator to conceptualize both the individual variations and regularities to be found in various African countries. (See, for example, Przeworski and Teune, 1970.) But the choice of such a method of study also betrays a political position—or, as others would call it, a political preference or agenda—the preference being a political unity of a *potential* basis for economic development. The empirical evidence relating to Africa's political economy that will be presented and synthesized in this study suggest that unless African development problems are viewed on a broader regional political perspective, the economic malaise that African countries have historically suffered, and continue to face, will not go away. Something drastic at the political level will have to be undertaken in order to alleviate bottlenecks in the development process. The statement suggests that in the final analysis, solutions to the developmental crisis in Africa will have to be political in nature.

This is not to suggest, however, that regional political solutions are the only viable alternatives to, or the panacea of, Africa's development problems. Several competent studies have demonstrated theoretically the potential for small political economies to cure their economic ills and to develop successfully, given certain political conditions (Thomas, 1974; List, 1856). The key to such a proposition, nonetheless, is the *political* basis for the resolution of the fundamental questions in a country's or a group of countries' political economy. This argument will be more fully developed in chapter 6 "Alternative Futures in Africa." The initial argument here is simply that, given the right political conditions (but especially the nature of the state, state power, and the distribution of power in society), larger political economies have an enhanced potential for successful development; hence our interest in dealing with such issues as the relative size of the economy and regional bases of economic organization, as opposed to single (mostly miniature) economies such as the ones found in sub-Saharan Africa. The argument also implies a *political* solution to the economic crisis, predicated on the nature of class relations and state power in society. Although a regional solution to the development crisis is suggested, this study will argue that such regional economic organizations as the Economic Organization of West African States (ECOWAS), Southern African Development Coordinating Conference (SADCC), or the defunct East African Community (EAC), etc., have not been and cannot be serious vehicles for eliminating underdevelopment. The breakup of East African Community in 1977 and the inability of ECOWAS to get off the ground in a substantive way are *prima facie* cases against such institutions. Internal political disagreements within SADCC based on simple national interest, and the apparent penetration of South African economic interests in SADCC, are further evidence of the unviability of regional economic organizations in Africa today.

Because our preferred political solution is based on larger political units, the data that will be presented in this chapter on Africa's economic conditions are essentially macro in character and mostly comparative within the sub-Saharan context. Most of the data are drawn from IMF, World Bank, and United Nations publications because, as already stated, these institutions seem to have more reliable data on Africa than African governments themselves. However, we will also provide examples from studies on individual countries from various sources to reinforce our arguments.

AFRICAN ECONOMIES: A SUMMARY OF CONTEMPORARY TRENDS

The Sub-Saharan Economy in General

A summary of Africa's economic performance based on data from the World Bank and other international agencies indicates that, in all important categories, the African economy has either stagnated or declined in the past decade. The World Bank (1985: 148) shows that, for the low-income countries of Africa (table 1.1), the only period since 1965 in which these countries experienced some form of growth was between 1965 and 1973, when the average annual growth of gross national product (GNP) per capita was 1.3 percent, a shortfall of 3.7 percent from the rate envisaged by the United Nations in 1960. In the period 1973–1980, low income countries in Africa had zero growth. In subsequent years, that is, 1981, 1982, 1983, and 1984, these countries had a cumulative decline in growth of − 1.7 percent, − 2.6 percent, − 2.6 percent, and − 1.5 percent, respectively. The middle-income countries of Africa (with more than $400 GNP per capita) had growth rates of − 4.1 percent, − 4.8 percent, − 5.4 percent, and − 5.4 percent, respectively in 1981, 1982, 1983, and 1984. These figures suggest that Africa's political economy is in serious trouble.

Toward the end of 1984 and the beginning of 1985 as industrialized capitalist countries of the West began to recover from the worst recession since the great depression of the 1930s it became clear that the recovery would bypass Africa. The gravity of the situation was exacerbated by the fact that the effects of the world recession of 1980–1982 were felt more by African countries than any other region of the world. Thus, while other areas of the Third World, such as West Asia, had higher rates of decline in growth of gross domestic product (GDP) per capita between 1980 and 1983 (table 2.2), the effects of the decline were not as strongly felt because of a slightly higher initial base in levels of production. A report by the World Bank placed the economic plight of African countries in a wider global context.

While sub-Saharan countries' growth suffered along with others during 1980-82, the recent recovery seems largely to have bypassed sub-Saharan Africa, even in those countries with the best earlier records. For oil importers, per capita output fell by 0.9 percent in 1981 and 1.7 percent in 1982, but there was no recovery in 1983—per capita output fell by a further 2 percent. Neither did oil exporters benefit from the 1983 recovery. Their per capita output fell about 11 percent in the two years 1981–82 and a further 7 percent in 1983. *For sub-Saharan Africa as a whole per capita output in 1983 was 11 percent below the 1980 level, more than offsetting all of the very modest gains of the 1970s.* (World Bank, 1984b: 10) (Emphasis added.)

Compared to other regions of the world, the same report pointed out that since the recession of 1980-82, the world economy has started to recover. In 1983, gross national product (GNP) in industrial countries rose 2.3 percent, after a fall of 0.1 percent in 1982; in developing countries, growth picked up from 1.1 to 1.3 percent. World trade, which had declined by 2.5 percent in 1982, grew by 2 percent in 1983; dollar prices of nonoil primary commodities, which had been falling since 1981, climbed by 7 percent in 1983. (p. 10)

There are two crucial questions that must be raised with regard to the above-quoted figures relating to Africa's economic performance. First, is the slow response to the world recovery a peculiarly African problem? Second, why did the world recession have more impact on Africa than on other regions? It seems to us that the answer to the first question is a relatively simple one. Examination of data on the world capitalist economy[4] suggests that the slow response to the world recovery by African countries is not peculiar to the continent, but rather it is a reflection of generally observed trends in the global economy. The only industrial countries that seem to be doing relatively well in the post-recession period are the United States, Japan, and, to a lesser extent, Australia. The United Nations (UN), for example, has shown that, while a reversal of world recessionary trends began in 1983, recovery has not been general. Even for historically strong capitalist economies of Western Europe, the recovery has been weak and sluggish. At any given point since 1980, more than 10 percent of the total European labor force has been unemployed, reflecting serious structural problems in European economies. According to the UN, "it is a mark of the weak and uneven character of world economic recovery in 1983 that world trade failed to pick up" (table 1.2). More profoundly, however, the failure of Western industrial economies to recover fully is a reflection of a general crisis of global capitalism, as several studies have indicated. (See for example, Brett, 1984.) As the subtitle to Brett's International Money and Capitalist Crisis suggests, reliance on an economic system that can no longer efficiently sustain itself presents a clear choice in terms of policy (i.e., whether it is still advisable to remain within a system which is constantly in crisis)—a subject we will return to in the next chapter.

The answer to the second question should also be relatively simple; however, the simplicity of the answer has not facilitated a better understanding of the African crisis in the West, especially within the International Monetary Fund (IMF) and other IMF-influenced lending institutions, both public and private. The issue of IMF policy prescriptions for Africa's economic development problems will be dealt with in detail in the following chapter. However, we should make the initial point here, based on available data, that the world recession has had more (negative) impact on Africa than on any other region because of the historically weak base of Africa's economy and its relatively weak position in international trade, especially given its position as a supplier of raw materials and other primary goods. The following two observations by the UN and the World Bank, respectively, should shed some light on this critical situation.

Table 1.1
Africa: Basic Indicators

	Population (millions) mid-1983	Area (thousands of square Kilometers)	GNP per capita[a] Dollars 1983	Average annual growth rate (percent) 1965-83[b]	Average annual rate of inflation (percent) 1965-73	1973-83[c]	Life expectancy at birth (years)
Low-income economies	2,333.4t	31,603.0t	260.0w	2.7w	1.4w	5.4w	59.0w
China and India	1,752.3t	12,849.0t	280.0w	3.2w	0.9w	3.7w	62.0w
--Other low-income	583.0t	18,754.0t	200.0w	0.7w	4.8w	13.8w	51.0w
Sub-Saharan Africa	245.2t	15,451.0t	220.0w	-0.2w	3.9w	17.5w	48.0w
Ethiopia	40.9	1,222.0	120.0	0.5	1.8	4.4	43.0
Mali	7.2	1,240.0	160.0	1.2	7.6	10.3	45.0
Zaire	29.7	2,345.0	170.0	-1.3	18.7	48.2	51.0
Burkina Faso	6.5	274.0	180.0	1.4	2.6	10.8	44.0
Malawi	6.6	111.0	210.0	2.2	4.5	9.8	44.0
Uganda	13.9	236.0	220.0	-4.4	5.6	62.7	49.0
Burundi	4.5	28.0	240.0	2.1	2.9	12.4	47.0
Niger	6.1	1,267.0	240.0	-1.2	4.0	11.8	45.0
Tanzania	20.8	945.0	240.0	0.9	3.2	11.5	51.0
Somalia	5.1	638.0	250.0	-0.8	3.8	20.1	45.0
Rwanda	5.7	26.0	270.0	2.3	7.7	11.2	47.0
Central African Republic	2.5	623.0	280.0	0.1	3.0	14.4	48.0
Togo	2.8	57.0	280.0	1.1	3.1	8.3	49.0
Benin	3.8	113.0	290.0	1.0	3.6	10.8	48.0
Guinea	5.8	246.0	300.0	1.1	3.0	4.0	37.0
Ghana	12.8	239.0	310.0	-2.1	8.1	51.6	59.0
Madagascar	9.5	587.0	310.0	-1.2	4.1	13.9	49.0
Sierra Leone	3.6	72.0	330.0	1.1	1.9	14.7	38.0
Kenya	18.9	583.0	340.0	2.3	2.3	10.8	57.0
Sudan	20.8	2,506.0	400.0	1.3	7.2	18.0	48.0
Chad*	4.8	1,284.0			4.5	8.3	43.0
Mozambique*	13.1	802.0				46.0	

Middle-income economies Sub-Saharan Africa	148.2t	5,822.0t	700.0w	1.9w	4.8w	12.4w	50.0w
Lower-middle income	665.1t	18,446.0t	750.0w	2.9w	5.6w	17.9w	57.0w
Senegal	6.2	196.0	440.0	-0.5	3.0	8.9	46.0
Lesotho	1.5	30.0	460.0	6.3	4.4	11.9	53.0
Liberia	2.1	111.0	480.0	0.8	1.5	7.2	49.0
Mauritania	1.6	1,031.0	480.0	0.3	3.9	7.8	46.0
Zambia	6.3	753.0	580.0	-1.3	5.2	10.3	51.0
Ivory Coast	9.5	322.0	710.0	1.0	4.1	11.9	52.0
Zimbabwe	7.9	391.0	740.0	1.5	3.0	9.7	56.0
Nigeria	93.6	924.0	770.0	3.2	10.3	13.3	49.0
Cameroon	9.6	475.0	820.0	2.7	5.8	12.6	54.0
Congo, People's Republic	1.6	342.0	1,230.0	3.5	4.6	12.4	63.0
Angola	8.2	1,247.0				43.0	

aGross National Product: The total domestic and foreign output claimed by residents. It comprises gross domestic product adjusted by net factor income from abroad. Factor income comprises receipts that residents receive from abroad for factor services (labor, investment, and interest) less similar payments made to nonresidents abroad. It is calculated without making deductions for depreciation. Because data for the entire period are not always available, figures followed by an asterisk are for periods other than that specified.
cFigures with an asterisk are for 1973-82, not 1973-83.

Source: World Bank, World Development Report (New York: Oxford University Press, 1985): 174-75.

Table 1.2
Growth of World Output and Trade, 1978–1982 (percentage)

	1978	1979	1980	1981	1982	1983a	1984b	1985c
Gross Domestic Product								
World	4.5	3.4	2.0	1.7	0.8	2.2	4	3.5
Developing countries	4.1	5.0	3.2	1.6	0.5	0.0	3.5	3.5
Developed market economies	4.0	3.1	1.2	1.5	-0.2	2.0	4	3
Centrally planned economies	6.2	3.1	3.7	2.4	3.7	4.3	4	4
International Trade								
World Imports	5.5	5.2	1.2	1.6	-0.7	0.6	4	5

aPreliminary estimates
bForecasts
cNet material product

Source: United Nations, *World Economic Survey: Current Trends and Policies in the World Economy*
(New York: U.N. Publ., 1984): 1.

The sub-Saharan African countries have been particularly vulnerable to the impact of recession. Given the low level of income of most of these countries, decreases in output and employment cause great hardship. The average per capita income of the 45 countries in the region is only half that of developing countries as a whole. Among the group, 26 are least developed countries with a per capita income below $300 per annum. Even in the mineral exporting countries, rarely less than two thirds of the population works in agriculture, half of whose output is derived from subsistence production. (UN, 1984: 15)

For export crops, Africa's total volume expanded by about 1 percent a year over 1980–1982 period—an improvement over the decline during 1970–1980. However, for most crops, the fall in world market shares that started in the 1970s continued in the 1980s. *These declines have occurred in commodities in which Africa has a comparative advantage and which are likely to remain its potential source of foreign exchange earnings.* (World Bank, 1984a: 11) (Emphasis added.)

These observations suggest that the negative impact of the global recession on Africa not only should have been expected, but its (long) duration viewed as inevitable. Data such as those presented in table 1.3 have more meaning when viewed from the historical and contextual perspective of a lower economic base. Most significant, perhaps, are data showing a decline of 0.9 percent in total GDP for the entire sub-Saharan region in the period 1981-1984 (table 1.3).

Agriculture and Food Production

One obviously cannot find comfort in the data presented in table 1.3. Of particular concern are the data for trends in both overall agricultural production per capita and in food production where there was a decline of − 1.7 percent and − 1.8 percent, respectively, in the period 1981–1984. Further reports furnished by the United Nations are even more revealing.

Growth in sub-Saharan Africa [during 1984–1985] continued to be constrained by the weak expansion in agriculture in most countries in the region. The weakness was particularly severe in the 20 countries for which a drought-related food emergency has been declared. Since domestic and external impulses for growth in developing countries are not going to change markedly in the near future, growth rates will remain generally weak. *Thus, even by the second half of the decade, the large majority of developing countries will not have recovered fully from the dramatic set-back suffered in the early 1980s.* (UN, 1985: 3) (Emphasis added.)

A World Bank report indicates that the average index of food production per capita (AIFPPC) for each country in sub-Saharan Africa varied considerably between 1974–1976 and 1981–1983 (table 1.4). For example, in the lower-income group (less than $300 GNP per capita) of sub-Saharan countries, the weighted average for 1981–1983 was 94 percent of the 1974–1976 period.

Table 1.3
Developing Countries in Sub-Saharan Africa:
Average Annual Ranges of Increase in Key Variables, 1971–1984

(Percentage)	1971-1975	1976-1980	1981-1984
Real GDP			
Total	4.4	2.6	-0.9
Energy importers	2.6	1.9	0.1
Energy exporters[a]	5.9	3.1	-1.8
Agricultual production			
Total	1.3	1.9	1.5
Per Capita	-1.7	-1.3	-1.7
Food production			
Total	1.3	2.1	1.4
Per Capita	-1.7	-1.1	-1.8
Cereals			
Total	1.3	1.8	-2.1
Per Capita	-1.7	-1.5	-5.2

[a]Angola, Cameroon, Congo, Gabon, and Nigeria

Source: United Nations, *World Economic Survey* (New York: UN Publ., 1985): 17.

However, within this group of countries we have Niger, whose AIFPPC increased by 22 percent, while that of Ghana declined by 35 percent. Similarly, for middle-income countries of the region, the weighted average for 1981–1983 was 93 percent of the 1974–1976 period. In this group of countries, the sharpest decline was recorded by Senegal (29 percent) while Ivory Coast (8 percent) had the highest increase. The critical point to remember, however, is that with both increases and declines in food production in Africa, the initial base of production has historically been low, which makes any decline a most unwelcome proposition.

Virtually every recent study on Africa's food situation has predicted catastrophe if drastic measures are not undertaken to alleviate the problem. Michael Watts (1983), for example, in his well researched and voluminous book, emphasizes the seriousness of the situation relating to Africa in general and specifically to Nigeria.

All attempts to project Africa's food situation conclude that major changes in domestic trends are required to avert a further deepening of the crisis in the 1980s. The International Food Policy Research Institute (IFPRI) estimates that historical rates of growth in domestic food production in Africa, coupled with a constant 1975 level of per capita income, would produce a 1990 cereal import of 17 million tons—roughly three times the 1979 level. Estimates by the Food and Agriculture Organization (FAO) and the United States Agency for International Development (USAID), based on more optimistic trend analysis, suggest a food deficit of roughly 12 million tons by 1990. The projected food import bill still leaves a significant calorie gap, namely , the difference between food demand and the quantity necessary to meet minimal caloric intake requirements. The IFPRI, for example estimates this calorie gap will be equivalent to 13 million tons by 1990. (1983: a)

Subsequent estimates, however, have projected the calorie deficit at a much higher level, especially in the aftermath of the 1983–1985 drought on the continent. In 1983 alone, in just one country—Ethiopia—more than three million people depended on external emergency food supplies for their survival. In 1987, external emergency food still accounted for a substantial portion of Ethiopia's food consumption. Another study draws a gruesome picture of Africa's food situation.

Although essentially agrarian, Africa is losing the ability to feed itself. In 1984, 140 million of its 531 million people were fed from abroad. In 1985, the ranks of those fed from abroad, already nearly half as large as the population of North America, will almost, certainly increase. A mid-February [1985] assessment of Africa's food situation by the United Nations reported that 10 million people had left their villages in search of food, many of them crowded into hastily erected relief camps. In late April [1985], the Economic Commission for Africa reported that starvation deaths had passed the one million mark, reminding people everywhere that space-age technologies and famine coexist. (Brown and Wolf, 1985: 8)

Food Production, Population Growth and Employment

It would be a gross omission if the discussion on food production were not directly related to the most important factor in the development equation: the population. Most studies on Africa's population growth have made the obvious Malthusian point regarding population growth outstripping food production in Africa. However, we need to point out that the Malthusian scare per se does not capture the significance of the imbalance between population growth and food production. Several factors—historical, political, social, economic, ecological, etc.—have played a role culminating in the current crisis: a crisis that need not have happened in the first place. The point here, however,

Table 1.4
Sub-Saharan Africa: Agriculture and Food Production

	Value added in agriculture (millions of 1980 dollars)		Cereal imports (thousands of metric tons)		Food aid in Cereals (thousands of metric tons)		Fertilizer consumption (hundreds of grams of plant nutrient per hectare of arable land)		Average index of food production per capita (1974-76=100)
	1970	1983[a]	1974	1983	1974/75[b]	1982/83[b]	1970[c]	1982	1981-83
Low-income economies of Sub-Saharan Africa			2,232t	3,277t	765t	1,969t	23w	42w	94w
Ethiopia	1,663	1,971	118	325	59	344	4	26	106
Mali	403	606	281	183	114	88	29	30	106
Zaire	1,503	1,866	343	273	(.)	110	8	8	93
Burkina Faso	444	517	99	59	0	45	3	42	100
Malawi			17	21	(.)	3	52	138	101
Uganda	2,579	2,614	37	19	16	14	13		91
Burundi	468	585	7	20	6	7	5	10	97
Niger	851	649	155	45	75	12	1	8	122
Tanzania	1,583	1,888	431	214	148	171	30	44	103
Somalia	434	570	42	246	110	189	31	9	72
Rwanda			3	23	19	12	3	10	114
Central African Republic	241	325	7	29	1	5	11	4	94
Togo	212	238	6	61	0	5	3	19	99
Benin		415	8	67	9	14	33	17	95
Guinea		755	63	112	49	25	18	17	85

Ghana	2,323	2,265	177	285	43	58	9	98	65
Madagascar	1,111	1,171	114	240	7	141	56	52	90
Sierra Leone	261	312	72	119	10	29	13	6	98
Kenya	1,223	2,253	15	160	2	165	224	289	86
Sudan	1,610	2,318	125	435	50	330	31	44	94
Chad	339		50	54	13	36	7	17	101
Mozambique			62	287	34	166	27	130	68
Middle-income economies of Sub-Saharan Africa			1,521t	4,859t	111t	411t	40w	91w	93w
Lower middle-income			16,776t	29,831t	1,491t	3,999t	176w	398w	105w
Senegal	603	702	341	591	28	91	20	35	71
Lesotho	94		49	91	14	28	17	151	76
Liberia	235	334	42	126	3	57	55	35	92
Mauritania	259	258	115	227	48	71	6	5	102
Zambia	444	562	93	247	1	83	71	185	74
Ivory Coast	1,733	2,670	172	562	4	0	71	85	108
Zimbabwe	557	673	56	124		6	466	532	79
Nigeria	17,186	16,001	389	2,336	7	0	3	65	98
Cameroon	1,492	1,955	81	178	4	6	28	57	84
Congo, People's Republic	147	164	34	90	2	9	112	19	99
Angola*			149	287	0	60	45	14	82

aFigures with an asterisk are for 1982, not 1983. bFigures are for the crop years and 1982/83. cAverage for 1969-71.

Source: World Bank, *World Development Report* (New York: Oxford University Press, 1985): 184–85.

15

is not to dismiss population growth as a critical variable in explaining the crisis, but rather to look deeper into the processes and forces that produced the crisis, since population control in itself—the Malthusian solution—cannot resolve the crisis (Mamdani, 1972; Meek, 1971). As Michael Watts has correctly pointed out:

The famine–poverty syndrome is not to be analyzed as a mechanical reflex of overpopulation or simply a precipitate of a predatory and hegemonic world capitalism. Rather, much of [Africa] is transitive, moving from precapitalist to capitalist relations of production, and accordingly displays a unique synthesis of the old and the new; food supply resides in this complex conservation and dissolution of peasant economy—in the subsumption a peripheral forms of production by international capital. (1983: 10)

Watts goes on to argue that the current food crisis in Africa is based in the production and productivity constraint of an emerging and changing peasant commodity production system, exchange relations, and the role of the state (both colonial and postcolonial) in the production process. Although one may argue with Watts on the variations of "the subsumption of peripheral forms of production by international capital," the main point of his argument regarding the *process* of peasant production and its incorporation in the international capitalist system is a critical one. However, it is also critical to remember that total incorporation of the peasantry into international capitalist relations is a theoretical and empirical proposition that has generated a spirited debate, which our study joins hoping to clarify some central issues. The first point revolves around the questions of whether a discussion of capitalist relations of production in rural Africa is significant to the understanding of the current crisis, and whether the understanding of the assumed capitalist development in rural Africa is relevant to the understanding of Africa's relation to international capitalism. The raw figures on Africa's population growth and future projections illustrate the need for immediate policy action in Africa and emphasize the magnitude and the immediacy of this crisis (table 1.5).

It is now acknowledged that Africa currently has the highest rate of population increase in the world, with a regional average of 3.3 percent yearly increase. Within sub-Saharan Africa, there is a variation in population increase rates with a range of 1.6 percent (Mauritius) and 4.4 percent (Kenya). Only five countries in table 1.5 have an average increase in population growth of less than 2.5 percent. The significance of these data on population growth has been made clear by the Economic Commission for Africa (ECA).

Africa's food situation is . . . the single most critical area of concern in the region for the whole decade of the 1970s when the African population was expanding at an average rate of around 2.8 percent, total food production in the region as a whole was rising by no more than 1.5 percent. By 1980, food self-sufficiency ratios had dropped from 98 percent in the 1960s to around 86 percent implying that, on average, each

Table 1.5
Sub-Saharan Africa: Population Growth and Projections

	Average annual growth of population (percent)			Population (millions)			Hypothetical size of stationary population (millions)	Assumed year of reaching net reproduction* rate of 1	Population momentum 1980
	1960-70	1970-82	1980-2000	1982	1990a	2000a			
Low-income economies	2.4w	2.8w	3.3w	217.0t	278.0t	386.0t			
Low-income semiarid	2.5w	2.6w	2.7w	31.0t	37.0t	48.0t			
Chad	1.9	2.0	2.5	5.0	6.0	7.0	22.0	2040.0	1.8
Mali	2.5	2.7	2.8	7.0	9.0	12.0	42.0	2040.0	1.8
Burkina Faso	2.0	2.0	2.4	7.0	8.0	10.0	35.0	2040.0	1.7
Somalia	2.8	2.8	2.4	5.0	5.0	7.0	23.0	2045.0	1.8
Niger	3.4	3.3	3.3	6.0	8.0	11.0	40.0	2040.0	1.9
Gambia, The	2.2	3.2	2.3	1.0	1.0	1.0	3.0	2045.0	1.9
Low-income other	2.4w	2.9w	3.4w	186.0t	241.0t	338.0t			
Ethiopia	2.4	2.0	3.1	33.0	42.5	57.0	231.0	2045.0	1.9
Guinea-Bissau		2.3	2.3	1.0	1.0	1.0	4.0	2045.0	1.8
Zaire	2.0	3.0	3.3	31.0	4.0	55.0	172.0	2030.0	1.9
Malawi	2.8	3.0	3.4	7.0	8.0	12.0	48.0	2040.0	1.9
Uganda	3.0	2.7	3.4	14.0	17.0	25.0	89.0	2035.0	2.0
Rwanda	2.6	3.4	3.6	6.0	7.0	11.0	47.0	2040.0	1.9
Burundi	1.4	2.2	3.0	4.0	5.0	7.0	27.0	2040.0	1.9
Tanzania	2.7	3.4	3.5	20.0	26.0	36.0	117.0	2030.0	2.0
Benin	2.6	2.7	3.3	4.0	5.0	7.0	23.0	2035.0	2.0

Table 1.5 Continued

	Average annual growth of population (percent)			Population (millions)			Hypothetical size of stationary population (millions)	Assumed year of reaching net reproduction rate of 1	Population momentum 1980
	1960-70	1970-82	1980-2000	1982	1990a	2000a			
Central African Republic	1.6	2.1	2.8	2.0	3.0	4.0	13.0	2040.0	1.9
Guinea	1.5	2.0	2.4	6.0	7.0	9.0	28.0	2045.0	1.8
Madagascar	2.2	2.6	3.2	9.0	12.0	16.0	54.0	2035.0	1.9
Togo	3.0	2.6	3.3	3.0	4.0	5.0	17.0	2035.0	2.0
Ghana	2.3	3.0	3.9	12.0	17.0	24.0	83.0	2030.0	2.0
Kenya	3.2	4.0	4.4	18.0	26.0	40.0	153.0	2030.0	2.1
Sierra Leone	1.7	2.0	2.4	3.0	4.0	5.0	16.0	2045.0	1.9
Mozambique*	2.1	4.3	3.4	13.0	17.0	24.0	82.0	2035.0	2.0
Middle income oil importers	2.7w	3.3w	3.3w	57.0t	74.0t	101.0t			
Sudan	2.2	3.2	2.9	20.0	25.0	34.0	112.0	2035.0	1.8
Mauritania	2.3	2.3	2.6	2.0	2.0	3.0	8.0	2035.0	1.8
Liberia	3.2	3.5	3.5	2.0	3.0	4.0	12.0	2030.0	1.8
Senegal	2.3	2.7	3.1	6.0	8.0	10.0	36.0	2040.0	1.93
Lesotho	2.0	2.4	2.8	1.0	2.0	2.0	7.0	2030.0	1.8
Zambia	2.6	3.1	3.6	6.0	8.0	11.0	37.0	2030.0	2.0
Zimbabwe	3.6	3.2	4.4	8.0	11.0	16.0	62.0	2030.0	2.1
Botswana	2.6	4.3	3.6	1.0	1.0	2.0	6.0	2025.0	1.9
Swaziland	2.7	3.2	3.9	1.0	1.0	1.0	5.0	2030.0	2.0
Ivory Coast	3.7	4.9	3.7	9.0	12.0	17.0	58.0	2035.0	2.0
Mauritius	2.2	1.4	1.6	1.0	1.0	1.0	2.0	2010.0	1.8

Middle-income oil exporters

	2.4w	2.6w	3.4w	111.0t	144.0t	203.0t					
Nigeria	2.5	2.6	3.5	91.0	119.0	169.0	618.0	2035.0	2.0
Cameroon	2.0	3.0	3.5	9.0	12.0	17.0	65.0	2035.0	1.9
Congo, People's Republic	2.4	3.8	2.0	2.0	3.0	3.0	10.0	2025.0	1.9
Gabon	0.4	1.4	2.6	1.0	1.0	1.0	3.0	2035.0	1.7
Angola*	2.1	2.5	2.8	8.0	10.0	13.0	44.0	2040.0	1.9
Sub-Saharan Africa	2.4w	2.8w	3.3w	385.0t	496.0t	690.0t			
All low-income countries	2.3w	1.9w	1.7w	2269.0t	2621.0t	3097.0t			
All lower middle-income countries	2.5w	2.5w	2.4w	673.0t	816.0t	1023.0t			
All upper middle-income countries	2.6w	2.3w	2.1w	490.0t	588.0t	718.0t			
Industrial market economies	1.1w	0.7w	0.4w	723.0t	749.0t	780.0t			

Source: World Bank, Toward Sustained Development in Sub-Saharan Africa:
A Joint Program Action (Washington, D.C. 1984): 82.

19

African had around 12 percent less home grown food in 1980 than 20 years earlier. (1983: 8)

The same ECA study went on to show that between 1970 and 1980, the volume of total food imports increased by an average annual rate of 8.4 percent, with foreign food aid reaching 1.5 million tons in 1980. Imports of food grains, on the other hand, reached a total of about 20.4 million tons in 1980, costing the African region more than $5 billion excluding the heavy ocean freight costs. The ECA, however, saw a more threatening situation than simply the high dollar cost of importation: "the increasing reliance of the African region on food aid and imports threatens to create a new and dangerous structural dependence on cereals like wheat which cannot be easily grown in many parts of the African region" (1983: 9). Obviously, if this situation materializes, Africa will be perpetually held hostage by whomever will be in a position to supply the cereals.

Another crisis related to population growth in Africa is the issue of ecological balance. In their 1985 study, Brown and Wolf show that as Africa's population approaches 600 million, agricultural systems are breaking down— systems of shifting cultivation that evolved over centuries and that were ecologically stable as recently as the 1950s, when the population was barely 200 million. Brown and Wolf argue that, under the pressure of population growth, marginal land is being plowed and fallow cycles are being shortened. Frequent use of land, often without fertilizer, and erosion of topsoil are making land less and less cultivatable. For example, in 1978 the Ethiopian Highlands alone were losing over 1 billion tons of topsoil per year through erosion (Brown and Wolf, 1985: 110).

Employment, however, is perhaps the most critical aspect of Africa's population growth. Without a doubt, society's main asset is its people, but for the people to be an asset, they must engage in production which will enhance the capacities (both physical and intellectual) of that society. Available evidence suggests that while Africa has had a rapid increase in population growth, the population has not been fully utilized. The ECA, for example, reveals that

out of a total of 33 million people that were added to the African labor force during the 1970s as much as 15 million found no access to remunerative employment. The high level of unemployment is further compounded by an unequal distribution of already low income and by a high dependence ratio of nearly three persons per employed person. The result is that about 70 people, out of every 100 African persons were in 1980, either "destitute" or on the verge of poverty. (1983: 8)[5]

Examples from two countries—Kenya and Ghana—illustrate the ECA's conclusion.

Any individual interested in development issues in Africa probably knows that Kenya has the highest population growth rate in the world, exceeding 4 percent. The problem in Kenya today is not only what to do with the current high birth rate, but also what to do with the people who are already born. As Diana Hunt has recently shown in her comprehensive study of Kenya's population growth, "between 1976 and the year 2000, 8 million people are expected to enter the labor force. This in an economy in which in 1982 the total labor force was 7.6 million (in 1976 6.2 million). These labor force entrants are already born. Their numbers cannot be modified by any future successes in population control." (1984: 1) In 1984, Kenya's GDP grew at a frighteningly low rate of 0.9 percent thus further compounding the problem of labor absorption since both the industrial and agricultural sectors of the economy had come to a near standstill.[6] Diana Hunt's findings on levels of poverty in Kenya closely mirror the ECA's observation above.

Surveys have shown that a substantial proportion of Kenya's population are already living in absolute poverty, with incomes that fall below a stringently defined poverty line. Reflecting the overall distribution of the population about 90 percent live in the rural sector, the majority of them in that 20 percent of Kenya's land area that can be used for cultivation (1984: 2).

Thus in Kenya today, the policy problems which the government faces are not just to eliminate poverty among the 6.2 million people (labor force members plus their dependents) already living below the poverty live, but to prevent the spread of poverty to a large proportion of the 8 million new labor force entrants and their dependents by the year 2000. But estimates cited by Diana Hunt show that as many as 50 percent of the 8 million labor force increase may be unable to find productive employment, with a substantial number of the productively employed being variously *underemployed*.

Having shown the plight that Kenya faces in terms of population growth, we now turn to an even more severely strained country: Ghana's problems are much more serious. Between 1970 and 1980, Ghana's GDP grew a mere 0.2 percent. Between 1979 and 1982, however, GDP growth rate in Ghana was − 6.1 percent (World Bank; 1984: 3). While agriculture in general grew at − 1.2 percent between 1970 and 1980, the figures for food production are frightening. With 1974–1976 as the base period (= 100), in 1981–1983 food production in Ghana declined to 65 percent—a drop of 35 percent in barely half a decade. But much more seriously,

population growth continues unabated at 3.3 percent per year [with a projection of 3.9 percent per year between 1980 and 2000]. At this rate, Ghana can expect a population of over 50 million by the year 2020, compared to 12 million at present and 8.6 million in 1970. Unless the economy revives, it can be expected that there will be a steady decline in such social indicators as life expectancy, literacy, school enrollments, and access to food and clean water, as a growing population presses on a declining and deteriorating system of essential public sector services. Even at present, the declining resources of the Government have all but eliminated a once effective family planning program, and undercut the Government's announced population policy. (World Bank, 1984a: xvi)

The two examples (Kenya and Ghana) cited above illustrate in a comprehensive way the dilemma faced by African countries in dealing with issues of development—more precisely, the relationship between economic production and population growth. It is obvious that, for some time, population growth in most African countries has consistently outstripped economic production (table 1.5). Policies pursued by African governments have not worked because, we argue, their understanding of economic development problems (including population growth) has been inadequate. The African governments have sought to deal with the issue of population growth in terms of a numbers game, which leaves much to be desired. Population growth must be viewed within the overall context of increased production. Population is not the problem; it is a symptom of larger problems in the political economy. The issue of the inability of African governments to understand economic development problems forms the basis of chapter 2.

A discussion of the relationship between food production and economic development would be incomplete without consideration of the long-term effects of malnutrition. It is quite clear that there has been significant reduction in infant mortality rates in Africa in the past two decades; the ratio of population per physician and nursing person has significantly improved. For example, between 1965 and 1983, infant mortality rate (for age 1 and under) for low-income sub-Saharan Africa improved from 156 to 119 per thousand, while that of children between ages 1 and 4 improved from 35 to 23. At the same time, between 1965 and 1980, the ratio of population per physician and nursing person improved from 38,263 to 27,922 and 4,627 to 3,148, respectively (World Bank, 1985b: 218–221).

However, critical to the survival rate of children is the *quality* of life led thereafter. The availability of food is central to the quality of life. The World Bank estimates that as much as 60 percent of the population in sub-Saharan Africa eat fewer calories each day than are estimated to be necessary for survival. The United Nations estimates that 5 million children die in Africa every year and another 5 million children are crippled both physically and mentally by malnutrition and hunger. The physical and mental crippling of Africa's younger population has grave consequences for the future development of the continent. There is no doubt that a mentally incompetent population cannot perform the necessary developmental tasks of the future, because the capacity to think critically and creatively (central ingredients for a dynamic population) will not be there. A young population with limited physical abilities cannot attend school properly, let alone think critically and creatively. Unless the survival rate for children is tied to the quality of their lives as adults, a substantial portion of Africa's population will be mentally incapacitated. This is by no means an alarmist position. A visit to the many refugee camps on the African continent will bear out this proposition.[7]

Industrial Development in Africa

Africa's principal industrialization strategy after independence was characterized by Import Substitution Industrialization (ISI), a policy similar to the one adopted by many Latin American countries in the early 1950s based on the advice of the Economic Commission for Latin America, (ECLA), (Evans, 1979; Stewart, 1977; Rweyemamu, 1973; Baer, 1972; Leys, 1975). All problems associated with ISI have afflicted African economies: the creation of technological dependency of African countries; monopoly of production by a few transnational corporations; high import content in both raw materials and technology; the introduction of inappropriate technology (e.g., sophisticated bread bakeries designed for winter climates); nonconvergence between what ISI factories produce and the consumption patterns of the general population; the problem of capacity utilization, given the high import content of raw materials and the shortage of foreign exchange to purchase them; the increasing external indebtedness of African countries resulting from their quest for industries that have little relevance to the developmental effort; and the creation and exacerbation of social inequalities as members of the "petty bourgeoisie" struggle to maintain their privileges and consumption habits as the general population recedes further into poverty.

However, despite its disproportionately large impact on the general production structure and social relations in society, the manufacturing sector in Africa remains small and enclaved, accounting for only 7.5 percent of the region's GDP. In fact, for the low-income countries of sub-Saharan Africa, the share of manufacturing to GDP declined from 9 percent to 7 percent between 1965 and 1983, while for the remainder of countries the sector stagnated at 8 percent of GDP (World Bank, 1985: 178). Compared to other regions of the world, Africa is still the least industrialized continent, according to a 1983 ECA study.

As of now, the industrialization process in Africa has relatively speaking failed to provide the dynamic forces for the structural transformation of the African economy to attain self-sustainment. . . . Relative to world manufacturing output, Africa had a share of manufacturing value added of only 0.9 in 1980 as compared to a share of 2.7 percent and 6 percent for South and East Asia and Latin America respectively. Thus, Africa was by 1980 still the least industrialized region in the world. (1983: 11)

Even for such countries as Ivory Coast and Nigeria (which, in the past two decades, have substantially increased their manufacturing sectors through ISI, prompting the application of the (problematic) concept of *dependent development* to these countries (Marcussen and Torp, 1982)), industrialization has actually stagnated in the past few years. Both countries are facing serious problems in capacity utilization of already built factories. Nigeria's factories have been operating at less than 50 percent capacity since 1983. The Ivory Coast economic "miracle" is now a burst bubble of optimism; the country has slipped further into debt accompanied by gross social inequalities, precipitating talk of an impending social crisis (Campbell, 1985). By 1987, both Nigeria and Ivory Coast had instituted retrenchment measures advocated by the IMF.

Problems faced by Ivory Coast's and Nigeria's manufacturing sectors are microcosmic realities of the sub-Saharan manufacturing sector in general. In fact, Ivory Coast and Nigeria represent the relatively "better-off" group of countries in the region. In some countries, such as Zaire and Guinea, the manufacturing sector has declined so drastically that it accounts for less than 2 percent of the GDP. Such statistics lead one to speculate on the possibility of the total collapse of some economies—an unwelcome proposition, but a very probable one.

Perhaps the grimmest picture regarding Africa's industrial development is provided by the ECA. The following quotation is presented in full so as not to weaken the impact of its message.

The overall picture of the projections of industrial product groups on the basis of a continuation of present trends in Africa's industrialization process shows that the region as a whole will, by the year 2008, continue to be highly dependent on the industrial products of other regions. This disturbing situation is projected without taking into account the rate of technological change in the industrialized countries which, if accounted for, would imply an even worse dependence. According to the projections, if the present industrial trends persist for the next 25 years, the African region would still have to import over 97 percent of its tractor requirements, over 98 percent of the region's projected demand for passenger and commercial vehicles, 37 percent of fertilizers, 12.3 percent of cement and 59 percent of iron and steel. This situation would, no doubt, imply that the African region would, if present trends continue without drastic industrial changes, remain unindustrialized even by the year 2008. (1983: 35)

Analysis of current strategies of development by African governments suggest that little is being done to change course drastically, which implies that ECA's predictions (and projections) may well be realized.

THE LIMITS OF MACRO DATA

Having presented data that describe what we called "the African condition," we need to point out at this juncture the obvious limitations of that data. First and foremost, should be said that while the data describe the African condition, they in no way explain why these conditions exist. Thus in a way the data is itself static, although the difference in time periods—that is, 1960 to 1985—provides a basis upon which directional change and evolution of Africa economies can be analyzed. The limits of descriptive data can also be said to be the limits of empiricism in general, with the latter's emphasis on "observed facts" as the basis of knowledge. Although useful as a first step in the social investigation process, a stress on the "hard facts" (e.g., percentage of manufacturing in relation to GDP) and an adherence to a purported neutral empiricism often leads to superficial, mechanistic, and, more often than not, erroneous interpretations of socioeconomic processes. Empiricism at its crudest is usually just an exercise in the collection of "facts."

For our purposes, however, we will attempt to go beyond the simple presentation of observed facts in order to comprehend fully the phenomenon of the decline of Africa's political economy. We adhere to the principle that science involves not only facts but theorizing as well. As Arnold Brecht observed, our method is

designed to explain something with reference to data or interrelations not directly observed or otherwise manifest. Mere "description" is not theory. Nor are "population" or goals, of policy, or of evaluations. Only the explanations, if any, offered for descriptions or proposals may be theoretical; the description or proposal as such is not. On the other hand, theory does include "prediction" provided that it follows from an explanation. (Quoted in Sills, 1968, vol. 12: 307)

Thus for us, issues such as the theoretical understanding of transitions of modes of production will be as important as the hard facts of malnutrition and declining food production in explaining the African condition. So will the nature of class relations in society. It is our contention that unless social forces that are not easily observable are understood in relation to what can be easily observed, our understanding of the African condition will be incomplete.

CONCLUSION: SUMMARIZING THE AFRICAN CONDITION

The data that we have presented in this chapter suggest that Africa is in serious trouble if nothing drastic is undertaken to improve the economic conditions in the region. The data having been presented, however, we need to pause and reflect upon what it means to the everyday existence of the people on the continent. Richard Sandbrook has done so in one specific case.

[In Ghana,] (t)he human dimensions of the economic crisis were tragic. A laborer had to work for more than a day to buy a beer, and almost two days to buy a loaf of bread. In 1983, a yam sufficient for a family meal cost as much as 200 cedis, or two weeks' wages for a laborer. In addition, households were obliged to waste a great deal of time each day locating supplies, as food and other essential commodities were scarce. (1985: 3)

The following observation by the World Bank, however, probably presents the most graphic characterization of the "human condition" in Africa in general.

No list of economic or financial statistics can convey the human misery spreading in sub-Saharan Africa. A special study by the United Nations Children's Fund... has documented how children have been the victims of economic decline. In Zambia's poorer northern regions, [for example,] height-for-age ratios have fallen in all age categories under . . . fifteen years. Child mortality in sub-Saharan Africa was 50 percent higher than the average of developing countries in the 1950s; now it is almost double the average. . . . The number of severely hungry and malnourished people is estimated to have increased from close to 80 million in 1972–74 to as many as 100 million in 1984. (1984b: 9)

Or, as Reginald H. Green has written:

In order to hold any overview to manageable length, it is necessary to describe the economic malaise in sub-Saharan Africa in macro—or mega—economic terms. The picture is therefore grossly misleading and insufficiently disquieting because it fails to convey the real human misery these figures symbolize. . . . [The] human dimension of the crisis is not reflected primarily in data on current account deficits or inflation rates but in rural clinics without pharmaceutical drugs, schools without books, broken water supply systems without spare parts and workers without employment or access to productive self-employment. Development is about human beings. They are its end and its actors, its evaluators and its justification. By that test, even more than by that of economic aggregates, sub-Saharan Africa is failing. (1985: 9–10)

The failing suggested by Green is supported by the World Bank study just quoted. In its observations, the World Bank demonstrates that even with some fundamental improvement in domestic economic management, per capita incomes in sub-Saharan Africa will continue to fall during 1985-1995. In the more pessimistic scenario drawn by the World Bank, GDP in sub-Saharan Africa is expected to grow at 2.8 percent a year and population at 3.5 percent, involving an annual fall in per capita GDP of 0.7 percent. On this basis, real African incomes in 1995 will be so low that between 65 and 80 percent of the people will be living below the poverty line, compared with roughly 60 percent in 1985.

The prognosis for a continent could not be any bleaker. However, there are a few concerned Africans and Africanists who do not think that the current pessimistic prognosis for sub-Saharan Africa necessarily makes a logical step toward catastrophe. Two such Africanists are Timothy M. Shaw and Olajide Aluko, who state in the preface of their book that although the prospects for most of Africa's countries and peoples based on short- as well as long-term trends are depressing, "the future is not just the extension of such circumstances or cycles. Rather, the crisis may produce its own dialectic, its own antithesis. Notwithstanding existential and ideological differences, optimism is not to be denied altogether" (1985: xv).

Shaw and Aluko should not be denied their optimism, given their apparent adherence to positive dialectic theory, but it should be remembered that dialectic theory also has a negative equation. Our contention is that—although optimism should not be denied altogether—if current "development" of African governments is not radically altered, World Bank projections may turn out to be optimistic.

NOTES

1. The Berg report has been subject to heated debate within circles of scholars and other professionals who deal with issues of African development. For the most part, the report has been criticized for its inappropriate policy prescriptions based on unwarranted if not ideologically induced assumptions on the causes of the African crisis. We will deal with the fundamental aspects of the report in chapter 2, but suffice it to say that the general thrust of the critique of the report has been that if African governments decide to follow the report's prescriptions to the letter the crisis on the continent will continue and predictably get worse. The various reports and studies relating to the Berg report have appeared in the following (among others): C. Allison and R. H. Green, eds., "Accelerated Development in Sub-Saharan Africa: What Agenda for Action?" *Institute for Development Studies Bulletin* 14, 1/2 (1983); James C. N. Paul, ed., "The World Bank's Accelerated Development in Sub-Saharan Africa: A Symposium," *African Studies Review* 27, 4 (1984); David F. Gordon, ed., *Rural Africana* 19/20, (Spring–Fall 1984), special double issue; and Browne and Cummings, *The Lagos of Action vs. The Berg Report* (1984).

2. See, for example, World Bank, *Sub-Saharan Africa: Progress Report on Development Prospects and Programs* (1983); and *Toward Sustained Development in Sub-Saharan Africa: A Joint Program of Action* (1984).

3. The African crisis of underdevelopment manifests itself in various ways. For example, it is generally acknowledged that in most cases international institutions such as the IMF, the World Bank, and the United Nations have more complete and reliable data on African countries than those countries themselves. Thus African negotiating teams, whenever they go to the IMF and to the World Bank for loans, are not infrequently embarrassed when IMF or World Bank teams have more information about Africa than have African negotiators. There are reasons for this state of affairs, some of which will be apparent in chapter 2 in our discussion of political choices and the African development experience.

4. For purposes of this study, the terms *world economy, international economy,* and *world capitalist economy* are used synonymously to refer to that part of the global economy that is dominated by the Organization for Economic Cooperatism and Development (OECD) countries.

5. The poverty line in Africa was equivalent to a per capita income of $115 at 1972 prices while those considered destitute had a per capita income of under $59.

6. Regardless of whether one agrees or disagrees with the Harrod-Domar model of the relationship between GNP growth and population growth, either way one looks at the Kenyan situation, the feeling is that Kenya is in serious trouble. A summary of the method of calculation of the Harrod-Domar model is derived from Joseph Spengler:

A rough rule of thumb enables us to estimate how much capital must be formed to offset a rate of population growth of 1 or more percent per year. Suppose that a country's wealth amounts to 3 to 4 times its national income and that a population is concerned only to maintain its wealth per capita, or wealth-population ratio unchanged. Then if a country's population is growing 1 percent per year, it needs to save 3 to 4 percent of its income, convert these savings into wealth, and thereby increase its wealth 1 percent. If this country's population were growing 2 or 3 percent per year, the required saving rate would have to be increased correspondingly; it would lie between 6 and 12 percent. (1964: 77)

7. As of mid-1985, Africa was home to about half of the world's estimated 10 million refugees. Many had become refugees because of the crippling drought of the early 1980s; but others were victims of political strife, such as those in Rwanda and Burundi, or in the Horn of Africa—that is, Ethiopia, Sudan, and Somalia.

2

The African Development Experience: History, Politics, Policy, and Choice

Self-reliance at the level of ideology and economic decline at the level of production are symptomatic of the African crisis.
—Timothy M. Shaw, *Towards a Political Economy for Africa: The Dialectics of Dependence*

The very strategies of development the African governments have been pursuing since independence have come from theories of economic development that were developed during the colonial and neocolonial periods to rationalize the colonial pattern of production in Africa. . . . The cumulative result is that, today, neither high rates of growth or diversification nor an increasing measure of self-reliance and self-sustainment has been achieved in the African economy.
—Adebayo Adedeji, "Development and Economic Growth in Africa to the Year 2000: Alternative Projections and Policies"

INTRODUCTION

This chapter will deal with the practical implications of the development policies that have been pursued by African governments since independence. It is an attempt to formulate, explain, and analyze the nature of the development crisis on the continent. For the most part, analyses of the current development crisis have fallen under two broad categories. First, there are those who believe that the crisis has been caused largely by constraints internal (or indigenous) to the African continent. These constraints include a lower initial socioeconomic base, excessive government interference in the production process, gross mismanagement and inefficiency in state-run institutions, excessive demand on resources, corruption, and, more often than not, sheer incompetence of African governments. The World Bank and its affiliate institutions are the most prominent proponents of this theory (World Bank, 1981). The second school of thought, largely associated with the progressive and liberal elements both in Africa and abroad, looks at external circumstances such as industrial recession in the West, the post-1973 oil crisis and the general secular movement of primary commodity prices in a downward trend to be the main causes of the crisis (Green, 1982; 1985).

This chapter will closely scrutinize the debate and offer some suggestions toward a better understanding of the crisis. It is our belief that for a scrutiny of the debate on Africa's development crisis to be of relevance, the logic of neoclassical international development theory (with particular emphasis on trade) and its historical application to the African situation in the postcolonial period must be reconstructed. The reasons for the reconstruction (and understanding) of the theory lie in the problematic of the critique of the theory itself by most African development practitioners (i.e., the various governments) and theoreticians (at universities—who frequently give advice to governments). Despite their dissatisfaction with the long-term implications of comparative advantage theory to the development process, governments and theoreticians have proceeded at full speed to apply its prescriptions in the planning and execution of development policy. It is the contention of this study that, unless theoretical criticism is synchronized with practical application, *politically,* such criticism does more harm than good by creating illusions and assuming possibilities for positive change. Thus the promulgation of various socialist ideologies and similar pronouncements intended for public consumption in Africa *may* represent reactionary politics and incompetence at their worst. It is with a critical eye, then, that policy pronouncements such as the *Lagos Plan of Action* (LPA) (OAU, 1982) are analyzed in this chapter.

Finally, this chapter will raise a political-ideological question that we feel is necessary if a meaningful change is to be made in the economic planning process. This critical political-ideological question relates to the issue of further incorporation and participation by Africa in the international economy while the prevailing international political-economic structure remains unchanged. The issue here is not a rhetorical pronouncement regarding the need or desire for independence and autonomous development in Africa, but rather the enumeration of practical steps for the attaining of that objective. These practical steps will be discussed in the chapter dealing with "alternative futures." However, our initial objective in this chapter is to demonstratively argue that the critical political-ideological questions regarding economic independence and autonomous development have *not* been raised, let alone seriously resolved. The demonstrative argument will be presented by examining what we view as the negative consequences of policies based on theoretical premises regarding the nature of the international system and African society in general, and specifically on the nature of the state in African countries. This study suggests that the *non-raising* of the basic political-ideological questions regarding the relationship between Africa and the world economy, to a great extent, summarizes the African predicament.

COMPARATIVE ADVANTAGE AS A DEVELOPMENT STRATEGY

Neoclassical theory of development through the concept of *comparative advantage* advocates international trade as a principle of specialization according to relative efficiency in production. Under the assumptions of the theory, a nation will tend to export those commodities which use the nation's abundant factor intensively, and will tend to import those commodities which use the nation's scarce factor intensively. Amplification of the comparative advantage theory would seem to suggest that international trade enables increases in the market for a country's products, which is a prerequisite for the kind of specialization and division of labor that allow an economy to make the best use of its factor endowments. Thus, logically, larger markets mean that more can be produced for sale, generating higher national income, resulting in a positive external balance of payments. A positive external balance of payments then enables a country to be relatively debt-free—which in turn allows for balanced growth internally without the pressure of external debt on national resources. (Kindleberger, 1956; 1962)[1] The premise, however, in the international movement of factors is the concept of "free trade."

The most famous of the original proponents of free trade in the twentieth century was the British political economist David Ricardo, whose book *Principles of Political Economy and Taxation* (1971) set forth a rigorous theoretical argument in support of the concept of free trade—which had been advocated by Adam Smith in *The Wealth of Nations,* first published in 1776. Ricardo argued that the pursuance of free trade under the notion of comparative costs and advantage would benefit British industry and, ultimately, all countries in the world who participated in international trade.

Under a system of perfectly free commerce, this pursuit of individual advantage is admirably connected with the universal good of the whole. By stimulating industry, by rewarding ingenuity, and by using most efficaciously the peculiar powers bestowed by nature, it distributes labour most effectively and most economically: while by increasing the general mass of production it diffuses general benefit, and binds together, by one common tie of interest and intercourse the universal society of nations throughout the civilised World. It is this principle which determines that wine shall be made in France and Portugal and that hardware and other goods shall be manufactured in England. (Ricardo 1971: 152)

British-Portuguese relations serve as the classic historical example of the practice of comparative advantage. It has been demonstrated (S. Sideri, 1970) that what passed as free trade, using comparative advantage in cost between the two countries, was actually a one-sided transaction overwhelmingly benefiting Britain. Sideri shows that indeed Britain became a net importer of food and primary products from Portugal. However, a closer reading of the relationship over the centuries demonstrates that British trade with Portugal was actually based on unequal treaties and not on "natural" international division of labor between equals. The treaties of 1642, 1654, 1661, and 1703 actually confirmed and formalized Portuguese dependence on Britain and, in effect, blocked Portuguese potential for any meaningful industrialization. The most telling example was the Methuen Treaty of 1703. The treaty created a specialization of production for the two countries, in wine and textiles, respectively, for Portugal and Britain. The expansion of English textiles under the Methuen Treaty involved a sacrifice by Portuguese producers which was intended to preserve the British advantage in textile manufacturing in exchange for Portuguese wine. Thus British wine imports from Portugal became the means by which British textile production could be expanded. In the process Britain stopped importing French wines, despite the fact that French wines were reckoned to be better. The giving up of French wines by Britain was regarded as a national sacrifice to further the course of industrialization. As Sideri states, "From this time the drinking of [Portuguese wine] was regarded as a patriotic duty by the English squire who later, after industrialisation had brought him affluence, reverted to drinking French wine" (1970: 8–9). However, Sideri points out further that the reciprocal privileges that Britain granted Portugal were essentially of little benefit to Portuguese merchants, because Portuguese merchants lacked sufficient competitive power to utilize fully the privileges stipulated in the treaty. In the meantime, the factories of the English merchants in Portugal put these privileges to "good use," in effect, further weakening the Portuguese merchant class:

Thus, in exchange for her concessions to England, Portugal obtained neither a real reduction of English import duties on wines nor the stabilization of those duties as (Portugal) had repeatedly demanded. The export of wine cannot be considered to have been very advantageous to Portugal. As we have already seen, trade was largely controlled by English interests which took most of the profits, while the Portuguese had to cope with unfavourable effects created by the expansion of such an "enclave" in which British investment soon reached the million pound mark. A trade "completely" in the hands of English merchants who did not hesitate to mercilessly sacrifice Duoro producers. (Sideri, 1970: 42-43)

In the early nineteenth century the Napoleonic wars further weakened the Portuguese economy, forcing the Portuguese King John V to flee to Brazil from 1807 to 1821. Britain, using its support for Portugal in the Napoleonic wars as a pretext, further pressed John V to open up Brazilian markets for British goods—in effect establishing British control of the Brazilian economy. A Portuguese economist pessimistically observed in 1810 that "the magical power of the steam engine, which has revolutionised the mechanical arts within the last few years, has provided the English with the means to produce manufactured goods so cheaply that nobody else can compete with them" (quoted in Sideri, 1970: 47).

The theory of comparative advantage has limited value, then, if one talks of two or more economies that are at two different levels of development. It is quite clear that Britain, in its relationship with Portugal, had a historically advantageous position in economic relations—which had the effect of diminishing the chances for Portuguese industrialization. In the mid-nineteenth century Frederick List, a German political economist (and a contemporary of Karl Marx), began to show how the theory of comparative advantage worked in favor of only one country—Britain. In examining the arguments between England on the one hand and France and Germany on the other, regarding the issue of comparative advantage, List chastised some French and German supporters of the theory for being oblivious to the qualitative difference between exports of an economy that is primarily agricultural and one that is industrial. In opposing proponents of free trade, List argued that

there is, for instance, no distinction made between the exportation of manufactured and of agricultural products; they believe they are promoting national interest by developing the latter at the expense of the former; they have not yet comprehended the principle of the industrial training or education of the country as a basis for the regulation of duties; they scruple not to sacrifice to foreign competition manufactures, which after enjoying protection for several years, and flourishing sufficiently to beget internal competition and a consequent large reduction of prices, they suffer to be destroyed, and with them the spirit of enterprise. (List, 1856: 68-69)

List further argued that the only reason Britain was pushing for free trade was that there were clear advantages to be gained from free trade by Britain. The relative merits of the comparative advantage theory, however, were clearly suspect to Frederick List.

Some [nations], favored by circumstances, having distanced others in manufactures, commerce, and navigation, and having early perceived that this advanced state was the surest mode of acquiring and keeping political supremacy, have adopted and still persevere in a policy so well adapted to give them the monopoly of manufactures, of industry and of commerce, and to impede the progress of less advanced nations or those in a lower degree of culture. The measures enforced by such nations, taken as a whole, the prohibitions, the duties on imports, the maritime restrictions, premiums upon exports [etc.] are called *the protective system.* (1856: 73) (Emphasis added.)

In other words, British advocacy for free trade in the nineteenth century was in effect a measure to protect British industry over less developed economies which at that time included the United States and countries in Continental Europe. Indeed, List demonstrated that in the mid-nineteenth century, following the opening up of United States ports to British manufactures, there was a marked decline in U.S. industrial production, suggesting that further opening of U.S. ports to British manufactures would have led to industrial disaster. The importance of Frederick List's work lies in the fact that his conclusions regarding issues of political economy were not simply based on theory but also in history and observation. It is through history and observation that he concluded that open economies based on comparative advantage reasoning were inherently injurious to late starters—to the course of industrialization in particular, and to national development in general. List noted that nineteenth-century Prussia had beaten the odds and industrialized, owing to its opposition to free trade.

> Alarmed by the consequences of [free trade] policy, nay, constrained by the convulsions it has occasioned, we have seen in our century, Prussia, a continental nation, as yet imperfectly prepared for manufacturing industrial, seeking her welfare in the prohibiting system so condemned by [free trade] theorists. And what has been her reward? *National Prosperity.* (1856: 62) (Emphasis added.)

The opposition to free trade, it must be noted, has nothing to do with radical economic theory. Indeed, in the nineteenth century, Frederick List was hardly a radical political economist. The strength of his argument was based on historical experience and logic. In the contemporary period, some conventional economists have argued against free trade. One such economist is Sir Arthur Lewis. In his famous 1950 article, "Industrialization of the British West Indies," Lewis convincingly and credibly argued that in the context of the West Indies, free trade (or laissez faire) policy created significant obstacles to industrialization, and hence to development. In the spirit of Frederick List, and in opposition to free trade, Lewis explained why it was only the British in the nineteenth century who insisted on free trade.

> [Free trade] views were never accepted outside England by persons responsible for the government of countries that were industrializing. Neither were they accepted by England herself in the long centuries from 1400 to 1850 when she was laying the foundations of her industrial greatness on the basis of vigourous fostering of new industries behind monopolistic grants, patents, subsidies and protective barriers. They have never been accepted by the rulers of any nation at the time when it was in the early throes of industrialization, whether by England, or the United States, or Germany, or Japan, or Russia, or any other country. It is only when England had become the leading manufacturing country in the world that she embraced *laissez-faire* views, and sought, unsuccessfully, to sell them to other nations. Independent nations, including the self-governing dominions, refused to buy them, but India and the rest of the dependent Empire were allowed no option. It has been the misfortune of the West Indies to be caught in the trap of these ideas. (1950: 34-35)

Unfortunately, sub-Saharan Africa also was caught in the trap of the idea of laissez-faire. We consider the above discussion to be important in introducing the issue of African development experience because of the parallel historical experiences of some European countries with those of contemporary sub-Saharan Africa. For example, understanding that Portugal's underdevelopment is not a historical accident, but rather a result of concrete traceable historical processes, is helpful to the analyst who sees similar patterns of development as they relate to Africa; however, this does not imply that Africa's contemporary problems can be understood solely through the Portuguese example. A concrete analysis of comparative advantage in relation to Africa must be done, for other historical examples to be relevant.

COMPARATIVE ADVANTAGE AND THE AFRICAN DEVELOPMENT EXPERIENCE

Although we will not concentrate too much on the historical relationship between Africa and the original centers of modern capitalism, it is nonetheless important to recognize the role that this historical relationship has played in bringing about the product specialization that today is the trademark of African economies.[2] Thus West Africa, for example, after an initial period of trade with Europe in commodities other than slaves, was forced to become a source of slaves, to the exclusion of other commodities. As Geoffrey Kay has remarked,

West Africa was reduced to a slave market and no society escaped without being turned into a corrupt parody of its former self. The degree of social incoherence that arose would have made the establishment of industrial capitalism impossible even if this had been historically practical. What it did allow, in fact what it made essential, was external colonial domination, either direct or indirect, and in this way it gave a spurious basis to the hypocritical claims of the colonizing powers that they brought civilization and order to a world of barbarism and chaos. (1975: 99)

The process of dominance and product specialization in Anglo-Portuguese relations from the seventeenth century onward also manifested itself in Anglo-African relations; therefore, we choose to call the beginning of African product specialization—even in the era of slave trade—the "Portugalization" of Africa. We contend that this process of product specialization proved to be historically significant in the later pattern of economic development (and underdevelopment) in Africa. In summarizing the work of John Flint (1974) and Christopher Fyfe (1974), Immanuel Wallerstein (1985: 41) has shown that with the decline of slave trade in the nineteenth century, especially in West Africa, the colonial economic relationship was intensified based on product specialization which was essentially injurious to African economic development. The negative impact of the colonial economic relationship became apparent with the steady increase in the volume of manufactured imports from the expanding factories of Europe, pushing the frontier of import-export trading inland and bringing more African peoples into the European trading sphere. According to Wallerstein:

The growth of this trade began to affect the structure of production in West Africa. Some previous economic activities—blacksmithing, iron smelting, even the mining of iron—declined, ruined by the competition of cheaper and purer iron bars imported from Europe, as well as by "increasing quantities of cheap European imports of iron basins, matchets, knives, hoes, wire and other metal goods turned out by the expanding mass production techniques of the industrial revolution." (1985: 41)

Wallerstein further points out that even the textile industry, which was one of the most advanced industries on the continent, was not spared the ravages of European competitive advantage based on mass production.

In the seventeenth and eighteenth centuries, the African producers had effectively resisted European intrusion because of product differentiation, but this began to change once the English mills began to mass produce cheap cotton cloth after the mid-eighteenth century. (1985: 42)

What was more devastating, however, was the fact that, once the old industries were destroyed by European competition, Africans were not able to establish new industries because of colonial demands for raw materials. Attempts by Africans to establish factories, such as those that occurred in Freetown, Sierra Leone and in Senegal, were quickly closed down by the British and French respectively. "In short, West Africa was being made to conform to the 'true principles of Commerce,' i.e., the export of British manufactures in return for African produce" (Wallerstein, 1985: 42).

The above story, which we call the "Portugalization" of Africa, is not necessarily new or novel. Dozens of studies have dealt with the subject. However, as one examines recent studies on the contemporary problems of African development, one is struck by the lack of historical analysis which should always accompany or inform contemporary analysis. Thus studies such as the ones prepared by the World Bank (1981, 1984a) or scholars (Price, 1984) for the most part neglect or minimize the importance of the historical dimension regarding the issue of product specialization. The fact that the integration of Africa into a wider international economic system was accomplished on terms that were largely unfavorable to her is given only secondary mention, requires critical response. The establishment of colonial rule in Africa and the cementing of "unequal" relationships in the international economy, we suggest, still warrant emphasis. As Wallerstein has summarized:

What is striking in [the] early period of colonial rule is that the larger needs of metropolitan economic institutions for expanded cash-crop production in Africa coincided with the administrative needs of the colonial officials. Export production was needed to provide a tax base sufficient to cover the costs of administration. And export production provided an ideological reinforcement. It was seen as part of the "civilizing" process, as well as an alternative to the slave trade. (1985: 46)

The policy emphasis on free trade and comparative advantage, it has since been shown, was a convenient way for European countries to manipulate the international system to their advantage. In the case of Britain, this manipulation was clearly evident at the turn of the century in her dealings with her colonial possessions. According to Geoffrey Kay:

The colonial commitment to free trade was more apparent than real. What it meant in practice was not free trade between the colonies and the rest of the world as much as free trade between British capital in the colonies and capital in Britain. It was a policy aimed to serve narrow sectional interests dressed up in general terms. . . . Whenever free trade threatened British interests as happened on occasions when a group of colonial producers were able to compete effectively with British enterprise [see for example the case of Ghana in Kay, 1972], allegiance to the holy grail (i.e. free trade) was either forgotten or carefully avoided. (1975: 107)

The point here is that free trade was never a viable policy, even for European countries that were much more developed than Third World countries. Indeed, the system of colonization itself was designed to ensure political and economic monopoly of respective European powers in the African territories they controlled. The nature of production was primarily geared toward the satisfaction of metropolitan colonial interests.

Thus, as we trace the evolution of twentieth-century production systems in Africa, we are struck by the strict product specialization that the colonial powers introduced to the continent. The Germans, for example, introduced sisal and cotton production in Tanganyika in the 1890s. Sisal production was specifically introduced to counter the long established monopoly of Britain in the rope and twine industry at a time of fierce maritime competition between the two countries. In Kenya and Uganda, the British introduced coffee, cotton, and tea production on a massive scale. The French encouraged the production of groundnuts in Senegal, while promoting coffee and vanilla production in Madagascar. Zaire and Zambia became specialists in the production of copper and other minerals.

Significant, however, is the fact that African labor was being made to produce directly in a system that was essentially alien in origin and objective. The direct (objective) *production* relations that were being created between foreign capital and the African producer (in his/her capacity as an independent producer or laborer on a plantation owned by Europeans) were to have an everlasting impact on the Africans. Those sectors of the African economy that were effectively penetrated by foreign capital became part of the international capitalist system with its well-known asymmetrical distribution of power and resources (Amin, 1974; 1977; Duvall et al., 1981).

The historical evolution of product specialization acknowledges the importance of the international factor in the explanation of the crisis facing African economies and thus helps us illuminate one side of the crisis equation. The second side of the crisis equation (i.e., the internal dimension) cannot be properly understood unless the first side is understood, and vice versa. An understanding of the dialectical relationship between the two sides of the equation is therefore critical to our analysis.

Table 2.1

Africa: Evolution of Commodity Concentration[a] 1960–1981

	1960	1965	1970	1981
Angola	50.0	56.3	55.1	99.3
Benin	65.6	67.3	48.6	76.3
Botswana	93.9	75.0	75.0	36.4
Burundi		89.6	96.1	92.8
Cameroon	70.6	58.5	54.8	40.1
Cape Verde	14.5	20.2	20.3	23.9
Central African Republic	74.8	37.0	55.7	50.2
Chad		93.0		99.2
Comoros	56.5	56.1	44.9	52.0
Congo, People's Republic			93.5	
Dijibouti			0.4	
Equatorial Guinea		97.8	96.0	87.6
Ethiopia	71.9	82.0	75.0	
Gabon	69.8	80.7	83.0	64.8
Gambia, The	99.6	75.2	88.7	68.7
Ghana	84.5	81.9	84.0	59.0
Guinea-Bissau		83.9	92.1	64.0
Ivory Coast	81.2	80.2	75.1	55.5
Kenya	34.2	50.5	49.7	64.4
Lesotho		90.1	65.2	18.3
Liberia	85.5	93.3	91.1	88.9
Madagascar	46.9	48.0	41.3	72.3
Malawi	93.8	73.6	70.3	91.6
Mali		93.2	92.2	93.8
Mauritania	89.6	96.4	98.7	81.1

Mauritius	91.6	92.2	92.4	55.2
Mozambique	46.9	33.9	34.2	37.3
Niger		97.2	83.6	
Nigeria	49.5	44.6	77.5	91.6
Reunion	79.0	80.3	88.7	76.7
Rwanda			78.7	100.0
Sao Tome & Principe	84.3	92.9	94.3	49.4
Senegal	82.9	79.1	50.2	20.8
Seychelles	95.0	54.0	46.8	18.0
Sierra Leone	26.3	28.3	25.9	18.4
Somalia	94.8	88.5	75.5	73.7
South Africa	17.1	15.5	16.2	8.5
Sudan	65.3	65.6	75.4	43.0
Swaziland	30.6	42.2	49.4	38.8
Tanzania, United Republic of	49.2	52.5	43.4	47.3
Togo	60.6	85.6	83.4	51.5
Uganda	69.8	86.3	85.4	44.1
Upper Volta		84.2	59.8	69.4
Zaire	52.0	60.1	73.0	92.7
Zambia	93.9	93.8	98.5	98.6
Zimbabwe	58.8	37.1	26.3	34.3

aPercentage contribution of three major commodities in total merchandise exports.

Source: The World Bank, *World Tables, Third Edition* (Baltimore/London: John Hopkins University Press, 1983): 542.

What is so remarkable about African economies in the post-independence period is the commitment to the principle of comparative advantage which was handed down to Africa during the colonial period. The evidence of this commitment, which in essence entails the emphasis in primary commodity production, can be seen in table 2.1, which outlines the evolution of commodity concentration in African countries since 1960, and in table 2.2, which shows the share of leading single-commodity export of all leading exports of African countries.

The two tables clearly show that since independence, on the average, African countries have increased their specialization to fewer and fewer products. The conventional wisdom has been that, through foreign exchange earnings derived from the exports of primary products in which Africa has a comparative advantage, African countries will be able to pursue economic development plans that will, among other things, reduce their dependence on imported manufactured goods. This will be accomplished through the establishment of import substitution industrialization (ISI), and will improve the general welfare of the population through the diffusion of new patterns of consumption that are presumed to be desirable.[3] On the issue of commodity concentration, the worst case is represented by Angola, whose commodity concentration (in oil) increased from 50 percent in 1960 to 99.3 percent in 1981. Countries such as Zambia and Burundi consistently have maintained high levels of commodity concentration (98.6 percent and 92.8 percent, respectively) over the past 20 years. Declines in agricultural production in Nigeria have resulted in oil accounting for over 90 percent of exports. The average commodity concentration for sub-Saharan Africa (except for South Africa) is 62 percent.[4]

The consequence of primary export commodity concentration is easily discernible; it can be seen in the poor performance of the export sector of the African countries in the past decade. Part of the problem in the export sector has been a general decline in export production due to adverse weather conditions and internal mismanagement, as has been observed by the World Bank (1981) and others (Shao, 1985). However, the external economic environment has had a substantial impact on export production, due to declines in world primary commodity prices.

F. Gerard Adams and Jere R. Behrman (1982), in a comprehensive study regarding difficulties associated with commodity problems, have suggested that there are two basic problems associated with dependence on primary commodities as a basis for acquiring foreign exchange, which in turn influence decisions regarding development planning. First, fluctuations in international primary markets exacerbate problems in pursuing both public and private ends, due to uncertainty in returns. Second, the secular movements in the terms of trade of many primary products, predominantly in a downward direction over the past two decades, have left their producers in a weakened economic position (1982: 3). In a 1984 report, the World Bank conceded as much.

For export crops, Africa's total volume expanded by about 1 percent a year over the 1980–82 period—an improvement over the decline during 1970–80. However, for most crops, the fall in world market shares that started in the 1970s continued in the 1980s. These declines have occurred in commodities in which Africa has a *comparative advantage* and which are likely to remain its potential source of foreign exchange earnings. (1984b: 11) (Emphasis added.)

A United Nations study in 1984 confirmed the World Bank's observation. The UN study showed that the prices of cocoa, coffee, copper, groundnut oil, and sugar, which constituted the main export products of many African countries, had experienced a significant decline after 1980; and by 1983 they were still below their 1979 levels. (See table 2.3.)

The present study suggests that the current panic, which characterizes the reaction of both the African governments and the international financial institutions regarding declining primary commodity prices, is difficult to understand. Why, for example, in 1985 would the government of Tanzania—in clear agreement with the International Monetary Fund—cry aloud that falling commodity prices were ruining Tanzania's economy; when, as early as 1966, the Tanzanian government had seen the price of sisal fall from 2,094 s. per ton in 1964 to 1,507 s. per ton in 1965, with the value of sisal exports falling by nearly 35 percent during the same period despite a moderate increase in volume?[5] In the subsequent development plans, Tanzania made a commitment to diversify production away from sisal, but the diversification was not qualitative—it was simply diversification from sisal production to other primary commodities such as tea, coffee, and cotton.

The transition from colonial rule to post-independence rule shows no qualitative change in the structure of production of African countries, despite earlier claims to the contrary (Kilby, 1969). Product specialization, the trademark of colonial production, still predominates Africa's production landscape. The continuation of primary product specialization by African economies to a significant extent helps to explain the continuing crisis of production on the continent, because African governments lack the capacity to control the international environment—an environment they are nonetheless committed to for ideological reasons. It is difficult to conceive of the African crisis without the international dimension, although some analysts are attempting to do this.

One such analyst is Robert Price. In his analysis of Ghana, for example, Price has flatly stated that

the international factor...cannot be considered decisive in the analysis of Ghana's economic demise. Neither the empirical evidence [sic] nor the logic of the situation sustain an analysis that attributes Ghana's condition to adverse trends in world commodity prices. (1984: 179)

Table 2.2

Share of Leading Single-Commodity Export and of all Leading Exports in Exports of African Countries

Country	Leading Single-Commodity Export as Percentage of Total Exports (1979-1979 Average)	Number of Leading Commodity Exports (IFS) 1979	Leading Commodity Exports as Percentage of Total Exports (1975-1979 Average)
Algeria	92	1	92
Gabon	77	3	91
Libya	100	1	100
Nigeria	93	2	97
Egypt	26	2	29
Benin	23	4	49
Burundi	89	2	93
Cameroon	29	4	61
Central African Republic	7	6	89
Chad	61	1	61
Congo, People's Republic	67	3	82
Ethiopia	62	4	85
Gambia	82	1	82
Ivory Coast	15	3	65
Kenya	28	3	59
Liberia	64	3	83

Madagascar	49	3	63
Malawi	49	4	80
Mali Republic	48	2	95
Mauritania	82	2	95
Mauritius	74	1	74
Morocco	38	2	95
Niger	62	2	64
Rwanda	70	3	87
Senegal	36	2	51
Sierra Leone	58	4	84
Somalia	70	3	88
Sudan	56	4	83
Tanzania	30	4	55
Togo	50	3	83
Tunisia	41	3	60
Uganda	88	3	96
Zaire	42	4	85
Zambia	93	1	93

Source: Reprinted by permission of the publisher, from Commodity Exports and Economic Development by F. Gerard Adams and Jere R. Behrman (Lexington, Mass.: Lexington Books).

Table 2.3
Sub-Saharan Africa: International Trade and Reserves 1978–1983

	1978	1979	1980	1981	1982	1983
Merchandise exports (billion $)	26.6	39.0	52.1	38.8	34.4	29.5
Energy importers	13.3	16.5	19.0	15.2	13.6	12.5
Energy exporters	13.5	22.5	33.1	23.0	20.8	17.0
Merchandise imports (billion $)	32.6	32.3	44.9	42.9	39.4	32.3
Energy importers	17.1	18.9	24.0	20.9	18.9	16.1
Energy exporters	15.1	13.4	20.9	22.0	20.5	16.2
Gross reserves (end of period) as a percentage of imports	9.5	16.7	18.3	12.3	9.1	11.2
Energy importers	11.1	10.6	7.5	9.1	9.5	13.7
Energy exporters	7.7	25.4	30.6	15.6	8.7	9.2

Prices of main export commodities (1970=100)

Cocoa	79	74	59	47	40	48
Coffee	65	74	65	46	49	55
Copper	104	151	166	132	112	121
Cotton	101	108	131	117	101	118
Groundnut Oil	126	104	100	122	68	83
Sugar	121	145	179	169	147	143
Energy importing countries (a): unit value of imports (1977=100)	110	128	156	155	150	152
Real net Official Development Assistance (ODA) disbursements (b) (billion $)	4.7	5.1	5.5	5.7	5.6	–

(a) Includes Cameroon, Congo, Gabon and Angola
(b) In 1977 prices and exchange rates. Deflated by the ODA of DAC member countries

---

Source: United Nations, *World Economic Survey*, (New York: U.N. Publ, 1984): 18.

But what does the evidence suggest? The following three examples from Ghana, Zambia, and Zaire are intended as a response to Price and to similar arguments.

The Effects of Product Specialization: Three Examples from Africa

The devastating negative effect of international price fluctuation of primary commodities on African economies, in terms of reduced export earnings, can be specifically demonstrated with the following three examples from Ghana, Zambia, and Zaire. T. K. Morrison in his 1979 study of Ghana—whose analysis can be generalized to apply to most African countries—points out that the most serious consequences of export instability are related in an immediate sense to its impact on the government budget. According to Morrison:

No automatic stabilizers cushion the effect of an export shortfall on government revenue. In many developing countries, the central governments play dominant roles in their economies and a revenue shortfall can therefore cause serious disruptions. (1979: 159)

In the specific case of Ghana, Morrison shows that between 1961 and 1974 the stability index for cocoa (Ghana's major export) was 31, compared to 47 for government cocoa revenues, 17 for total government revenues, and 31 for total export earnings. These figures indicate that the fluctuation in cocoa prices (31) was the actual instability index for total export earnings. With regard to government revenues, the data supplied by Morrison shows that three declines in government revenue—in 1962, 1966, and 1972—followed three export shortfalls (1979: 161). Robert Price and the World Bank, in studies already cited, argue that, despite the fact that Ghana has been plagued by insufficient export earnings because of international price instability, the data do not support the thesis that adverse terms of trade are chiefly responsible for Ghana's foreign exchange position and have slowed her economic growth.

The World Bank (1984a: 10) prefers to argue that it is the institutional, technological, and policy environment for agricultural growth in Ghana that had become adverse over time—foremost among these factors being a massive appreciation of the real effective exchange rate which, if 1973 is considered as a base year (= 100), by 1981 saw the cedi overvalued by 816 percent—thus reducing the export value of cocoa internationally and making foreign goods dearer. What we are not told, however, is the cumulative effect of declining export prices beginning in the early 1960s, which forced some cocoa farmers to abandon their farms or refuse to plant new trees. This is not a denial of the vast mismanagement of the state sector in Ghana, which grew at a relatively fast pace in the mid-1960s. It is an acknowledgement of a two-pronged assault (one external, the other internal) on Ghana's productivity, an acknowledgement which casts serious doubts on the viability of IMF prescriptions regarding devaluation and other issues, as we will see later.

In the case of Zambia, Robert L. Curry, Jr., has shown that the reliance on copper for over 90 percent of export earnings has had an unfavorable impact not only in terms of reduced government revenue but also on the overall performance of the economy and its effect on the working population (1979a). According to Curry, the decline in the price of copper has been reflected in the decline in the country's export sector, with the result that Zambia's GDP declined from K998 million (lK = US 1.20) in 1970 to K185 million in 1978. This means that there was an absolute decline in the living standards of the people. In the meantime, imports rose from K328 million to K565 million over the same period. However, the real value of imports stagnated due to import inflation. The export/debt service ratio of Zambia at the end of 1982 was 195 percent, an indication of the seriousness of the problem (*Time*, Jan. 10, 1983). A subsequent econometric study of the copper industry in Zambia (the industry that provides virtually all export earnings), by F. Gerard Adams and Jere R. Behrman (1982), confirms both the earlier argument on the perils of commodity concentration and the point made by Robert L. Curry, Jr., on the effects of declining returns on export earnings. The following lengthy quotation from the econometric study is necessary to make the point. (Table 2.4 is adapted from the Adams/Behrman study to further elaborate on the quotation.)

The transmission mechanisms from the copper sector to the rest of the economy are several. Copper workers reduce their expenditures on domestic and imported goods because of their drop in income. Their decline in wages reduces wages elsewhere in the economy because of their pace-setting role, with a decline as large as − 1.8 percent below the base path in year two [see table 2.4]—although the cycle above the base path in years four and five means that the average decline over the first quinquennium is only − 0.4 percent. . . . Government revenues fall from copper and from other depressed activities and induce an average decline of − 2.9 percent in government expenditures. The balance on the current account drops precipititously in the first year and then cycles around the base path. Due primarily to the resulting depletion of foreign exchange reserves, the money supply drops an average of − 3.1 percent. Of course, many of the variables interact with feedbacks throughout the economy. (1982: 211)

More recent reports of the Zambian economy are even less encouraging. *Africa Confidential* reported the increasing misery generated by the consequences of export production.

The ever widening balance of payments deficit, the almost built-in recurrent expenditure deficit and a chronic shortage of foreign exchange are now pushing up prices of basic commodities and goods to a critical level. For the low wage-earners (80-100 Kwacha a month), the purchase of food alone accounts for all earnings. Across-the-board, real earnings have fallen by at least 30% over the past five years. Inflation is set to ac-

Table 2.4
Simulations of the Impact of Sustained Changes in the London Metal Exchange Copper Price on Zambia Goal Attainment (percentage deviations for major variables)

| | 10-Percent Sustained Change in LME Copper Price | | | | | |
| | Average Decrease for Years | | | | Average Increase for years 1 - 9 | |
	1 - 2	1 - 3	1 - 5	6 - 9	1 - 5	1 - 9
Copper sector						
Value added	-1.9	-2.4	-3.5	-6.1	3.1	4.9
Wage bill	-2.8	-3.9	-4.4	-6.4	4.2	5.7
Zambians	-3.4	-4.7	-5.3	-7.4	5.2	6.5
Expatriates	-1.7	-2.0	-2.4	-3.5	2.2	3.2
Total employment	-0.9	-1.9	-4.3	-10.4	4.1	9.3
Nonwage bill	-17.0	-17.3	-22.6	58.9b	23.3	-40.9
Overall Economy						
GDP	-1.2	-1.6	-1.9	-2.8	1.8	2.6
Agriculture	.0	-.1	-.2	-.4	.2	.4
Secondary	-1.9	-2.6	-3.7	-6.2	3.4	5.5
Tertiary	-.7	-1.0	-.8	-.5	.8	.6
Aggregate Demand						
Gross investment	-6.6	-9.4	-10.3	-13.9	10.3	14.0
Imports	-3.4	-5.0	-5.7	-8.4	5.7	8.6

Income and employment						
Wage rate	-1.7	-2.1	-1.6	-.2	1.6	.4
Employment	-.4	-.7	-1.1	-1.6	1.1	1.6
Price (GDP deflator)	-5.7	-5.7	-5.1	-4.0	5.1	4.3
Balance of current account	-102.2	-87.1	-51.2	-15.0	51.8	15.6
Fiscal and monetary policies						
Current revenues	-16.2	-14.0	-8.0	-6.9	8.2	7.4
Current expenditures	-7.4	-9.6	-11.4	-5.7	11.7	6.1
Money supply	-5.0	-8.6	-10.0	-9.6	10.2	9.9

Note: The percentage deviations are from a base simulation which is identical except for the indicated change. All variables are in real terms unless otherwise noted.

aBecause this variable is the difference between almost equal flows, a comparison of the percentage deviation across years is not very meaningful.

bIn years eight and nine the base nonwage income is very small. Also there is cycling to the other side of the base path in these years. The result is the problem noted in note a, with a misleading sign in regard to the absolute deviations as opposed to the percentage changes.

Source: Adams, F. Gerard and Jere R. Behrman, *Commodity Exports and Economic Development*, (1982): 209–210.

celerate to over 50%. But employers, often on the verge of insolvency, cannot afford to grant wage increases of even half the rate of inflation. . . . Lack of foreign exchange is so serious that . . . no vital industrial plant is spared. Dunlop Zambia, [for example] which has the capacity to produce enough tyres for the whole country, is closed because it has run out of imported raw materials. Without tyres, transport companies are progressively reducing operations. Literally, the country threatens to come to a standstill. (1985: 1)

The roots of the crisis in the Zambian economy, like many other African economies, clearly can be traced to the excessive reliance on the notions of comparative advantage which were handed down during the colonial era and faithfully implemented by the succeeding post-colonial state.

Zaire, in the past few years, has been referred to as Africa's economic basket case. This is due to its poor performance in the international economy and to the increased internal economic dislocation and deterioration. Scholars are now writing about "The Rise and Decline of the Zairian State" (Young and Turner, 1985) to emphasize the current crisis. Since copper is Zaire's most important product, accounting for approximately 70 percent of its export earnings, its predicament is not too different from that of Zambia. Thus, for example, in 1974 the price of one ton of copper on the world market was US $3,000. In 1975, the same ton sold for only U.S. $1,000, a decline of over 66 percent. In 1982, one metric ton of copper at the London Metal Exchange sold for just £684. In the meantime, prices of imported goods were rising steadily as a result of inflation in the industrial countries, evidenced by the cost of petroleum products which increased from $50 million to $200 million in only one year: 1974–75 (Europa Publications, 1981: 1135). Since 1970, the balance of Zaire's government account has been continuously in the red, with no relief in sight.

It would not, however, be accurate to state that the international economic system is the sole contributor to Zaire's economic crisis. It is obvious that the now-legendary corruption in the Zairian government has not helped the problems of deficits in any way. J. Ph. Peemas (1975) has shown that as the deficit problem began to take its toll on the economy, the initial reaction of the state was to finance the deficit partly by internal monetary mechanisms, which multiplied five-fold in the early seventies, and by external borrowing, which multiplied over twelve-fold in the same period. In 1982, Zaire's ratio of debt service to foreign exchange was 83 percent.

With mounting foreign debt and internal economic dislocation, Zaire had to endure two serious political/military crises in 1977 and 1978, which threatened to topple the Mobutu regime. In the first half of 1985, two serious attempts to dislodge Mobutu from power were reported. The effect of the economic decline on the Zairian masses has been devastating, with both urban and rural poverty reaching unprecedented levels. David J. Gould (1977: 355) has estimated that, in some areas, the standard of living has declined 100 percent.

Ghana, Zambia, and Zaire are not particularly unique cases. This pattern can be observed throughout the continent. Due to increased economic difficulties, most African governments have been forced to accede to IMF prescriptions in terms of how to run their economies. As of 1987, the Ghanaian cedi had been devalued almost 3000 percent (1973 = 100). The economic conditions, however, do not seem to have improved. The state is becoming more and more oppressive as the population attempts to disengage from it. (See chapter 5.)

THE CASE AGAINST COMPARATIVE ADVANTAGE IN AFRICA: A FURTHER ELABORATION ON ITS NEGATIVE CONSEQUENCES

In 1841, Frederick List defended his opposition to the free trade concept advocated by the followers of Adam Smith.

If the author [List] had been an Englishman, he would probably never have entertained doubts of the fundamental principle of Adam Smith's theory. It was the condition of his own country [i.e., Germany] which begot in him, more than twenty years since, the first doubts of the infallibly of that theory. It was the condition of his own country which, since that time, determined him to develop, first in anonymous articles, then in more elaborate treaties, not anonymous, contrary opinions. At this moment, the interests of Germany alone give the courage to publish the present work. (1856: 69-70)

The same argument can be applied to Africa today, given the negative consequences free trade and comparative advantage arguably have had on the region's economies. The deteriorating economic situation of the African countries, due to their reliance on raw materials and the latter's decline in value on the world market, should serve as a prima facie case against the theory of comparative advantage—as demonstrated by the degree of commodity concentration (table 2.1) despite the systematic decrease in international prices of those commodities.

Furthermore, African government planners, through their primary lenders—the International Monetary Fund and the World Bank—have not sought to change their development strategies to counter the flawed theoretical and practical premise upon which their development planning is based. More fundamentally, there is a presumption which needs closer examination: with the increased international exposure and globalization of African economies, do these countries have any alternative but to follow the advice of these lending institutions? This practical dilemma is summed up in a critical analysis of Africa's relations with international lending institutions by A. M. Babu, a former minister of economic development and planning in Tanzania.

There is a limited scope for the expansion of demand for our tea, coffee, cashews, and other products, in that the population which consumes these primary commodities in the Western World grows at less than 2% annually. How many more cups of tea can a

British worker consume beyond what he is already consuming, however prosperous Britain becomes? He has already reached saturation point in the consumption of tea and there is just no room for more. No British importer would import an additional 7% of our tea when the demand at home was rising by less than 2%. *The World Bank knows about these hard facts of business life. Why then does it recommend us to borrow more in order to increase the production of crops whose development potential is so limited?* (1981: 43) (Emphasis added.)

Despite such obvious difficulties with the export-led strategy of development, the World Bank in both its 1981 and 1984 reports was still suggesting that Africa should seek to improve its international trading position by increasing exports of its primary products.

The agriculture-based and export-oriented development strategy suggested for the 1980s is an essential beginning to a process of long-term transformation, a prelude to industrialization. It is not a permanent course for any country, but one that in Africa generates resources more quickly [sic] than any alternative and benefits more people.
. . . .
A strategy focused on agriculture and exports is thus open-ended, a necessary beginning. It will help generate the resources Africa needs to consolidate its political and administrative forces, educate and improve the health of its people, and find out what will work and what will not. It will bring forth human talent now neglected and uncover physical resources not yet imagined. And it will open the way to a future whose shape we cannot yet see. (1981: 6-7)

We only need to point out (again) that it is exactly the same policies that the World Bank is suggesting that have been pursued by African countries since independence. In any case, the obvious consequence of the dilemma pointed out by A. M. Babu is that African economies are finding it increasingly difficult to remain afloat. In 1981, African earnings were $1 billion less than they were the previous year. The period between 1981 and 1985 showed very few signs of improvement (UN, 1985). There is no relief in sight; prices of most primary commodities are at their lowest level in 30 years. With the cost of imported goods soaring, propelled largely in recent years by the rising value of the dollar, the basic currency for most imports, African governments have been forced to borrow heavily from outside sources. Currently, the average debt service ratio to export earnings in Africa is about 50 percent. Table 2.5 is a summary of the evolution of Africa's external debt between 1974 and 1983.[6] Robert L. Curry, Jr., using United Nations statistics, estimated that between 1973 and 1977 the undisbursed external debt for African countries rose from $9.5 billion to $21.0 billion. Furthermore, "the outstanding disbursed debt to gross continental product increased from 72.5 percent to 95.8 percent in relation to export receipts, each proportion being relatively high contrasted to elsewhere in the Third World" (1979: 15). Although he went on to point out that the ratio of debt-service payments to export earnings remained a constant 10 percent in the period 1977–1979, due to the relatively higher grant com-

Table 2.5
Sub-Saharan Africa: Public and Private Debt (1971–83) (US $ million)

	1974	1976	1978	1979	1980	1981	1982	1983
Debt Outstanding Disbursements Only	12,524.1	17,745.0	29,204.4	36,585.6	42,903.8	47,864.7	53,741.8	58,506.6
Disbursements	3,023.1	4,099.0	7,786.8	8,655.6	10,243.9	10,096.8	11,439.9	11,479.1
Principal Repayments	839.5	1,212.1	1,492.8	1,963.1	2,598.0	2,958.3	3,195.4	3,814.5
Net Flows	2,183.7	2,183.7	2,887.7	6,294.0	7,645.7	7,138.5	8,244.4	7,664.4
Interests Payments	405.9	522.5	958.5	1,395.6	2,129.6	2,178.4	2,657.5	2,839.3
Net Transfers	1,777.8	2,365.3	5,353.5	5,296.8	5,516.1	4,960.1	5,587.0	4,825.3
Total Debt Service	1,245.4	1,734.6	2,451.3	3,358.7	4,727.6	5,136.7	5,852.9	6,653.8

Source: *World Bank, World Debt Tables: External Debt of Developing Countries, 1984–85 edition* (Washington, D.C., 1985): 29.

ponent in official development assistance to Africa, recent figures indicate that the situation has grown much worse. A comparison between 1985 data and a 1982 IMF study should be instructive here.

A 1982 study by the International Monetary Fund showed that in 1981 the public and publicly guaranteed long-term external debt of African countries increased by $4.4 billion to about $45 billion, following a similar increase in 1979. The same study projected Africa's debt to be $60 billion by the end of 1982. The study traced these debt figures directly to the decline in the value of exports which, in 1981, had declined 10 percent for Africa as a whole, but 40 percent in Ghana, 24 percent in Zaire, and 20 percent in Ivory Coast, Kenya, and Zambia (IMF, 1982: 96). As we have already noted, any decline in the value (and volume) of export earnings inevitably has negative consequences on economic development. Thus, in the period under study, the IMF stated that:

the non-oil developing countries of Africa [minus South Africa] experienced considerably lower growth in 1982 than in 1980, together with much the same rate in inflation and, once again, a very large current account deficit in the balance of payments. Real GDP in these countries grew in 1981, on average, by only about [1.5] percent—even less than the average for the period 1978-80. In combination with population growth rate of about 2.5 percent per annum, this record implies that real per capita income has stagnated during the whole period 1978-81. (1982: 6)

We have already pointed out that there was further stagnation during 1980-1983. The IMF study concluded that to make matters worse, consumer prices were accelerating at an annual rate of 27 percent for the whole continent while per capita output was declining. The worst case was represented by Ghana, which had an inflation rate of 200 percent in 1981–1982.

It has been necessary to review data on Africa's economic performance in the 1970s because it helps to bring to the fore the magnitude of the current problem, especially when we see, that instead of improving, African economies have been declining. The irony of the African situation now is that whenever an economy *stagnates,* it is cause for celebration, because a stagnating economy is better than a declining one!

AFRICA AND INTERNATIONAL FINANCIAL INSTITUTIONS: THE HIGH PRICE OF INTERDEPENDENCE

It should be clear by now that Africa has paid a high price for its incorporation into the international capitalist system. As prices of the export commodities have declined, the balance-of-payments situation of African countries has worsened considerably; this includes even energy-exporting countries such as Nigeria and the People's Republic of the Congo. As a result of the balance-of-payments crisis, roughly a dozen sub-Saharan countries have been compelled to enter into standby arrangements with the IMF for Fund-supported adjustment programs each year since 1979 (UN, 1984). Fund-supported adjustment programs have drawn criticism from various quarters for their inappropriateness and for their irrelevant and biased notions regarding what the fundamental causes of the balance-of-payments crisis in Africa. In a speech sharply critical of the IMF, at the Royal Commonwealth Society in London on March 20, 1985, Julius Nyerere, former president of Tanzania, accused the IMF of a variety of misdealings.

There is one International Agency ... which is now increasingly being used to back up anti-internationalist actions. The I.M.F. was established to bring stability to world trade, and to encourage its expansion. Its decision making is virtually controlled by five major industrialized countries; for some purposes the U.S.A. alone can at least veto a decision by all other I.M.F. members. The I.M.F. has virtually ceased to concern itself with the economic problems of the Rich Countries for which it was originally conceived. It has become largely an instrument for economic and ideological control of poor countries by the rich ones. Thus, for example, when poor countries are in deficit—for whatever reason—they turn to the I.M.F. They need foreign exchange urgently, and the World bank as well as bilateral creditors and Aid Donors become very reluctant indeed to continue their support in the absence of an agreement with the Fund.

Yet in practice the conditions on which I.M.F. credits can be obtained are inappropriate to the circumstances of Africa—probably of the whole Third World. The I.M.F. is not designed to deal with structural imbalances; its credits are short term, and very expensive, at 9% interest, 3 years grace period and 3 years repayment. It uses its conditionality as a means of rationing its decreased resources in proportion to World trade. And every Third World country knows the litany of conditions with which it will be confronted. (Nyerere, 1985a: 8-9)

Nyerere's views about the IMF seem to be universally accepted in Africa, if not in the entire Third World. The IMF, on the other hand, has consistently argued the appropriateness of its measures in attempting to put Africa's economic house in order. The IMF, for example, has argued that the balance-of-payments difficulties result from excessive domestic demand and poor fiscal and monetary management—problems that can be resolved by balancing the budget, curbing the money supply, cutting subsidies, and establishing a realistic exchange rate (Nowzad, 1982: 9-10). As can be seen, the IMF's position clearly suggests that the paramount origins of the crisis are domestic.

In the already-cited and much-debated Berg report, the World Bank (1981) attempted to draw a balanced assessment of the sources of the economic crisis in Africa. The report raised three fundamental issues.

1. Internal constraints based on structural factors that evolved from historical circumstances or from the physical environment. These include underdeveloped human resources, the economic disruption that accompanied decolonization and postcolonial consolidation, climate and geographic factors hostile to development and rapidly growing population.
2. Adverse trends in the international economy, particularly since 1974. These include "stagflation" in the industrialized countries, higher energy prices, the relatively

slow growth of trade in primary products, and—for copper and iron ore exporters—adverse terms of trade.

3. Domestic policy inadequacies, of which three are critical. First, trade and exchange-
rate policies have overprotected industry, held back agriculture, and absorbed much
administrative capacity. Second, too little attention has been paid to administrative
constraints in mobilizing and managing resources for development; given the widespread weakness of planning, decision-making, and management capacities, public
sectors frequently become overextended. Third, there had been a consistent bias
against agriculture in price, tax, and exchange-rate policies. (World Bank, 1981: 4)

Adverse international trends notwithstanding, it is common knowledge that
both the IMF and the World Bank have emphasized domestic policy inadequacies more than historical internal constraints and "adverse trends in the international economy" as the basis of the current economic crisis; this theory is at
the center of the continuing disagreement between these two institutions and
African countries regarding adjustment. African countries have argued that
most of their deficit problems can be traced to three basic developments: the
two (1973–1974, 1979) oil price shocks, which more than quadrupled the cost
of energy—all payable in foreign currency; the slow growth in world trade in
primary commodities, as already discussed in the previous section; and the
persistently rising prices of imported manufactured goods, especially after the
floating of the dollar in 1973 (Rwegasira, 1984: 451). Due to these factors,
Rwegasira, among others, estimates that the external debt for the non-oil African region rose from $42 billion in 1978 to about $75 billion in 1983, at a
time when the cost of loans was rising rapidly. There is no precise figure representing how much sub-Saharan Africa currently owes because of the different ways in which debts are calculated. Thus, the $90 billion figure that for-
mer president Nyerere cited at the beginning of 1985 could be grossly
underestimated (Nyerere, 1985b: 1). In any case, the demonstrable weakness
of the African economies makes any figure approaching $100 billion in debt
too much to absorb.

For its part, however, the IMF has rightly argued that in some African countries, a rapid but inefficient growth of the public sector has contributed to the
deficit problem and directly to inflation, with increases in money supply. As
we have pointed out, Zaire has done exactly that. But again, the case of Zaire
and its corrupt government cannot be generalized to apply to the rest of the
continent. For example, in the now familiar case of the dispute between Tanzania and the IMF (*Africa Report,* November–December 1985), Tanzania,
while acknowledging problems in its public sector, has argued that the nation-
alized industries were not as inefficient and unproductive as the IMF claimed.
Furthermore, Tanzania, on its own initiative, had undertaken serious steps to
curb corruption and eliminate unproductive public corporations. Indeed, Tanzania has argued time and again that the IMF should seriously look at the high
interest rates that Africa and the rest of the Third World have been saddled
with since 1973, when the world entered the era of the "floating exchange."

The problem of the floating exchange needs more emphasis than it has been given up to now. Bahram Nowzad and others who have discussed the problem have only given it cursory emphasis or have been apologists for the IMF position.

Given the differential rates of inflation that have been characteristic of the post-1973 era and the divergent policies followed in the major countries, a worldwide regime of flexible rates has been the only realistic option. Unfortunately, there seems to be no viable and generally acceptable alternative in present circumstances. *And whatever relative merits of fixed and floating rates, exchange-rate developments reflect world economic and political conditions—in particular the degree of stability in the economies of major countries—and the Fund has little influence over them.* (1982: 6) (Emphasis added.)

But that is precisely the point. If the Fund admittedly has little influence over exchange rate development, and since exchange rate development is at the core of increased indebtedness, it is ironic that the Fund should impose the conditionalities that are its current trademark. It is evident that the Fund tends to assume that any country that needs to borrow must have been incompetent or careless and therefore would benefit from its guidance, at a price. As we have seen, the IMF also works on the assumption that most balance-of-payment problems are caused domestically. This latter view is vehemently disputed by an international banker who is familiar with the African situation. Antonio-Gabriel M. Cunha (1985: 21-24) notes that of the six main factors which contributed to the long-term African structural problems, five were external, and one natural:

1. Crushing commodity prices, often aggravated by restricted access to western markets
2. Drought-triggered falls in output levels
3. The prolonged recession abroad
4. High interest rates internationally
5. An ever-rising dollar and
6. A squeeze on the flow of credit.

Cunha concludes that "under the burden of these factors, the long-standing weakness—not failures—of sub-Saharan Africa's economic structures became more apparent" (1985: 21).

Nonetheless, the Fund rejects the idea that the origin of a deficit should be taken into account in determining the degree of conditionality imposed. As Sidney Dell comments, the IMF has justified its position with the argument that

both internal and external factors may be present in many situations. [However] in terms of adjustment, it is suggested, a more important consideration is whether the imbalance is transitory, and therefore self-serving, or is likely to persist. If it is likely to persist, the country will need to undertake adjustment regardless of the internal or exogenous character of the deficit. (1981: 19)

Given the position adopted by the IMF regarding the nature of the deficit problem, it is not surprising that some African countries (among them Tanzania and Nigeria) have taken an increasingly confrontational attitude in their dealings with the IMF. The position taken by Tanzania and Nigeria, among others, regarding conditionalities makes political and economic sense in an indirect way. African countries that have adopted IMF conditionalities have not fared any better, as the cases of Ghana (1983), Uganda (1980–1981), and Zambia (1982–1983, 1985) clearly demonstrate. All these countries accepted the IMF conditionalities; they also represent some of the worst economic sinking ships on the continent. As of early 1986, the devaluation of the Ghanaian cedi had brought it down to around C100 to the dollar (*Africa Confidential,* January 15, 1986). Since 1983, the cedi has collapsed from a rate of less than three cedis to the dollar, a fall of over 3000 percent, although doubts have always persisted regarding the implementation of IMF sponsored devaluation. The Ghanaian government under Jerry Rawlings—and Milton A. Obote in Uganda—had counted on this dramatic devaluation and other IMF austerity measures as the key to reversing Ghana's economic decline. But in 1985 exports valued at $630 million still lagged $95 million behind imports, which at $725 million were less than half the level needed to put factories back into production. Raw materials and spares for industrial processes, as well as fertilizer and implements for agriculture, were still in seriously short supply.

In the immediate sense, as devaluations have been implemented in Ghana, the effect has been severe liquidity problems with importers unable to open up lines of credit supplied as overseas aid. In 1985, for example, a total of $517 million had been pledged as foreign aid. However, local businessmen could not find enough local currency to take advantage of the pledged aid. The result was that in 1984 imports were less than 50 percent of the 1969 figure.

In addition, while devaluation led to equally high cost-of-living increases, the producer price of cocoa—Ghana's principal cash crop—rose only 366 percent between 1983 and 1985, which suggests that, for peasant farmers, it was unprofitable to grow and harvest the crop. As a result, aging cocoa trees are not being replaced. In one sense, however, reduction in cocoa production may prove beneficial for Ghana in the long run because the government will have to rethink its investment policies. Obviously even in the good years, when production was at its highest, peasant farmers were not getting their due share because of international prices and bureaucratic interference in the form of cocoa marketing boards, which appropriated a substantial portion of profits from cocoa (Price, 1984). The suggestion that reduced cocoa production may be a blessing in disguise for Ghana will be discussed in chapter 6.

As 1986 wore on, external debt was becoming more of a burden for Ghana as more loans fell due, including some of the debts repudiated by the Acheampong regime in 1972 and reinstated on relatively easier terms in 1974. In 1985, debt servicing took up 67 percent of Ghana's export earnings, although was not immediately apparent because Ghana utilized its IMF drawings. However, the IMF payments were themselves to be reimbursed beginning in 1986. It is not quite clear how Ghana will manage to repay $600 million to the IMF, as the economy continues to show signs of serious strain, bordering on catastrophe. The Ghanaian example can probably be applied to Zambia, Zaire, Sudan, etc., thus further raising the question of the nature of the relationship between African countries and international financial institutions.

How about the politics of implementing IMF conditionalities in Africa? In recent years, the IMF has been accused, among other things, of being insensitive to politics. But that accusation is largely inaccurate. It is common knowledge that the voting power in the IMF reflects the realities of economic and financial power in the world because the countries with the largest economies make the greatest contribution to the financial resources of the Fund (Nowzad, 1982: 3). The political leadership of these large economies in recent years has reinforced the IMF position regarding both the causes of and solutions to the economic and financial crisis in the Third World. Thus, the familiar demands of the IMF, such as reduction in the size of public spending (less government), and inflation reduction (credit control, devaluation), have been the same themes officially advocated by countries such as the United States and Great Britain.

Ironically, the position adopted by industrialized countries today regarding IMF conditionalities (with the exception of the United States) does not reflect their own position after World War II when their economies had been wrecked by the havoc of World War II. Sidney Dell, for example, has pointed out that there is

startling similarity between the views held today by developing country members of the Fund and the views that were being vigorously advocated by the Europeans at a time when they, too, had to face major balance-of-payments pressure of a structural character. (1981: 14)

For that reason, continues Dell, citing the example of Great Britain, Churchill's war cabinet had instructed British negotiators at Bretton Woods to adopt the position that

a deficit country should not be required to introduce a "deflationary policy, enforced by dear money and similar measures, having the effect of causing unemployment; for this would amount to restoring, subject to insufficient safeguards, the evils of the old automatic gold standard." (1981: 2)

Whether or not the IMF and its supporters agree on the negative effects of its programs, there is ample evidence to suggest that its conditionalities have been devastating to countries which have implemented them. For example, a recent book (Wionczek et al., 1985) catalogues failure after failure of IMF programs in Latin America and points out that "issues raised [by industrial countries] almost look exclusively at the economic and financial aspects of the crisis, ignoring the critical issues of how long countries in the southern hemisphere can endure the painful IMF-tailored adjustment programs" (xi).

Another study by the Economic Commission for Latin America and the Caribbean (ECLAC, 1985) concurs with the observation of Wionczek et al. The ECLAC points out that both the adjustment process and the renegotiation of the external debt have proved very costly for the countries of the region. According to the ECLAC, between 1981 and 1983 the Latin American and Caribbean countries achieved a substantial reduction in the deficit on the balance-of-payments current account, thus meeting the basic objective of the adjustment policies; but this was due almost exclusively to the tremendous reduction in the volume of imports. Under such circumstances, the adjustment was sharply recessive in nature and in many countries had gone hand-in-hand with a considerable slowdown of domestic activity and a deterioration of the employment situation, thus further depressing the economy. At the same time, the debt-renegotiation agreements, which had enabled these countries to avoid even more serious balance-of-payments crises, also contributed to a sharp increase in the cost of external financing, and overwhelmingly benefited the creditor banks from the developed capitalist world.

Because of the increasing debt burden, Latin American countries (at an economic conference held in January 1984 in Quito, Ecuador) proposed that debt service not exceed a *"reasonable"* proportion of the debtor countries' export earnings. However, President Nyerere of Tanzania was more blunt: "If the rich refuse to discuss methods by which the Third World can repay its debt should we continue to try and pay on the terms set even at the cost of letting our people starve?" (*West Africa,* April 1, 1985: 604) President Nyerere's public statement only reflects the attitudes of many Third World countries that have privately raised the issue of nonpayment (or postponement of payment) of interest rates in times of financial difficulties. The problem, however, is that neither the African nor the Latin American and Caribbean countries have seriously examined an alternative beyond the current international economic structures; thus their complaints regarding the IMF are little more that the cries of the defeated.

Most of these countries have sought to solve their economic problems through the so-called New International Economic Order (NIEO)—a forum under the auspices of the United Nations which proposes, among other things, the institution of a framework for the transfer of technology from the developed to the underdeveloped world and support for better terms of trade more favorable to Third World countries. Since its inception in the early 1970s, the NIEO has achieved very little, partly because many of the proposals advanced by Third World countries were unrealistic with lists that reflected very little of the global economy. Thus a more important consideration against a pro-

NIEO stance, however, is the structural change in the international economic system itself. As many studies have shown (Shaw, 1985: 6; Ruggie, 1983), there has been a profound change in the dialectic of the world capitalist economy in the sense that it has become more global and more hierarchical. A few countries in the Third World (such as Brazil and Taiwan in terms of industrialization, or Malaysia and Indonesia in terms of agriculture) are being elevated to more prominent status. Most African countries, on the other hand, have been relegated to what Shaw calls "historical irrelevance." The latter group of countries are those which produce primary products no longer considered essential to sustain industrial life in developed countries (such as sisal in Tanzania and cocoa in Ghana). This structural shift, for example, has meant that Nigeria, which was a leading source of palm oil in the 1960s and early 1970s, has been replaced by Indonesia, while Liberia has been supplanted by Malaysia's rubber exports. Nigeria and Liberia have, therefore, been further peripheralized in the world economy, making the concept of the "Fourth World" more credible.

The consequence for Africa of this structural change in the world economy is enormous. It means that Africa is increasingly becoming marginal to international commodity exchange (not to mention its loss of strategic value). As peripheralization of the African economy continues, the strategy of comparative advantage becomes more and more suspect. For how can comparative advantage work when your products are no longer in demand despite low-cost production? How can one effectively negotiate a NIEO when the cards to bargain with are constantly eroding in value?

WHAT IS TO BE DONE? AN INTROVERTED LOOK AT AFRICA'S ECONOMIC CRISIS

All the above having been said, it's imperative that the most fundamental point regarding development should be raised. The point is simple. In the final analysis, Africa is ultimately responsible for what happens to her *herenow* and *hereafter.* History cannot be forgotten or ignored in assessing Africa's condition, and indeed a substantial portion of this chapter did just that, tracing the historical evolution of product specialization in Africa's international economic relations. While the structural constraints had already been placed on various countries on the continent, it is not totally correct, or even desirable, that we dwell on those historical characteristics as the sole basis for assessing the potential economic future of the continent.

Without hesitation, we contend that the blind acceptance of comparative advantage by African countries at the time of independence signaled the beginnings of the current crisis. By adopting comparative advantage as a basis for development, the African leadership boxed itself into an untenable position, *for comparative advantage/product specialization required that problems emanating from that specialization be resolved internationally.* By accepting and emphasizing product specialization, African countries lost the initiative, indeed the entire basis, for independent economic action. Therefore, it is not surprising that, as economic conditions have worsened, African countries (along with others in the Third World) have sought to resolve these problems through international fora such as the New International Economic Order (Rothstein, 1977; 1979) and the Lome Conventions (Ravenhill, 1985). Both Rothstein and Ravenhill have shown how these fora have failed to alleviate the basic problems associated with international economic interdependence: the commodities problem, transfer of technology and industrial goods, and generalized debt relief. The industrial countries, to a large extent, have not been willing to give up their advantage in the structural relationship; and primary export production lies at the center of the crisis for the nonindustrialized countries. In the specific case of Lome, Marcussen and Torp have argued that

the new aspects of the Lome Convention (the STABEX Scheme and the chapter on industrial co-operation) do not . . . contribute basically to new tendencies in the international division of labour. With regard to STABEX [Agreement on Stabilization of the Export Earnings], it seems that the countries already most integrated in the world market are those which primarily benefit from the scheme, while, for example, the landlocked countries in West Africa, with a relatively substantial inter-regional trade and only a few exportable products, cannot take advantage of the scheme . . . [furthermore,] the Lome Convention cannot *in itself* secure the creation of capitalist development processes.

The two authors conclude their argument by reiterating a point we made earlier.

The Lome Convention is not a model for a new international economic order, but rather has to be looked at in its historical perspective: as a partly modified but nevertheless continuous effort to preserve an already established international division of labour. (1982: 62)

The authors, however, also point out that despite the difficulties associated with implementing the Lome Conventions, or the NIEO in general, the possibility should not be excluded that a few relatively well-off peripheral economies can take advantage of the different elements in the Conventions in a development strategy combining the activities of international capital. It should be apparent, however, that the number of countries that can possibly take advantage of the schemes is so small that, in overall terms, both Lome and NIEO arrangements are largely more symbolic than substantive.

In clear recognition of their dilemma, African governments, through the *Lagos Plan of Action* (LPA), have sought to establish a new pattern of development based on four basic guidelines that will presumably lead to self-reliance and self-sustained development:

1. The use of Africa's vast resources to meet the aspirations of the people

2. A change from total reliance on export of a few raw materials to a growth path based on a combination of natural resources, entrepreneurial, managerial, and technical resources, and the restructuring and expansion of the domestic market

3. The mobilization of Africa's human and material resources for industrial development, the outside contributions being only supplementary to domestic efforts, and

4. The promotion of African economic integration in order to create a continent-wide framework for economic cooperation for development based on collective self-reliance. (OAU, 1982)

These guidelines clearly stand out as highly desirable ideals. But the record regarding their implementation is different. To put it simply, the rhetoric contained in the *Lagos Plan of Action* (LPA) has not been matched by implementation because, again, most African countries instead of looking for internal solutions to their economic problems, have sought extracontinental sources to implement their plans. Furthermore, "Member States [of the OAU] have failed to reflect in their national development plans the decisions they have taken collectively in other (multinational) fora" (Browne and Cummings, 1984: 59). Browne and Cummings go on to state that

genuine cooperation . . . amongst the countries of Africa has very shallow roots. Most economic relationships run from Africa to the former colonial powers in Europe, a pattern which was firmly fixed during the colonial era. Inter-African telephone and telegraphic communications as well as postal services and even air travel are often most expeditiously accomplished by routing via Europe rather than directly from one African capital to another, thus enhancing the isolation of the African countries from one another. Politico-economic commercial arrangements such as the Lome agreements effectively tie Africa to Europe. . . . In the absence of . . . a continental outlook, . . . the LPA is not likely to be achievable, especially when one realizes that the LPA requires its participants to veer dramatically from the economic path which they are currently pursuing and to link their economic futures to that of their equally fragile neighbours. (1984: 61)

A serious examination of LPA suggests that, qualitatively and substantively, the document is not very different from the Berg Report. Indeed, the Berg Report saw itself as complementary to LPA. This fact, by implication, points to the most fundamental issue regarding development policy in Africa today: The African *leadership* (both ideologically and politically) cannot transcend its historical role as successor to the colonial state, and has failed to evolve into a leadership capable of fundamentally transforming society. It is caught in a vicious circle of political and ideological contradiction through its insistence on the necessity of holding international interdependence sancrosant. In chapter 5, our task will be to show why and how the postcolonial state in Africa, along with the leadership, has failed to perform the basic tasks of transforming society. Chapter 6 will attempt a theoretical construct of an alternative future for Africa, which will incorporate suggestions regarding a different outlook to the international system, and a necessary change in leadership. Whether we call it a revolution, or simply a change of guard, a new leadership must evolve to take over the tasks of development which will have, as a minimum objective, reduction in international interdependence (since current interdependence is really dependence), and new class realignments internally. Contrary to others, we do not believe LPA is the answer. It is not even a beginning.

CONCLUSION

In this chapter we have argued that the nature of the development crisis in Africa can be partly traced to the historical structural relationship between African and the developed capitalist world, which evolved through several centuries. Basic to this structural relationship was the evolution of product specialization, which has been injurious to the African economies by exposing them to a wider system beyond the control or meaningful influence of African actors. The weakness of African countries/economies in the international system derives from its specialization of primary, raw material production. In relative terms, African raw materials historically have not fared very well against industrial goods in international trade. For that reason, we suggested that Africa must get out of that historically determined specialization if a solution to the current crisis is to be found. How Africa may begin to get out of that specialization will be the subject of chapter 6.

We have also argued that the historical structural relationship between Africa and the developed capitalist world is not the only problem. Classes that have monopolized state power since independence are equally to blame, since these classes have not sought ways to alleviate the economic crisis. Indeed, the most concerted effort by African governments in the past decade to solve the economic crisis has been in the proclamation of the *Lagos Plan of Action*. But due to the ideological predisposition of the classes that control state power, African governments do not see a solution to the economic crisis outside the international framework. For all practical purposes, LPA is a dead letter. The lessons of history obviously have not had an effect on the actions of the leadership in Africa. In the next chapter we seek to elaborate on the nature of the evolution of development theory in order to analyze the current stalemate in the theorizing regarding the crisis in underdevelopment.

It is apparent that the relationship between sub-Saharan Africa and the international capitalist economic system is very real and that for the most part, the distribution of rewards in the system is highly skewed against Africa. However, the decline of African economies should also be viewed in terms of the internal historical constraints that may have little to do with the international capitalist system. In light of recent theorizing about the "World System" as an integrated whole (Wallerstein, 1974 and others), our alluding to "internal historical constraints" may prove controversial. But unless we examine (1) the internal dynamism (or lack of it) of a good portion of the sub-Saharan economy, and (2) whether indeed the whole of Africa forms part of a world capitalist system which has been fully penetrated and incorporated, we may be missing a crucial explanation for the economic stagnation of the continent.

We suggest that the most fruitful way to do that would be to examine the evolution of capitalist relations in Africa, not only in those centers which obviously have direct or indirect links to the international economy—that is, coffee plantations or import substitution industries jointly owned by multinationals and African governments—but also the kinds of social relations that prevail in the rural areas, distant from the obvious centers of capitalist development. We seek to do this in chapter 4, a process we call "disaggregating capitalism in Africa."

NOTES

1. Reformulation of *comparative advantage* theory has been attempted by advocates of *free trade* who make the assumption that an international economic system based on the free movement of commodities and financial resources remains the only chance for maintaining an equilibrium of sorts in the system where demand and supply of resources (both commodity and finance) act upon each other much as they do in the domestic economy. Attempts to refine the theory, however, have been relatively unsuccessful, because the underlying weakness in the original formulation of the theory is that it emphasizes *equilibrium* in the international movement of relevant factors—capital, labor, commodities—other things being equal. The problem is that other things are never equal. (See, for example, Meir, 1963.)

2. There are several studies that have dealt with the long-term historical origins of product specialization in African-European relations. See, for example, Rodney, 1972; Wallerstein, 1974; 1980; Brett, 1972.

3. This position was strongly advocated by earlier modernization studies of the late 1950s and 1960s. A sample of these studies which emphasized diffusion of new consumption pattern and culture included Almond and Coleman, 1960; Binder et al., 1971; Rostow, 1960.

4. Calculated from figures in table 2.1.

5. United Republic of Tanzania, *Background to the Budget 1966–67,* 35–42.

6. The World Bank's Debtor Reporting System (DRS), which is the basic source for most data, does not capture the total external indebtedness of developing countries. The two principal omissions are short-term debt, meaning external liabilities with original maturity, and the debt of developing countries that do not report formally under the DRS, such as the use of IMF credit. (World Bank, 1985b: vii)

The omission on the reporting system partly accounts for the glaring difference between the officially reported debt level of African countries—$170 billion in July 1985 (*West Africa,* July 29, 1985)—and the estimated $300 billion suggested by other estimates.

3

Evolution of Development Theory and Its Application to African Development

INTRODUCTION

This chapter builds upon the discussion in the previous chapter in one important way. It attempts to place the theory of comparative advantage within a wider discussion regarding the evolution of development theory in general, especially after World War II. By tracing the evolution of development theory since World War II, one cannot help but recognize the political forces that shaped the ideology of development (or developmentalism) and the opposing political forces that were associated with the emergence of the self-proclaimed socialist world under the tutelage of Soviet leadership. While most theorizing about Third World development took place in the capitalist West, the preferred solution to the perceived condition of low socioeconomic development was geared toward challenging a socialist development alternative for the Third World. The ideological current of anti-Sovietism, especially by American authors, made it possible for subtitles such as "A Non-Communist Manifesto" (Rostow, 1960) not only palatable, but ideologically necessary. This followed the recognition of the Soviet Union as a world power inimical to the interests of the West.

The challenge to the West posed by the ascendance of the Soviet Union was understood to be multifaceted—the obvious challenge being military, especially in light of a divided Europe. But subsequent to the initial postwar resolution of the problems in Europe, the other challenge was for the minds and hearts of Third World peoples. Indeed, the ideological competition between the West and the East made it possible for political independence to occur in most of the colonized Third World. It became increasingly clear that the West could not maintain any decent moral-ideological stand under conditions of colonialism. It is partly within the context of the ideological competition with socialism that Franklin D. Roosevelt's insistence upon the self-determination clause in the Atlantic Charter of 1941 can be understood. The other context in which Roosevelt's insistence upon the implementation of the whole Atlantic

Charter can be understood is the general ascendance of American capitalism, and America's philosophical opposition to the closed markets of European colonies in the Third World. Either way, the end of World War II, coupled with the emergence of the United States as a world power, colonialism in its rudimentary form had seen its day.

The end of colonialism serves as a convenient starting point for the study of the evolution of development theory in general and its application to Africa specifically. It should be pointed out, however, that development theory, especially in the way it came to be applied to Africa, had historical roots in the study of development in Latin America. Latin America has served as a laboratory for development theories due to its relatively longer period of independence, beginning in the nineteenth century. In our discussion of development theory, therefore, it is inescapable that the influence of Latin America should be discussed.

This chapter thus attempts to do three things. First, it surveys the premises upon which the modernization theory of development are based, and offers a general critique of the approach. Second, it traces the emergence of dependency theory as a countervailing paradigm to the modernization approach. Dependency theory is examined in detail with a formal model of basic assumptions. And finally, we attempt to show how scholars and theoreticians in general have attempted to move beyond the dependency approach having realized its weaknesses. In this regard, the notions of *dependent development* and *internationalization of capital* are closely examined in order to assess the current status of development theory and and to determine whether dependent development and internationalization of capital are useful (or even valid) concepts in relating development theory to Africa's development experience.

In recent years, a number of studies have appeared dealing with a general synthesis of the evolution of development theory. This chapter in part summarizes and synthesizes those studies. With the exception of Marcussen and Torp, however, none of the cited studies specifically deal with Africa. One of our tasks, therefore, will be to relate the general theorizing about the internationalization of capital and dependent development to the African development experience.

MODERNIZATION THEORY: A GENERAL OBSERVATION

Modernization theory was partly stimulated by the experience of the countries that gained independence after World War II and by the emergence of the United States as a leading Western power. By the latter token, Western (but especially American) interest in the Third World was not merely academic, but had the distinct political objective of countering Soviet influence. As Eugene Staley stated in 1961:

The future of underdeveloped countries is a vital matter for the future of Western civilization, including the security and the way of life of the American people. Should the communist power bloc succeed in bringing most of the underdeveloped countries into its orbit and cutting their links with the West, the effect on U.S. security would be disastrous. (1961: 3–4)

Elsewhere, Staley argued that the challenge of Communism posed a decisive test for Western civilization because

the Communists offer a competing system which borrows the industrial technology of the West but repudiates Western political freedom.... Communism now directs its main drive toward the underdeveloped countries. The choice of these countries between taking the Communist path or modernizing with Western aid and friendship will probably determine our own security and the course of world civilization. (1961: 3)

Staley's arguments were not isolated opinions of a single academician; neither were such arguments confined to academia. Samuel Huntington and Jorge Dominguez have pointed out that American scholarship followed the U.S. flag in the Cold War against the Soviet Union. Expansion of area studies in American universities went hand in hand with the expansion of American presence in Asia, the Middle East, Latin America, and Africa (1975: 1). The shared anticommunist concern between the academicians and the United States government is reflected in the 1957 *Report to the President by Vice President Nixon on his trip to Africa*. In the report, Nixon speculated that, similar to other parts of the Third World,

Africa is a priority target for the international communist movement. I gathered the distinct impression that the Communist leaders consider Africa today to be as important in their designs for world conquest as they considered China to be twenty-five years ago. (Emerson, 1967: 7)

It is through the close affinity between Western academicians and politicians' interests that modernization theory was variously accused of being a tool of "imperialism." Representative of this position is P. W. Preston's criticism that

"modernization theory" is the ideological child of the "cold war." The US theorists operating within the ambit of the notion of "containment" seek to secure allies for the US within the Third World. Competition with the USSR necessitates that self-interest be disguised; thus, in reply to offers of "socialism," the US presents "modernization" and membership of the "free world"; this I take to be the moral core of "modernization theory." (1985: 18)

Below are sets of assumptions and premises which seem to have guided modernization theorists in their study of underdeveloped countries.

Modernization Theory: Inventory of Premises

First, at a general level, modernization theory regarded underdeveloped countries as those that remained agricultural and rural, and whose populations were held in thrall by archaic social organizations and outmoded attitudes not compatible with sustained growth in production. Development would occur with industrialization, which would bring a massive shift of the labor force out of agriculture and other primary production sectors into processing and manufacturing. Of primary importance, however, was the emphasis of modernization theory on the change of values—from consummatory to instrumental—as expressed in the works of Daniel Lerner (1958), David Apter (1965), and to some extent Leonard Doob (1960). Development (or positive change) was conceived of as a gradual movement on a continuum of consummatory and instrumental values, with the latter as the ideal (or desired) objective—represented by Western society. Thus, according to Doob, "civilization refers to the culture, or the way of life, possessed by modern literate and industrial nations in Europe and America." (1960: 2)

Daniel Lerner made the same point two years earlier when he wrote that "Western society still provides the most developed model of societal attributes (power, wealth, skill, rationality) which Middle East spokesmen continue to advocate as their own goal." (1958: 47) According to Lerner, in order for development to take place, the village has to be replaced by towns, illiteracy by enlightenment, resignation by ambition, and piety by excitement. All these changes, it must be added, focus on the personal meaning of social change which Lerner calls "the transformations worked into the daily lifeways of individuals." Lerner operates on the assumption that increasing urbanization has tended historically to raise literacy; rising literacy has tended to increase media exposure; increasing media exposure has gone with wider economic participation (increase in per capita income) and political participation (voting and emergence of voluntary organization). He concludes that "the same basic model reappears in virtually all modernizing societies on all continents of the world regardless of variations in race, color, creed . . . indeed [Third World] modernizers will do well to study the historical sequence of Western growth." (1958: 46)

The *second* set of premises was purely economic. It was assumed that industrialization, because it requires high capital investment and a shift from animate to inanimate sources of energy, would bring about higher productivity, which would translate into higher national income. This, in turn, would make possible capital accumulation through savings, which would be reinvested in factories, machines, and infrastructural facilities. This would produce a multiplier effect, moving the economy progressively to higher and higher levels of development. Modernization theory advocated (and presumed) the vigorous participation of the West in helping the Third World to achieve the objective of rapid economic development because, without such help, the West would stand to lose in a political contest with the Soviet Union. As Eugene Staley noted, "it is not societies with a mature industrial capitalism that are most susceptible to the Communist brand of revolutionary dictatorship. Rather, it is those which have begun to stir out of centuries-old poverty and ignorance but have not yet attained living conditions tolerable by modern standards." (1961: 383)

Third, on the social and psychological level, universal education was necessary because industrialization, unlike traditional agriculture, requires a population with higher skills, literacy, and creativity. As Daniel Lerner and Leonard Doob suggest, a new system of social values supportive of industrial growth—namely, personal discipline, punctuality, hard work, and responsiveness to monetary incentives—would be part of universal education.

Fourth, an important element of modernization theory was the benign role it conferred upon developed countries with regard to the elimination of underdevelopment in the rest of the world. Underdevelopment was seen primarily as a product of causes internal to the countries concerned. To help these countries out of the vicious circle of poverty, ignorance, and disease, the developed countries were required to extend assistance in the form of technical expertise, loans, and credits, and to train local entrepreneurs, technicians, and managers. The basis for this lay partly in the relative success of the Marshall plan in the rebuilding of postwar Europe; and it was hoped that similar success would be repeated in the Third World.

Of more significance, however, was the active involvement of U.S. policymakers in the administration of foreign assistance. Joan Spero (1981: 147–81) has shown how important foreign assistance was considered to be in the late 1950s, not only for its economic dimension, but also for its political role as a tool in the Cold War. Thus, according to one United States Senate study quoted by Spero:

A comprehensive and sustained program of American economic assistance aimed at helping the free underdeveloped countries to create the conditions for self-sustaining growth can, in the short run, materially reduce the danger of conflict triggered by aggressive minor powers, and can, say in two to three decades, result in an overwhelming preponderance of societies with a successful record of solving their problems without resort to coercion or violence. The establishment of such a preponderance of stable, effective and democratic societies gives the best promise of a favorable settlement of the Cold War and of a peaceful progressive world environment. (1981: 154)

Such assistance was thought important since development was considered to be the result of the innovations and changes generated in the developed countries and diffused or transferred (unilinearly) to the underdeveloped countries.[1] Such diffusion was assumed to be beneficial in its effect, serving to modernize whole countries (or regions) and raising the level of the more backward periphery to that of the central regions or urbanized areas. This assumption was also tied to the conception of a dual society in the Third World where one part of society was considered to be modern, developed, and urban, and the other was backward, feudal, and rural (Rostow, 1960).

Fifth, once diffusion had taken place, the underdeveloped societies would evolve democratic institutions similar to those found in the West—competitive political parties, periodic elections, representative institutions (parliament), constitutional governments, and judicial systems that would guarantee political liberties. These political developments, however, would be dependent on the transformation of the socioeconomic system (Almond and Verba, 1963; Lipset, 1961).

The Analysis

All the assumptions of modernization theory are based on the premise that underdevelopment is a condition all nations have experienced at some time in history. While some nations have managed to develop, others have not. According to A. F. K. Organski, an exponent of the "stages of growth" thesis,

the path of each nation through [the] first stage of [development] is unique . . . all were . . . "economically underdeveloped" nations, that is to say, preindustrial. All have had governments we call inefficient and undemocratic. And all have had to struggle with the problems of unification. (1967: 8)

Thus, according to Organski, underdevelopment is the absence (or low level) of development. Similar to others in the modernization tradition, Organski holds the notion that societies develop in a unilinear fashion from lower stages of development to higher ones. The titles to both W. W. Rostow's and Organski's books are indicative of this notion.

Rostow's five stages are listed as follows:

1. *The traditional society,* characterized by limited productive functions
2. *The preconditions for take-off stage,* characterized by a transformation in the traditional society in the ways necessary for it to exploit the fruits of modern society
3. *The take-off stage,* characterized by a steady economic growth based on effective investment and savings of about 5 to 10 percent of the GNP
4. *The drive to maturity,* characterized by a shift from relatively narrow complex of industry and technology to more complex processes—for example, a shift from coal and iron industries to machine tools, chemicals, and electrical equipment
5. *The age of high-mass consumption,* where in time, the leading sectors shift towards durable consumer goods and services—for example, automobiles, television, and refrigerators. (1960: 4–11)

The movement from one stage of growth to another is not characterized by any major conflict; rather, the transition is supposed to be a matter of course. So confident was Rostow in his theory of development that he came "to the view that it is possible . . . to break down the story of each national economy—and sometimes the history of regions—according to a [set of stages of growth] (1960: 1). He further argued that it was possible to fit any society into one of his five categories (1960: 4).

In modernization theory, no distinction is made between growth and development. Development is regarded as almost synonymous with industrialization, although it would be unfair to say that every author within this tradition treats the two concepts as one. Nonetheless, for the most part, industrialization is considered as a prerequisite for development, both political and economic. According to Organski, with the coming of industrialization, the shape and work of the nation change: "The early stages of economic development . . . can be measured in a rough way by the percentage of workers engaged in agriculture; a nation [is] considered economically developed when more than 50% of its economically active men have moved out of agricultural work into other pursuits" (1967: 6). According to this reasoning, the smaller the labor force engaged in agriculture, the more industrialized the nation (and, presumably, the more developed).

The fallacy in this argument is an obvious one. There is *no* necessary relationship between urbanization, industrialization, and "development" as such. All these variables can occur independent of each other. This is not to say, however, that they could not happen simultaneously. It is the theoretical linkage that we question.

While industrialization is easy to characterize as a shift from the use of animate to inanimate sources of energy, and the establishment of a factory system in society, modernization (or modernity) in its usage seems to be so wide-ranging as to include the totality of change. As James S. Coleman suggested in the conclusion to one of the most influential books on development in the 1960s:

A *modern society* is characterized, among other things, by a comparatively high degree of urbanization, widespread literacy, comparatively higher per capita income, extensive geographical and social mobility, a relatively high degree of commercialization and industrialization of the economy, an extensive and penetrative network of mass communication media, and in general, by widespread participation and involvement by members of the society in modern social and economic process. (Almond and Coleman, 1960: 532)

C. E. Black, another important author within modernization theory, characterized modernization as

the process by which historically evolved institutions are adapted to the rapidly changing functions that reflect the unprecedented increase in man's knowledge, permitting control over his environment that accompanied the scientific revolution. . . . [This revolution involves] a worldwide transformation affecting all human relationships. (1966: 7)

From the above characterization of modernity, we could disaggregate the concept of modernity into three analytical categories—the economic, socio-psychological, and political components. The economic component would involve the industrialization process and a general increase in the material output of society (GNP). The GNP could be used in an abstract way to measure the national wealth (Rostow, 1960: ix). The sociopsychological component would involve a change in societal values and attitudes, making them more compatible with changes in the economic sphere. Daniel Lerner, for example, saw the *mobile personality* as an essential attribute of development. He argued that a mobile society encourages rationality because the calculus of choice shapes individual behavior and conditions its rewards. As a result of mobility, individuals perceive social future to be manipulable and, in a way, control their own destiny (1958: 49).

David Apter (1965: 96–99), on the other hand, was particularly interested in the change of values. He treated modernization not in terms of the entire process of transformation from tradition to modernity, but more particularly in terms of the transitional phase between traditionalism (preindustrial) and industrialization. Apter was more concerned with *process* than with distinctions between relatively modernized and nonmodernized societies; and he focused his attention on *ideology, motivation* and *mobility,* as reflected in the changing roles of the members of modernizing societies. It was Apter's belief that a transformation of values was necessary (if not mandatory) for economic modernization to take place.

Political development, as already noted, was expected to result from economic development. Modernization theory, however, had difficulty in defining what political development entails, besides a resemblance to Western political systems. Thus in a search for a definition of political development within modernization theory, Lucian Pye found *ten* different usages (1966: 63–67). The confusion and uncertainty in defining political development was the beginning of a general crisis in modernization theory in general, as the reality of Third World development continued to defy the theory's assumptions. The confusion and uncertainty of modernization theory regarding political development was demonstrated by Huntington and Dominguez:

Political development is] in effect, a shorthand way of referring to the politics of the developing countries, that is, the poor or less industrialized countries of Asia, Africa and Latin America. In this sense, almost any study of aspects of the politics of these countries could be termed a study in political development even though the subject, concepts, and methods employed might be virtually identical with those that are used to study the politics of a "developed" country. (1975: 3–4)

Thus a survey study of the attitudes of citizens of Tanzania toward their government would often be called a study in political development, while the same questionnaire or study applied to Great Britain would not. Huntington and

Dominguez advised that, since the concept of political development was used in so many different ways, it was necessary to associate it with economic development, since political development derived from economic development. For Huntington and Dominguez, if any one definitional approach has priority, it is political development, conceived as the political consequences of modernization (1975: 5). Perhaps the most comprehensive characterization of political development was given by James S. Coleman whose structural-functional bias can be seen in the following definition:

The most general characteristic of [a modern political system] is in the relative high degree of differentiation, explicitness, and functional distinctiveness of political and governmental structures, each of which tends to perform for the political system as a whole, a regulatory role for the respective political and authoritative functions. (Almond and Coleman, 1960: 532)

The above discussion of modernization summarizes the assumptions of the theory. It cannot be denied that the theory had great appeal to Western (but especially American) theorists who saw a chance to transform whole societies according to the image of the West. Its unilinear assumption was breathtaking in its simplicity. The solution to underdevelopment was seen simply as a matter of infusing capital from the West. As one looks at modernization theory closely, one is struck by the inherent belief that England serves as an example for the development of backward areas elsewhere, and that England's historical transition from feudalism to capitalism represents the route which Third World countries should follow. As Ronald Chilcote has observed:

In the terms of definition employed by the diffusion model, medieval England was underdeveloped. National integration was lacking, poverty and illiteracy were the normal conditions of the serf. . . . Today England is seen as a success story of gradual progress from underdeveloped island to the developed national-state. (Chilcote and Edelstein, 1974: 5)

By the late 1960s and early 1970s, modernization theory had come under such strong criticism both from within and without, that it lost its appeal to most sectors of the academic community—both in the developed and underdeveloped countries. The most damning indictment against modernization theory was that despite some form of infusion of Western capital, development as such had not occurred in the Third World. The little development that occurred was beset by problems of increased inequality, inappropriate technology, etc. to make the whole theorizing laughable. Furthermore, the sociopsychological "determinants," à la Lerner and Apter, had not accompanied attempted industrialization. Finally, political development of the Western variety had not taken root. Instead of democratization, most Third World political systems became one-party or military dictatorships. Samuel Huntington's (1968) and others' attempts to grapple with problems of establishing "political order" in these societies signaled the failure of the theory to fully comprehend and explain the reality of Third World development. It is not surprising, therefore, that modernization had to be supplanted by another theory: dependency.

Modernization Theory: A General Critique

Modernization theory has been criticized on several grounds. The basic criticism, however, lies in the nonoccurrence of the anticipated results: the development of (Western-type) democratic institutions in the Third World, and the elimination of poverty through an overall increase in material wealth in those countries. The second major critique concerns the theory's treatment of Third World countries as autonomous units, operating in a world of their own without an external dimension—that is, the international economy. For that reason, the theory has been criticized as ahistorical. We elaborate on both criticisms below.

From within modernization theory itself, C. E. Black (1966: 191), for example, criticized Rostow's work for not accounting for the differences represented by traditional institutions in the Third World. Black argues that Rostow appears to be a liberal economic determinist who believes that the achievement of "high mass consumption" will tend to dissolve institutional differences among societies and orient them toward the model represented by the earlier modernizing societies, especially Britain. A. F. K. Organski fares no better because he also presents a periodization of politics—primitive unification, industrialization, national welfare, and abundance—in an almost perfect reflection of Rostow's economic stages. Thus Organski's scheme is essentially economic in its determinism.

Economic determinism leads to another criticism, that of lack of historical specificity. Modernization has been criticized for treating underdevelopment without any awareness of the historical reality of the world capitalist economy out of which, arguably, most conditions of underdevelopment have emerged (Wallerstein, 1974; Frank, 1967). Without the international dimension, modernization theory became amazingly simple and an easy way to explain underdevelopment. As Robert Rothstein has observed:

In retrospect, the economic growth theories of the 1950s oversimplified responses to complex problems. This is usually attributed to two factors: The need for a clear and attractive alternative to the Soviet Model of development and the tendency to use the relatively uncomplicated [sic] history of Western economic growth as a relevant analogy for the less developed countries . . . most of the available theories stressed easy stages of growth in which, once a missing link had been provided (finance or technology), economic growth would follow more or less automatically. (1977: 80–81)

Rothstein further points out that modernization theory said very little about the international economic system itself. Implicitly, the model rested on the notion that the system—that is, the pattern of relations established by the major economic powers, for example, the concept of free trade, the International Monetary Fund, the World Bank, General Agreement on Trade and Tariffs, etc.—would have a benign effect (Rothstein, 1977: 81). By adopting this posture, modernization theory was avoiding the discussion of the specific historical position that underdeveloped countries occupy within the polarized structure of the world capitalist economy.

In our discussion on comparative advantage in the last chapter, we pointed to the many obstacles that African countries face in their attempt to continue trading with advanced industrialized countries. With the continued evolution and change in international production through a New International Division of Labor (NIDL), with the geographic shift of most primary production to more productive regions such as the Pacific Basin, and with a technological revolution that is increasingly rendering raw materials from Africa redundant, expensive, and "unwanted," the African continent is becoming more and more peripheralized in world economic production. The external component of modernization theory, i.e., comparative advantage, has thus been proven ineffective. The combination of internal and external weaknesses of modernization theory made it inevitable that it should lose credibility in development theorizing. Magnus Blömstrom and Björn Hettne have aptly summarized the critique of modernization theory:

Methodologically neo-evolutionism is based on comparative statistics which neglect both the sources and the route of change. From a *logical* point of view there is, for example, the mistake of equating serialism with causal explanations of transitions. *Empirically,* it is easy to point out that any effort to classify societies using indicators of tradition and modernity soon breaks down. From a *moral* point of view, finally, the most clear-cut objection is the unabashed ethnocentricism implied in the modernization approach. (1984: 24)

DEPENDENCY THEORY: A GENERAL OBSERVATION

As we have argued, modernization theory emerged out of the desire by Western academicians to explain and to come to grips with new developments in the Third World, and also with the emergence of the United States as the leading world power—whose preeminence was being challenged by the Soviet Union. Dependency theory emerged in the mid-1960s as a challenge to modernization propositions, because the latter were seen as not only inadequate but also inappropriate explanations of the Third World experience. Much of the earlier history of dependency theory related to Latin America.

Economists and other social scientists working with the United Nations Economic Commission for Latin America (ECLA) under the famous Brazilian economist Raul Prebisch in the 1950s were among the first scholars to associate underdevelopment with the worsening terms of international trade. Thus these scholars paid closer attention than modernization theorists to international influences upon Third World development. By adopting the international perspective, these theorists were offering a pointed criticism of modernization theory, which had regarded these regimes as isolated from the international economic system.[2]

However, as numerous studies have shown (Blömstrom and Hettne, 1984; Duvall et al., 1981; Rothstein, 1977; Gereffi, 1983), the ECLA school concentrated upon *terms of trade* rather than the production structure, both external and internal. Eventually, the ECLA formulation reached an impasse when, even after substituting trade for domestic production through import-substitution industrialization, underdevelopment continued. Thus, in essence, the ECLA program had been a reified modernization theory with international structures being pushed to the fore. As Blomstrom and Hettne have pointed out:

The economic stagnation in Latin American together with the lack of confidence in the prevailing development theories created a sense of great confusion. The intellectuals were groping for alternative explanatory models. There were certain limitations to the extent to which ECLA could provide assistance in this area: first, since ECLA focused its attention on purely economic problems, social and political problems were excluded from the analysis. Secondly, ECLA's dependence on conservative Latin American governments precluded the use of analyses and remedies that appeared too radical, such as land reforms. (1984: 56)

Dependency theory as it evolved in the 1960s and 1970s was a reaction to what it saw as the inadequacies of both modernization theory and the strategy of import-substitution industrialization (among others) adopted by the ECLA. It is important to note that while most of the work done on dependency theory has come from Latin America, the basic framework has been variously adopted by scholars writing about Africa and other parts of the Third World. The adoption of the dependency approach by a large number of African(ist) scholars (e.g., Leys, 1975; Shivji, 1976; Onimode, 1982; Langdon, 1981; Amin, 1974; 1977; etc.) indicates a need for a closer look at the theory.

Dependency Theory: Inventory of Premises

It is difficult to say with any degree of accuracy that there is *a* theory of dependency as such. Rather, dependency is a framework of analysis that incorporates complex social, economic, and political processes taking place in the Third World. For purposes of our discussion, we will refer to this framework as *dependency theory*. The difficulty of identifying *a* theory of dependency has already been recognized by a number of scholars. For example, Duvall et al. have observed that

the label (dependency) signifies a broad set of contemporary discussions about imperialism, global inequality, and underdevelopment that focus on the economic, social and political "distortions" of peripheral societies which result from their incorporation into the global capitalist system. (1981: 312)

In dependency theory, the concept of underdevelopment is used to express a particular kind of asymmetrical relationship between developed and underdeveloped countries, largely to the former's advantage. Unlike *undevelopment,* underdevelopment acknowledges some kind of development, but a problematic kind of development.

The diversity of scholars and their intellectual backgrounds—political scientists, sociologists, economists, historians, etc.—also provides a breadth of perspective that would be difficult to assimilate into a single theoretical structure. All these factors not withstanding, Duvall et al. (1981: 313) were able to draw together five basic arguments that could be said to characterize dependency theory:

1. The financial and technological penetration of peripheral societies by the developed capitalist centers
2. The creation of an unbalanced economic structure both within the periphery and between the periphery and the center
3. Structural constraints on self-sustained economic growth in the periphery
4. The emergence of distinctive peripheral capitalist class relationships
5. The transformation of the role of the peripheral state.

It is the general view of dependency theory that the above characteristics are shaped through a *historical* linkage between the center (developed countries) and the periphery (the Third World) via three avenues: financial and technological penetration; cultural penetration; and trade, with the asymmetric incorporation in the international system being a reflection of the weakness of the dependent country as a buyer or seller of goods and services to the international market. For purposes of illustration, figure 1 reproduces the model of dependency theory developed by Duvall et al.[3]

Key:

A. The Periphery Economy

I. X_1 and X_2 refer to systemic financial and technological penetration. These two variables may be defined as the extent to which the effective capital stock of a given national economy has been supplied by foreigners.

X_3 and X_4 refer to cultural penetration. This variable refers to the principal shared attitudes and predispositions of the elite with respect to economic, political, and social means and ends.

II. X_5 deals with trade partner concentration.

Figure 1 A Simple Flow Model of Dependency

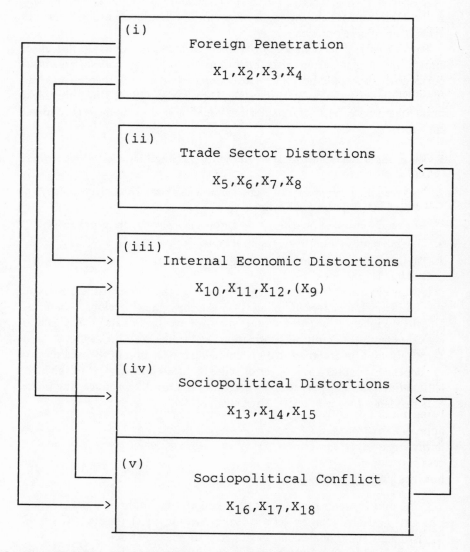

Source: Duvall et al. "A Formal Model of 'Dependencia Theory': Structure and Measurement." In Richard L. Merritt and Bruce M. Russett, eds., *From National Development to Global Community*. London: Allen & Unwin, 1981, 316.

X_6 deals with the concentration on a small number of products in the export profile in the peripheral economy. In many African countries, the largest commodity accounts for over 60 percent of total exports. See table 2.2.

X_7 deals with the relative economic importance of foreign trade.

X_8 deals with trade vulnerability as a result of X_5, X_6, and X_7.

III. X_9 refers to the level of economic activity. The level of economic activity is characterized by the extent of capital accumulation.

X_{10} refers to the extent to which different sectors of the economy are at different levels of economic activity and capital accumulation. In dependency theory, this process is known as *uneven development*—that is, the transformation of the peripheral economy toward a capitalist mode of production occuring at very different rates for different sectors of the economy.

X_{11} refers to the unconnectedness in the production and distribution within the national economy. In dependency theory, this process is known as *economic disintegration* or *disarticulation*—that is, goods and services produced for domestic consumption are used only in limited sectors of the economy.

X_{12} refers to sectoral heterogeneity in the returns of labor—that is, as financial and technological penetration takes place, it does so unevenly across economic sectors; as a result the returns depend on the level and character of penetration.

B. The Peripheral Capitalist Polity

IV. X_{13} refers to the extent of governmental involvement in the peripheral economy which, conceptually, includes both the relative size or importance of state-owned or controlled economic sectors, and the degree or pervasiveness of governmental regulations of economic activity.

X_{14} refers to *economic marginalization*—that is, the extent to which various classes, especially workers and/or peasants, are incapable of maintaining their economic position. This concept is especially important because it looks at the living standards of those actually working and the degree to which workers approach or remain at an economic "margin." The concept is also important in the sense that it appreciates the importance of labor in the productive process and observes the phenomenon of the reserve army of the unemployed and how the latter affects wages in the periphery.

X_{15} refers to *economic inequality*—that is, inequality in access to valued goods and services, substantially a function of inequality of income and in part a consequence of marginalization. X_{15} is closely related to X_{11}. A standard argument in social conflict theories, and one adopted by dependency theory, is that economic inequality fosters conflict, especially latent conflict; dependency theory sees the origins of conflict as primarily economic.

X_{16} refers to *latent conflict*—that is, the potential for civil strife. Class conflict as a result of X_{14} and X_{15} becomes a key variable in any understanding of the social and political consequences of dependence. Although latent conflict is not easily measurable, it is important to note its pervasive existence in the periphery.

X_{17} refers to *manifest conflict*—that is, general strikes, riots, demonstrations, and terrorism. As the state becomes more deeply and pervasively involved in the economy, conflict is frequently stimulated over access to state power.

X_{18} refers to *coercive authoritarianism of the regime.* This notion is related to the concept of government involvement in the economy, and deals with the apparent increase in peripheral societies of a statist class interest—that exist out of the bourgeois control of the state, but develop beyond that to a point where new class interests come to the fore and express themselves in coercive authoritarian policy. These class interests remain closely tied to those of the bourgeoisie but have their own basis in the apparatus of the state—in control of the means of coercion (Duvall et al., 1981: 338). So X_{18} translates itself as size × governmental control × social control, of the coercive forces of the state.

Thus, X_1 to X_{18} presents dependency theory in schematic form. Duvall and his colleagues have summarized it thus:

The main distinguishing feature of contemporary dependency theory,... is the argument that particular social and political "distortions" result from, or develop out of, capitalist penetration, trade dependence, and distorted economic development. These political and social "distortions"... include increasing governmental involvement in the economy, creating a particular form of state capitalism. (1981: 317)

It is our belief that, given the propositions outlined by Duvall et al., dependency theory's main arguments can be tested using specific criteria, in terms of either geographic region or economic sector in a particular country. Earlier attempts at testing dependency theory were not very successful because of the inability of those who performed the tests to comprehend fully the complexity of dependency arguments. Instead they resorted to establishing essentially useless statistical correlations to disprove the theory (Kleeimeier, 1978: 701–4). The present work, however, does not get into the problematic of testing dependency propositions.

Dependency Theory: The Analysis

It has already been pointed out that the point of departure for dependency theory was its divergence from the prevailing assessment of the problems of underdevelopment (ECLA's), especially the decrease in emphasis on the terms of trade as sources of bargaining weakness in international markets, and the resulting barrier to economic growth in in the Third World.

Dependency theory moved away from this position in two critical ways. First, dependency theory denied the appropriateness of an emphasis on trade to the exclusion of financial, technological, and cultural-political considerations. Second, it denied the theory of the fundamental causative nature of trade, seeing it rather as the derived effect of the other, more basic forms of penetration—financial, technological, and political-cultural. In the dependency model (figure 1) this aspect is represented as X_1 through X_4. The flow of assumptions explaining this phenomenon can be summarized as follows:

1. Concentration of a peripheral nation's value structure upon a metropolitan partner will produce concentration of trade.
2. Political and cultural values will shape consumption preferences and production habits and will increase demand for goods from the dominant metropolitan country.
3. The means of production obtained from that country will shape economic development to require further inputs from the source of capital, thus forming a "vicious circle of dependence."

The point to emphasize here is that the foreign connection is seen as having a negative impact on the development profile of the peripheral society. This is diametrically opposed to the modernization position, which considered the influence of foreign capital, technology, and culture as essentially positive. Modernization theory saw foreign influence as helping the peripheral society to evolve a modern socioeconomic system. Dependency theory, on the other hand, argued that foreign penetration created underdevelopment in the Third World. Furthermore, underdevelopment was being sustained by a perpetual dependence by the Third World on the developed countries. Theotonio Dos Santos, whose article on "The Structure of Dependence" helped to popularize dependency theory in the United States with its publication in *The American Economic Review* (1970), defined dependence in the following terms:

By dependence we mean a situation in which the economy of certain countries is conditioned by the development and expansion of another economy to which the former is subjected. The relation . . . of interdependence between two or more economies, and between these and world trade, assumes the form of dependence when some countries (the dominant ones) can expand and be self-sustaining, while other countries (the dependent ones) can do this only as a reflection of that expansion, which can have either a positive or negative effect on their immediate development. (1970: 231)

In strictly economic terms, dependency theory sees peripheral development as having no dynamism of its own, since the need for production in the periphery is triggered by forces external to it. The need to establish a historical link between present-day economic characteristics in the periphery and capitalist development in the metropole forms A. G. Frank's thesis on the "development of underdevelopment." Because of the amount of discussion generated by his works (1967; 1969; 1972; 1974; 1978), Frank is regarded as one of the leading theoreticians of dependency.[4]

Frank maintains that it is incorrect to consider contemporary underdevelopment a simple reflection of the economic, political, and social structure of the underdeveloped country itself. On the contrary, underdevelopment is in large part the historical product of relations between the underdeveloped periphery and the developed center countries. Therefore, the concept of underdevelopment is *relational*. These relations were an essential part of the structure and evolution of the worldwide capitalist system. Thus Frank writes that

to the extent the fruits of their labor through monopoly trade—no less than in the times of Cortez and Pizarro in Mexico and Peru, Clive in India, Rhodes in Africa, the "Open Door" in China—the metropolis destroyed and/or totally transformed the earlier viable social and economic systems of these societies, incorporating them into the metropolitan dominated world-wide capitalist system and converted them into sources for its own metropolitan capital accumulation and development. The resulting fate for those conquered, transformed or newly acquired established societies was, and remains their decapitalization, structurally generated unproductiveness, ever increasing misery for the masses—in a word, their underdevelopment. (1969: 225)

Frank and other adherents to the dependency model (and world-systems theory, especially Wallerstein, 1974; 1980; 1985) thus take a very long-term historical perspective extending back to what they see as the initial creation of a world system in the sixteenth century.[5] Beginning in the sixteenth century, the center countries (Spain, Portugal, Holland, Britain, and France) had created a world division of labor between themselves and the periphery. Commerce and manufacturing were established largely in the center, while the colonies took on the role of plantation agriculture and mineral extraction for the world market. The mechanism used to achieve these objectives was the subjugation of native populations, who were made into landless peasants in semi-slavery conditions. In some areas, such as the Caribbean, the native populations were fully exterminated and their places taken by slave labor imported from Africa (Rodney, 1972).

In the early 1970s, dependency theory was transformed as the paradigmatic shift from modernization to dependency became a foregone conclusion. At this time, a new element in dependency theory emerged, characterized by Dos Santos's contribution, among others. While Frank had concentrated on the long historical developments leading to the creation of dependent societies, Dos Santos (1970) concentrated his attention on new developments in the world capitalist economy with the rise of transnational corporations, the ascendance of the United States as a leading economic power, and the eventual economic domination of Latin America by U.S. transnationals.

Dos Santos identified two types of dependence, one in the pre-1945 period and the other after 1945. In the former, he pointed to *colonial* dependence, characterized by export trade in which commercial and financial capital in alliance with the "colonialist style," dominated the economic relations of the Europeans and the colonies by means of a trade monopoly—complemented by a colonial monopoly of land, mines, and labor. Dos Santos also identified a *financial-industrial* dependence, which consolidated itself at the end of the nineteenth century, which was characterized by the domination of big capital in the leading sectors of the economies of the center countries, and by its expansion abroad through investment in the production of raw materials. As a result of this investment, a productive structure devoted to the export of raw materials evolved in the periphery, resulting in external-oriented development. However,

in the post-war period, a new type of dependence has been consolidated based on multi-national corporations which began to invest in industries geared to the internal market of underdeveloped countries. This form of dependence is basically technological-industrial dependence. (Dos Santos, 1970: 232)

Dos Santos's analysis examined the results of the program of ISI, which had been advocated by Prebisch and the ECLA. ISI had sought to increase the share of total consumption satisfied by domestic production, involving an effort to take over the existing domestic market from foreign producers. The trouble with ISI, however, was that, first, it did not change the demand profile (i.e., income distribution) internally, and thus there was no qualitative change in the productive structure-affecting economies of scale. Second, Latin America had no technology of its own to match up the production requirements for the existing domestic market. The result was a further importation of finance and technology, leading to further dependence.

Dos Santos pointed out that this new form of dependence was conditioned by the exigencies of the international commodity and capital markets. The possibility of generating new investments depended on the existence of financial resources in foreign currency for the purchase of machinery, patents, and processed raw materials not readily available domestically. But such purchases were subject to two limitations:

1. The limit of resources generated by the export sector, reflected in the balance of payments, which include not only trade but service relations,
2. The limitations of monopoly on patents which lead transnational firms to prefer to transfer their machines in the form of capital rather than as commodities for sale. (See also Merhav, 1969; Baer, 1972)

These two limitations put a ceiling on what the peripheral countries can do on their own when development plans, especially regarding industrialization, are envisaged as independent of the international framework. Thus industrial development is strongly conditioned by fluctuations in the balance of payments leading to external deficits, and eventually to a huge foreign debt. The most important point, however, is that foreign control of the peripheral economy remains intact, especially in its most dynamic sector. Due to patent rights and agreements unfavorable to the periphery, transnationals are able to repatriate a high volume of profit (Barnet and Muller, 1974).

In retrospect, we can view Dos Santos's contribution as presenting a new notion of the international division of labor created by the evolution of ISI, in which the periphery was no longer exclusively made up of raw material—exporting enclave economies. The new dependence analysis suggests to us that the modern sector of the entire periphery was now fully incorporated in the world capitalist system, given its close relationship to transnational corporations. But the development remained partial, with no dynamism of its own, because of the negative dependence relations.

Another aspect of dependency theory that has received increased attention is what is generally known as *dependent development*. This aspect of dependency will be dealt with later in this chapter, but we intend here to present its basic theoretical features and to establish that the concept of dependent development builds upon the concept of the new dependence à la Dos Santos.

Chronologically, we have seen that Frank's notion of the "development of underdevelopment" formed the basis for the initial theorizing about dependency. Dos Santos's analysis, however, moved one step further and identified the infusion of finance and technology into peripheral production—from simple extraction to manufacturing of industrial goods, albeit still in a dependent form. Agricultural production still takes place, but so does manufacturing. Dependent development, on the other hand, is defined as

a special instance of dependency, characterized by the association of alliance of international and local capital. The state also joins the alliance as an active partner, and the resulting triple alliance is still a fundamental factor in the emergence of dependent development. (Evans, 1979: 32)

While the role of international capital in the production structure of the peripheral economy is fully recognized by both Frank and Dos Santos, there is no *explicit* recognition of the role of the state as an active participant in the organization of production. Therefore, the most significant element in the definition of dependent development is the role of the peripheral state in the economy. In the dependency model presented earlier, this aspect refers to variable X_{13}—that is, the extent of government involvement in the peripheral economy, which, conceptually, includes both the relative size or importance of state-owned or controlled economic sectors, and the degree of pervasiveness of governmental regulation of economic activity. Perhaps the most developed form of dependent development is found in Latin America—Brazil (Evans, 1979) and Mexico (Gereffi, 1983; Bennett and Sharpe, 1985). The issue of dependent development has only recently gained currency. We will return to it later in this chapter in discussing its adoption by scholars writing about Africa.

A Critique of the "Orthodox" Dependency Theory

The original (or orthodox) formulation of dependency has been criticized both from within the paradigm itself, and from without. The main criticism from without, essentially emanating from modernization theory, has been dependency theory's concentration on economic factors of underdevelopment and its assignment of the responsibility for underdevelopment to one external factor—the international capitalist system (Smith, 1979).

Smith, for example, argues that dependency theory in general substantially overestimates the power of the international system in the affairs of dependent countries today. In classic modernization form, Smith argues that the responsibility of underdevelopment lies within the Third World itself because, unlike the West, the Third World lacks entrepreneurship, efficiency in economic organization, and innovation. With the attainment of independence, Smith does not see how the West can continually be blamed for the inability of the Third World to escape underdevelopment.

The problem with Smith's argument and, indeed, with all the reified modernization arguments emanating from the IMF and the World Bank, is that first, it fails to appreciate history. The first two chapters of this work demonstrated the continuing link between Africa's economy and the international capitalist system. Chapter 2 shows that, even with political independence, the ideological affinity of African leaders to comparative advantage is one major obstacle to achieving autonomous development. But the ideological affinity to the West in and of itself does not necessarily perpetuate underdevelopment; it is the practice resulting from that ideology that becomes injurious to the production profile of African countries.

The second problem with the reified modernization argument, on the internal basis of underdevelopment, is its polemical nature. As we will later elaborate, in its quest to counter dependency theory's very strong arguments regarding trade dependence and overall distortion of the peripheral economy, the reified modernization theory fails to appreciate its own weaknesses and thus reverts to its original formulations, which were flawed in significant ways. It is futile, for example, to argue that trade dependence between African and Western countries does not exist, a dependence that even the conservative *Economist* of London acknowledges (December 6, 1985: 15). The *Economist* reported that in 1985 alone, because of declining prices of Third World raw materials, OECD countries paid $65 billion less than in the previous year, equivalent to 0.7 percent of the entire budget of all OECD countries. The *Economist* called this windfall the "poor man's gift."

Perhaps the most devastating critique of dependency has come from the left and from within progressive ranks who ordinarily would be politically sympathetic to the dependency position. Thus dependency theory has been criticized for adopting a "latent stagnation" thesis by emphasizing the negative consequences of dependency but providing no solution to the problem of un-derdevelopment (Leys, 1975: 18). Frank's insistence on the "development of underdevelopment," for example, simply looks at the continued expatriation of peripheral surplus, but does not appreciate the changing domestic produc-tive structure of some peripheral economies, such as those in Southeast Asia and Latin America. Wallerstein's modification of the dependency analysis, which appreciates the evolution of a "semi-periphery" to include some indus-trializing peripheral countries, nonetheless falters through lack of a rigorous defining criteria as to the meaning of the relationship between center, semi-periphery and periphery. The best definition of a semi-periphery is "that which lies between the capabilities of a 'center' and the incapabilities of a pure 'pe-riphery.' "

Thus the original dependency formulation has been criticized for moving too quickly from the proposition that capitalism is bound up with and sup-portive of continuing underdevelopment in large parts of the world

to the conclusion not only that the rise of underdevelopment is inherent in the extension of the world division of labor through capitalist expansion, but also that the "devel-opment of underdevelopment" is an indispensable condition for capitalist development itself. (Brenner, 1977: 27)

In the same vein, R. A. Fernandez and J. F. Ocampo, contrary to the standard view held in dependency theory, argue that

the basis for Latin American backwardness cannot be attributed to the capitalist char-acter of its economies and their integration within the world capitalist system, but rather, the *lack* of capitalist development and the persistence of feudal forms in agri-culture . . . underdevelopment is nothing more than backwardness: a retardation brought about by feudal, semi-feudal, and pre-capitalist remnants. (1974: 36)

Dependency theory, by concentrating on the negative consequences of capi-talist development, ignores possibilities for internal change. Since most de-pendency theorists consider themselves "progressive" or even "revolution-ary," the only assumed destination beyond dependency in the wake of a "revolution" is socialism. One may ask, for example, whether it is necessary (or even valid) to pose the issue of underdevelopment and change in the Third World in terms of capitalism versus socialism, and the expected triumph of the latter over the former? A simple understanding of dialectic theory would caution against such theorizing. The logical jump between dependency and socialism is not specified but assumed, and this is a major shortcoming that the theory still has to resolve.

Thus it is fair to say that dependency theory and the world-system approach make the mistake of defining the world capitalist system as the primary unit of analysis, and using analytic concepts that obscure significant historical actors in specific situations, these approaches make it difficult to understand evolutionary transformations in the very system that is their subject matter.

MODERNIZATION AND DEPENDENCY: INTELLECTUAL CONSEQUENCES FOR AFRICA

The Berlin Conference of 1884–1885, which formally partitioned Africa among European powers, signified the beginning of a new era for Africa's intellectual evolution. In a nutshell, theorizing about African society and development became a growth industry, but more so after 1945 when it became clear that sooner or later Africa would become independent. In both Europe and the United States, universities developed programs for African studies—for example, at the School of Oriental and African Studies in London, and in the 1950s at Northwestern University and Boston University in the United States. The study of Africa did not escape the intellectual evolution of development theory, from modernization to dependency.

Within modernization theory, there was an outpouring of studies on Africa (Almond and Coleman, 1960; Apter, 1955; 1961; 1965; Zolberg, 1966; Coleman and Rosberg, 1966; Kilby, 1969; etc.). As the development paradigm shifted to embrace dependency, the approach was embraced by Africanist scholars (for a summary, see Leys, 1977). With the paradigmatic shift from modernization to dependency, however, Africanist scholars seem to have stagnated with acceptance of dependency propositions.[6] One may argue that, in part, this is due to the fact that dependency propositions provided an easy scapegoat for Africa's current problems as long as the external element remained the main independent variable. It is within this framework that arguments by African scholars, such as Bade Onimode, can be understood. Writing about Nigeria's underdevelopment, Onimode argues that

it is impossible to understand the character of underdevelopment without investigating its history which is why [my] study has delved into the pre-colonial, colonial and recent neo-colonial history of Nigeria's underdevelopment. *This history is inseparable from the functioning of imperialism in all its stages as the single most important catalyst in the evolution of Nigeria from pre-colonial times,* and this prompted the exploration of the impact of imperialism on the country's underdevelopment. (1982: 1) (Emphasis added.)

Elsewhere he argues that "it must . . . be untenable to suggest that development occurred independently in any part of the world capitalist system" (1982: 8).

Onimode's arguments, valid as they may be, grossly underestimate the internal dynamics of African (and other Third World) societies and their ability to resist and adapt to change in a historically evolving way. Part of our task in chapter 4 will be to suggest the "untenable," by exploring the evolution and nature of capitalism in Africa. Thus we concur with Magnus Blömstrom and, Björn Hettne, who have concluded that "judging from the current debate in development theory, the demise of the dependency school has left an awkward theoretical vacuum. The critics are generally less successful in pointing out new theoretical directions" (1984: 163). Michael Bratton (1982: 333–72) has pointed out that many of the charges once leveled at modernization theory apply to dependency theory as well. For example, dependency theory's assumption of the unchecked spread of global production and trade relations implies that nothing of formative or lasting influence survives from the precapitalist experience—an issue that we treat at length in the next chapter. Another observation that Bratton makes is that, within dependency theory, change is strictly unilinear, only now in a direction away rather than toward an idealized conception of modernity. And finally, in viewing the processes of industrialization, a semblance of stages can be discerned in the shift from the export of primary commodities to dependent industrialization by import substitution.

BEYOND DEPENDENCY: DEPENDENT DEVELOPMENT AND INTERNATIONALIZATION OF CAPITAL

Introduction: General Observations

In the past decade or so there has evolved a school of thought associated with dependency theory which has advanced the theorization of industrialization in the periphery in the context of "internationalization of capital," that is, the export of both finance and machinery to the periphery for expanded reproduction of capital. Much of the theorizing regarding dependent development has been related to Latin America (Evans, 1979; Gereffi, 1983; Bennett and Sharpe, 1985; etc.) and to South and East Asia (Kaplinsky, 1984; Grieco, 1984). The only two studies on Africa unequivocally adopting "internationalization of capital" theses are Marcussen and Torp (1982) and Swainson (1980). The problem with Swainson's work, however, is that after making a case for the internationalization of capital, she concludes by denying its applicability to Kenya, her case study.

Perhaps the dean of the "internationalization of capital" school was the late Bill Warren, whose two contributions (1973; 1980), for the most part, shaped the debate on Third World industrialization in the 1970s. In his earlier work, Bill Warren argued that

it can now be seen that the elements inhibiting capitalist industrialization, which operated in the period of political control, were comparatively short-lived and that the post-war period is witnessing the full re-emergence of those elements of imperialism conducive to capitalist industrialization. (1973: 42)

Warren was recognizing what other dependency theorists, such as Dos Santos, had acknowledged regarding the changing character of production in the periphery through the export of machinery and finance capital. The difference between the two theorists, however, was that Warren regarded Third World industrialization through ISI as essentially positive.

In both his works, Warren argued that empirical data showed that there had been a substantial, accelerating, and even historically unprecedented improvement in the growth of productive capacity and the material welfare of the mass of the population in the Third World. Further, he argued, these societies had proved themselves increasingly capable of generating powerful internal sources of economic expansion and of achieving an ever more independent economic and political status. To "prove" his point, Warren presented a table of growth in real terms of GNP for countries with more than 1 million inhabitants between 1960 and 1973. Of the 87 Third World countries presented, however, only seven had growth rates exceeding 5 percent—Libya, Saudi Arabia, Singapore, South Korea, Hong Kong, Taiwan, Iran. Of these countries, three (Libya, Saudi Arabia, and Iran) were oil producing, and the rest were enclaves of capitalist production in Southeast Asia (Warren, 1980: 196).

Warren's arguments nonetheless need to be examined seriously. Evidence from Latin America, for example, suggests that since World War II the export of capital to that region has resulted in a significant shift in the productive structure of the region's economies. F. H. Cardoso (1972: 81–86) provides evidence on the increasing role of manufacturing in Brazil's GNP. Cardoso uses recent figures to argue that foreign investment in the Third World generally, but particularly in Latin America, is moving away from oil, raw materials, and agriculture, and toward industry with increasing acceptance of local participation in their enterprises. Cardoso's view is echoed in a recent observation by Douglas C. Bennett and Kenneth E. Sharpe:

Since World War II, investments by transnational corporations have been particularly critical in shaping situations of dependency. Whereas direct foreign investment was once confined primarily to mining and agriculture, and to activities closely connected with these, such as railroads, direct foreign investment in manufacturing has been dominant in recent decades. (1985: 7)

Cardoso, Bennett and Sharpe, Evans, Gereffi, and others have concluded that in some dependent economies, unlike in orthodox dependency, foreign investment no longer remains a simple zero-sum game of exploitation. Cardoso, for example, suggests that if only the purely economic indicators were considered, development and foreign monopoly penetration in the industrial sectors of dependent economies could be shown to be compatible—"in fact, dependency, monopoly, capitalism and development are not contradictory terms: there occurs a kind of dependent capitalist development in the sectors of the Third World integrated into the new forms of monopolistic expansion" (1972: 89).

Dependent development has been shown to rely heavily on the peripheral state's capacity to organize internal production and its willingness to enter into production ventures with foreign capital. In his study of Brazil, for example, Peter Evans observes that

the direct role of the Brazilian state in the process of industrialization has increased dramatically. The internalization of imperialism has given the state a new position of power from which to bargain with the multinationals. If classic dependence was associated with weak states, dependent development is associated with the strengthening of strong states in the "semi-periphery." The consolidation of state power may even be considered a prerequisite of dependent development. (1979: 11)

However, Evans and his co-theorists recognize that the image of the dependent capitalist state cannot be based simply on its role as an agent of accumulation, but rather, the state as an agent of social control as well. A particular state's ability to guarantee continued expanded reproduction of capital by extracting resources from society and deploying these to create and support coercive and administrative organizations are essential to dependent development. (Kay, 1975: 126; Evans, 1979: 47) The peripheral state's coercive apparatus forms part of its bargaining strength with transnational corporations considering investing in the periphery.

Dependent Development in Africa

Theorizing about dependent development in Africa has been striking by its absence. As already noted, only two major works (Swainson, 1980; Marcussen and Torp, 1982) have tried to systematically apply the concept to African development. Swainson's work ultimately showed the fallacy of applying the theory to Kenya. Henrik Secher Marcussen and J. E. Torp, on the other hand, have tried to apply the theory to the Ivory Coast with mixed results. In this section, we will closely look at Marcussen and Torp's work to assess its validity and applicability to sub-Saharan Africa.[7]

Marcussen and Torp clearly adopt the notion of dependent development as the title of their book, *Internationalization of Capital*, suggests. They primarily argue that

changing historical conditions for capital accumulation in the Western industrialized countries (the Centre) in the 1970s have led to new ways in which the developing countries (the Periphery) are integrated in the reproduction of the Centre's capital.... The consequence of this process is an increased differentiation among the countries in the Periphery. A few are for the first time in the process of establishing the basis for national capital accumulation within the framework of capitalist development. (p. 9)

More significant, however, is their conviction that their approach is better than that of dependency theory:

What distinguishes our study ... is that we have reached the conclusion that dynamic elements exist in the changing historical conditions for capital accumulation in the

Western countries, particularly the economic crisis since 1973, and that these elements are responsible for the creation of new reproductive structures in parts of the Periphery which may very well break with the "blocked development" situation. (p. 10)

Marcussen and Torp acknowledge that much discussion regarding dependent development (or newly industrializing countries) relates to Latin America and Southeast Asia. They claim, however, that "in the Periphery new examples are appearing of countries showing tendencies towards the establishment of advanced capitalist and reproduction process. In an African context, this may be the case in countries like Nigeria, Kenya, and the Ivory Coast" (1982: 29). But where is the evidence?

Theoretically, it is plausible that any increase in the manufacturing capacity of a peripheral economy may lead to more sectoral differentiation, and possibly to increased productivity in the economy via the multiplier effect. However, as one looks at the African economy in the past decade (see chapter 1), the economy has essentially stagnated or declined in significant sectors. Indeed, as table 1.6 shows, the manufacturing sector in Africa, overall, contributes to less than 10 percent of the GDP. This includes Nigeria, Kenya, and the Ivory Coast, countries that Marcussen and Torp project to be beneficiaries of internationalization of capital. Since dependent development substantially hinges on the ability of manufacturing to expand, the thesis is brought into serious question in the African context.

The Brazilian case illustrates the evolution of dependent development. It is estimated that in 1907 agriculture accounted for four-fifths and industry only one-fifth of Brazilian GDP. The proportion remained unchanged during the first two decades of the century. But then the balance began to shift in favor of industry until, by 1939, the proportion was closer to two-fifths industry and three-fifths agriculture (Evans, 1979: 70). Currently, manufacturing accounts for more than 50 percent of the GDP.

The evidence provided by Marcussen and Torp reveals the difficulty of applying dependent development theory to Africa. In the case of Ivory Coast, they point out that agriculture is still the backbone of the economy, contributing to two-thirds of the export earnings of the country. Two-fifths of the population derive their income from agricultural activities (1982: 74). Sectoral differentiation in the economy of Ivory Coast is at such a low level that it is difficult to talk of an integrated national economy with vertical and horizontal linkages:

In 1971, 75 percent of all industrial enterprises were situated in Abidjan [the capital]. These firms produced 70 percent of total industrial turnover and represented 60 percent of all industrial investments. Nevertheless, only 22 percent of industrial inputs came from Abidjan, while 26 percent came from other parts of the country. In addition to this, only 145 of the semi-processed goods purchased came from Abidjan. . . . This leads to the conclusion that, in spite of the existence of a large metropolis with more than 500,000 inhabitants and three-quarters of all industrial enterprises, it is not possible to speak of an industrial milieu, if we understand by this term the geographically concentrated existence of economic and technological exchanges and other interconnections between industrial units. Instead we see a new type of "dualism": an agricultural sector tied to the industrial sector, *but only limited linkages between the industrial enterprises themselves.* (Marcussen and Torp, 1982: 99–100) (Emphasis added)

More than anything else, Ivory Coast's industrialization characterizes the very early phase of ISI.

The rudimentary form of industrial production similarly characterizes Nigeria's manufacturing sector. Despite Nigeria's abundant oil wealth in the 1970s and early 1980s, it has failed to attract the kind of industries that have formed the basis for Mexico's or Brazil's dependent industrialization, despite a concerted effort by the Nigerian government to offer a favorable investment climate to foreign capital. The reluctance of foreign capital to invest in Nigeria has contributed to the continued outlook of the Nigerian economy as essentially agricultural and less dynamic (Schatz, 1977: 21).

It must be recalled that dependent development in part relies on the ability of local entrepreneurs or the state to provide resources that form the basis of a partnership between local and foreign interests. This precondition can only be met if local entrepreneurs or the state can show their ability to accumulate capital and sustain the momentum of accumulation over longer periods of time. There also must be a significant absorptive capacity in the peripheral economy to sustain any long-term investments in industries such as iron and steel to justify foreign capital's investments. The absorptive capacity of an economy is partly determined by effective demand and level of economic integration.

In Nigeria, despite the oil boom, the absorptive capacity of the economy has not expanded. D. Babatunde Thomas, for example, has argued that "in the Nigerian case ... limited information on profitable investment, limited technical capacity for technology and its effective utilization pose more formidable constraints on the development process than capital shortage per se" (1975: 3). A more recent study by Nicholas Balabkins (1982) corroborates Thomas's work. Balabkins has shown that Nigeria, in the past twenty years, has suffered from what he calls undigested economic growth, that is, inadequate absorptive capacity due to factor imbalance in the economy. Thus the structure and rapid growth of the oil industry in Nigeria have allowed only marginal linkage effects with the other sectors of the economy, particularly agriculture, the major source of national employment. In 1960, agricultural products constituted about four-fifths of Nigeria's total value of exports. By 1970, however, their value had dropped to 44 percent of the total export earnings and in 1978–1979 they accounted for only 6.6 percent of the total. These figures are significant for two reasons.

First, as Peter Matlon (1981: 324) has pointed out, during 1964–1965, agriculture accounted for 58 percent of GDP and employed 70 percent of the active work force. By 1974–1975, agriculture's share in GDP had fallen to only 23 percent while the proportion of the labor force remained relatively high at 64 percent. In contrast, during the same period, the petroleum and mining sector increased its share of GDP from 3 percent to 46 percent, while its proportion of total employment remained below 1 percent. Thus structural changes in the Nigerian economy led to few qualitative changes in either manufacturing or employment.

Second, as agricultural production declined in Nigeria, the government was forced to rely heavily on imported foodstuffs, spending one billion naira (1N = $1.20) in 1978 alone (*Europa Publications,* 1980–1981: 764). Agricultural decline generated rural unrest, while unemployment in the cities engendered urban unrest (Schatz, 1977: 31). The combination of the two factors contributed to the unattractiveness of Nigeria to foreign capital, as political stability was increasingly called into question.

In the case of Kenya, the evidence betrays Nicola Swainson's attempt to portray her economy as the target of an expanding internationalized capital. For example, as of the mid-1970s, the estimated book value of foreign investment in Kenya was only 130 million pounds sterling—approximately $170 million (1980: 215). It should be clear that $170 million worth of investment does not form a basis for dependent development, especially when collaborative ventures between indigenous capital and foreign capital involve the production of simple manufactured goods such as sugar, rice, maize, salt, soup, shampoo, sweets, matches, batteries, insecticides, cement, wire, and tools (Swainson, 1980: 187).

Kenya's manufactures should be compared with those of Brazil to illustrate the point. In 1980, manufactured goods made up more than 50 percent of Brazil's GNP of $242 billion. These manufactures included vehicles, ships, footwear, textiles, etc. Since the early 1980s, Brazil has exported weapons worth some $700 million or more annually. Much of the weaponry was developed in joint ventures with European companies. Future aims of Brazil include the production of nuclear powered submarines, surface-to-air and surface-to-surface missiles. Its aeronautical factories currently produce helicopters, passenger aircraft, tactical fighters, and military transporters, etc. Table 3.1 shows the limited amount of private capital that found its way to Africa in the 1970s, compared to the rest of the Third World.

Dependent development as a development strategy or prospect for African countries is too far-fetched a proposition to be taken seriously. Using Peter Evans's basic criterion for dependent development, none of the African countries fit the bill:

"Dependent development" will be used to refer to cases where capital accumulation and diversified industrialization of more than superficial sort are not only occurring in a peripheral country but are dominating the transformation of its economy and social structure. (1979: 32)

Table 3.1
Private Flows of Capital from DAC Counties to the Third World and to Africa

Total

	Net Direct Foreign Investment from DAC Members	Total Net Private Flows from DAC Members
Avg. 1970-72	2404.4	5139.4
Avg. 1973-75	5574.1	11348.2
1977	4130.1	17471.9
1978	6934.6	28379.0
Africa		
Avg. 1970-72	444.1	1004.5
Avg. 1973-75	111.3	1884.9
1977	373.6	5026.8
1978	414.7	6791.2

Principal[a] African Recipients of Direct Foreign Investment from DAC Countries

	Net Direct Investment from DAC	Total Net Pvt. Flows from DAC	Total Net Pvt.Flows From EC	EC/DAC %
Cameroon				
Avg. 1970-72	0.3	1.2	-	-
Avg. 1973-75	3.7	14.1	14.1	100.1
1977	-0.3	115.7	87.2	74.7
1978	-1.8	77.0	79.7	104.0

Gabon				
Avg. 1970-72	0.2	10.0	-	-
Avg. 1973-75	23.6	78.5	62.4	79.4
1977	25.6	248.2	241.37	97.3
1978	9.1	54.0	51.7	95.7
Kenya				
Avg. 1970-72	7.3	13.2	-	-
Avg. 1973-75	13.1	17.1	13.96	81.6
1977	6.1	298.8	234.96	78.6
1978	-0.6	64.4	39.17	60.8
Liberia				
Avg. 1970-72	14.6	63.7	38.69	60.7[b]
Avg. 1973-75	104.3	357.6	198.69	55.6
1977	170.4	678.5	282.87	41.7
1978	146.6	671.7	60.32	9.0
Nigeria				
Avg. 1970-72	119.4	125.9	-	-
Avg. 1973-75	51.3	95.5	121.4	127.1[c]
1977	32.2	83.3	104.41	125.3
1978	-14.3	377.4	332.48	88.1
Zaire				
Avg. 1970-72	7.5	89.7	-	-
Avg. 1973-75	26.3	260.5	168.76	64.8
1977	16.4	99.7	102.37	102.7
1978	93.8	203.8	110.28	54.1
Zambia				
Avg. 1970-72	13.2	19.4	-	-
Avg. 1973-75	21.2	106.0	96.82	91.3
1977	2.8	7.5	15.24	203.2
1978	0.9	47.9	55.97	116.8

Table 3.1 Continued

Note: DAC, the Development Assistance Committee of the OECD, is composed of the industrialized countries of Western Europe, North America and Japan.

a"Principal" is defined as net DFI of greater than $10 million for at least one of the designated time periods. North African countries, Rhodesia, South Africa, Somalia, and Niger, which meet these criteria are not included here.

bTo Liberia:

Total Net Pvt. Flows from (avg.)

	1973-75	1977	1978
U.S.	58.0	26.0	-63.0
Japan	101.9	337.0	669.2

cTo Nigeria:

Total Net Pvt. Flows from U.S.

1973	1974	1975	1976	1977	1978
-257.0	-220.0	+332.0	-194.0	-12.0	53.0

Source: Lynn Krieger Mytelka (1983), "The Limits of Export-Led Development: The Ivory Coast's Experience with Manufacturers." In John Gerald Ruggie, ed. *The Antinomies of Interdependence*. New York: Columbia University Press, 250–51.

A most important element in dependent development theory deals with the role of the state both in guaranteeing capital accumulation through its control of society's coercive instruments, and in participating in economic ventures through what dependent development theorists call the "triple alliance," that is, the collaboration between the peripheral state, the local bourgeoisie, and foreign capital. The collaborative effort, however, is an ambiguous proposition, which suggests that neither the local state nor the local bourgeoisie is in real control. As Peter Evans has noted:

Regardless of ambiguities in its relation to the national bourgeoisie, the centrality of state to accumulation on the periphery is incontrovertible. Imperialism as a process and the multinationals as organizations concentrate accumulation at the center of the international system. The local owning class has failed to achieve domination over local industry even in the most advanced peripheral countries. Unless the state can enforce a priority on local accumulation and push local industrialization effectively, there is no effective sponsor for peripheral industrialization. (1979: 43)

Economic decline in Africa in the past decade, however, has taken its toll on the state's ability to be an effective partner in organizing production. Neither has the state been effective in guaranteeing security. These two elements cast serious doubt on the dependent development equation that emphasizes the state's role in the "triple alliance." Chapter 5 of this study devotes itself to a critical analysis of the state's role in the economy and its ability to sustain capital accumulation in Africa. As we consider the obviously increased peripheralization of Africa in the global economy, the new international hierarchy based on structural changes not only makes the concept of dependent development less empirical, but also makes the consideration of comparative advantage in the export of primary products (as advocated by the World Bank) even more unrealistic.

Africa's lack of industrialization, hence a limit to dependent development, is captured by the OAU through the Lagos Plan of Action:

By [UNIDO][8] standards, in 1977 no African country was industrialized, 16 were in course of industrialisation, 21 were non-industrialised and the rest semi-industrialised. But even this comprehensive definition of industrialisation is unsound, as it relates to the national production of each country and does not specify the composition of industry. In fact very few African countries are in the course of coherent integrated industrialization; and where take-off stage is reached it is by industries whose production factors (equipment, machines and technology) are imported and hardly affect other sectors of the national economy, being concerned principally with assembly or industries linked with foreign companies exploiting natural resources. (OAU, 1982: vi)

Given developments since 1982 toward deindustrialization in many African countries (as a result of the overall economic crisis), the LPA sounds too optimistic.

CONCLUSION: DEVELOPMENT THEORY, DEPENDENT DEVELOPMENT, AND THE AFRICAN CONDITION

It should be clear that our study has a dim view of prospects for dependent development in Africa in the near or medium term. This conclusion is drawn from the analysis of changes in the structure of the global economy, which have increasingly peripheralized Africa from the center of economic activity, evidenced by declines in Africa's manufacturing sector. While Ivory Coast, Nigeria, and Kenya may have proved tempting cases for dependent development in a continent characterized by economic crises, these three countries have joined the rest of the continent in their quest to stave off economic decline.

Perhaps the optimism of the late 1970s and early 1980s regarding dependent development in these three countries may have been fueled by a noncritical look at the nature of the newly industrializing countries (NICs) of Latin America and Southeast Asia. In all the NICs, five critical factors converged to allow rapid industrialization—factors that have been conspicuously absent in Africa: geographical location to facilitate quick movement of whole factories by Transnational Corporations (TNCs)[9]; political stability; preexisting technological infrastructure from earlier ISI, coupled with full utilization of capacity; the role of the state as guarantor of investment and as active participant; the easy access to finance capital in the early 1970s with the emergence of transnational currency markets such as the Eurodollar (Schmitz, 1984: 9). Or, as Raphael Kaplinsky has noted:

It is often forgotten that the export and growth success of the NICs from the mid-1960s until the end of the 1970s occurred in a time-span which, by the experience of global industrialisation, must be considered as short-run. It also took place in an historically unprecedented period of reasonably full employment in the major advanced economies, high rates in industrial growth and a virtual explosion in global trade. Besides, it also occurred within a series of social formations which were country-, temporally- and geographically-specific. (1984: Preface vii)

So as one looks at the number of the NICs, the list is always the same: South Korea, Taiwan, Hong Kong, Singapore, Brazil, and Mexico. Together, these countries accounted for 62 percent of Third World manufactured exports in 1975 (Schmitz, 1984: 8).

Development theory is, therefore, in a state of confusion (if not crisis) because of its general inability to transcend successfully the modernization and dependency paradigms, especially as they apply to Africa. On the other hand, Africanists have been content, for the most part, to let dependency be their organizing analytical concept regardless of its glaring inadequacies and inconsistencies. While dependent development may have proved to be a step forward in examining some economies of Latin America and Southeast Asia, the concept has proved harder to apply to African development because of the latter's general economic decline. In the next chapter, therefore, an attempt is made to reconstruct development theory from a perspective of internally generated capitalist development forces in Africa by examining the evolution of the internal development structure. We call this process "disaggregating capitalism in Africa."

NOTES

1. Modernization theory is also known as *diffusion theory,* given the assumption that modernity as found in the West would form the ideal or objective of development in the Third World. This modernity would then be diffused to the rest of the world—hence the term *diffusion theory.* In this study and others, the concepts of modernization and diffusion are used interchangeably.

2. The critique that modernization theory had ignored the international dimension is not totally accurate. Modernization theory, through the concept of comparative advantage, had assumed a smooth flowing of commodities across international borders, based on production efficiencies for each participating country. Comparative advantage worked relatively well for the already-developed countries but was a disaster for the majority of Third World countries. However, this does not nullify the fact that modernization theory had an international dimension. Comparative advantage concepts may have been naive or even unrealistic; nonetheless they provided a theoretical linkage between internal modernization and external trade in the world economy.

3. Duvall et al.'s model of dependency theory is one of the best to be developed in the past 10 years, yet its adoption and usage has been less than systematic. Part of the problem, however, is the fact that the decision to adopt the model requires a systematic analysis of all the 18 variables employed in the model. Most dependency analysts are content to use only a few of the variables—hence the incomplete nature of many critiques and analyses of dependency. For exceptions to this see Russett and Starr, 1981: 452; Nyang'oro, 1983: 79–82.

4. Although Frank has attempted to make modifications to his original formulation of "development of underdevelopment," the fundamental premises of his arguments are still retained in his modified thesis. Hence, our decision to use his earlier works. For his new version, see Frank, 1974.

5. Wallerstein (1974) calls this period the *long* sixteenth century, extending conceptually (and historically) from 1450 to 1600.

6. There are exceptions to this general observation. See, for example, Shaw, 1985.

7. As we mentioned at the beginning of this study, our focus is on sub-Saharan Africa. South Africa could possibly fit the bill on dependent development, but it remains outside the scope of this study.

8. UNIDO—United Nations Industrial Development Organization—classifies countries in four major categories: industrialized (more than 30 percent of GNP accounted for by industry); semi-industrialized (20–30 percent of GNP accounted for by industry); countries in the course of industrialization (10–20 percent of GNP accounted for by industry); and non-industrialized (less than 10 percent of GNP accounted for by industry).

9. Broadly defined, a Transnational Corporation (TNC) is a large firm which undertakes direct foreign investment in two or more countries. For details about transnational corporations see: United Nations Center for Transnational Corporations, *Transnational Corporations in World Development: Third Survey* (1983).

4

Disaggregating Capitalism in Africa: Theoretical Issues

Development theory has reached some kind of impasse because it has been unable to explain the growing number of instances where several models co-exist and overlap in the same country. Instead of recognizing the merits and defects of all positions and trying to test their application on the basis of the concept of historical specificity, development theory tends to be fixed in typologies of universalism.

—Stanley Aronowitz, "Introduction"

Imperialism, through its different phases has produced a world capitalist system as a *single* economic and social system, which embraces all areas in the non-socialist world, including the most isolated subsistence farmers. The structure and functions of this world capitalist system prohibits the emergence of an independent national capitalist system.

Bade Onimode, *Imperialism and Underdevelopment in Nigeria*

INTRODUCTION

The two above quotations represent, in a nutshell, the current status in the theorizing about development in the Third World. The first quotation, by Stanley Aronowitz, represents the latest attempt at moving away from general (or universal) models of development to an assessment of specific regions, based on particular historical experiences that may have little or no relevance to any other region in the world. The second quotation, by Bade Onimode, is yet another attempt at establishing the universality of both capitalism and socialism as the only socioeconomic systems in the world today. Onimode's argument is an augmented Wallersteinian/Frankian world system/dependency theory formulation which the present study so far has found to be less than satisfactory.

World system/dependency theory formulations are especially vulnerable on two theoretically related propositions. The *first* relates to the conceptualization of capitalism as a worldwide system. As we stated in the previous chapter, Wallerstein and Frank (and their followers) argue that the world market was capitalist from its inception in the long sixteenth century, circa 1450–1600 (Wallerstein, 1974). Frank makes a forceful argument regarding the evolution of the world market from the sixteenth century, especially the subjugation of Latin America to this wider system of exchange (1967; 1969). To a large extent, Walter Rodney's 1972 study makes the same argument in relation to Africa. In this argument, the whole history of European colonialism in the Third World is seen as a totality of production relations where international capitalist enterprises substantively subjugated peasant and other forms of indigenous labor across the board. The problem with such a formulation is that it equates capitalism with a trade-based division of labor, where the dynamics of accumulation are assumed to operate through the imperatives of exchange rather than production. This argument has its roots in Adam Smith's work. We seek to demonstrate later in this chapter the fallacy of this argument, especially as it concerns Africa's production structure.

The *second* related theoretical concern deals with the issue of independent capitalist development in the Third World, given the theoretical subordination of the Third World to international capital within world system/dependency theory. Given the logic of international capitalism, dependency theory does not see any possibility of independent capitalist development in the periphery. Henry Bernstein and Bonnie K. Campbell, among others, have taken issue with such formulations and point

the dangers of a simple model of neo-colonial dependence (determination by "external" forces) which denies indigenous social forces their own dynamics—the expression of class and other social contradictions within the country. This effect of dependency theory is connected with its tendency (at least as applied to Africa, if not in the Latin American context) to deny the possibility of any significant indigenous capital accumulation. In turn this produces an instrumental version of the neo-colonial state as a mechanism of domination by international capital, in alliance with a strictly subordinated bureaucratic-military apparatus and/or comprador bourgeoisie. (1985: 9)

Such concerns, in the case of Kenya for example, have been expressed by Colin Leys (1977) and Nicola Swainson (1980). These two authors have favored an approach that transcends the preoccupation of dependency theory with the asymmetrical relationship between an apparently omnipotent international capitalism, and a local bourgeoisie that is overwhelmed by its subordination. The problem with such arguments, however, is that little empirical evidence is provided to support the contention of an existing ascending national bourgeoisie. One instance should help clarify the picture.

Swainson (1980), in reference to Kenya, has argued that we need to look at the embryonic development of capitalism in Kenya beginning in the 1920s, and the subsequent post-1945 internationalization of capital as the basis for local and international capital collaboration, culminating in a form of "independent" capital accumulation and capitalist development in Kenya. The problem with Swainson's formulation, however, is that she shows that it is international capital that still provides the basis for accumulation, and indeed provides the basis for further local subordination.

The extension of internal accumulation has been accompanied by an increased penetration of foreign capital in the Kenyan manufacturing sector. The investment of foreign firms in manufacturing during the 1960s and 1970s was partly in response to global conditions of accumulation which in general have given rise to a massive export of productive capital. This shift in emphasis of foreign capital away from the traditional plantation sectors into manufacturing has been a response to pressure from indigenous capitalists who have made land their exclusive preserve since independence. (1980: 17)

The question here is whether indeed there is a well established indigenous capitalist class in Kenya to warrant the adoption of Swainson's position. The evidence she further provides only shows that foreign capital has increased its stake in the Kenyan economy. Swainson's attempt to show an existing local dynamic bourgeoisie in Kenya fails for the simple reason that it does not exist. A recent work by John Sender and Sheila Smith (1986) makes the same mistake—essentially adopting a neo-Bill Warren (1980) thesis. The labored attempt by Swainson, Sender and Smith to prove the existence of indigenous African capitalism fails because any significant independent local capital accumulation is still lacking.

To us, therefore, the issue of whether the African production structure is predominantly capitalist as argued by dependency theory—or that African production systems are capable of producing indigenous capitalists, as argued by Swainson and Leys among others—has to be taken a step back to the first principle of investigation: that of definition of the problem. As a first step, we will attempt a brief definition and analysis of what constitutes capitalism and whether, on the basis of the definition, Africa can be regarded as capitalist. We believe it is through such an investigation process that issues of development can be better understood.

DEFINING CAPITALISM

Critical to the definition and analysis of any mode of production is an examination of the labor process and ultimately an examination of relationship between labor and the means of production, and the attendant social relations of production. It should be recognized that modes of production other than capitalism have historically existed, but for our purposes (at least initially) we are only interested in examining what constitutes the capitalist mode. Based on that examination, a determination then can be made as to whether Africa is a capitalist society, as suggested by dependency and other neo-Marxian formulations.

Despite its affinity for Marxist political economy, dependency/world-system theory is uncharacteristically un-Marxian in its ultimate characterization of what constitutes capitalism in the Marxist sense. As we have shown in the previous chapter, dependency theory assumes that trade and unequal exchange between developed capitalist economies and the Third World have historically provided the basis for capitalist production in the Third World, given the ultimate destination of the surplus (i.e., the developed capitalist world). But the ultimate destination of the surplus cannot constitute a determination of the mode of production, given the absence of an examination of the labor process at the point of production. This omission has always been dependency theory's Achilles' heel. The exchange process does not constitute capitalism.

Maurice Dobb (1963) has argued from a classic Marxian sense that the essence of capitalism has to be sought in a particular system of production under which labor-power has itself become a commodity and is bought and sold in the market like any other object of exchange. According to Dobb, the historical prerequisite of this system was the concentration of ownership of the means of production in the hands of a class, consisting of only a minor section of society, and the consequent emergence of a propertyless class for whom the sale of their labor-power was their *only* source of livelihood. This definition excludes the system of independent handicraft production where the craftsmen or other independent producers owned their own tools of production (petty as they were), and undertook the sale of their own products. According to Dobb:

What differentiates the use of this definition from others is that the existence of trade and of money-lending and the presence of a specialized class of merchants or financiers, even though they be men of substance, does not suffice to constitute a capitalist society. Men of capital however acquisitive, are not enough: their capital must be used to yoke labor to the creation of surplus-value in production. (1963: 8)

Although Dobb wrote his book in 1946 two decades before the popularization of dependency theory, he was well aware of the possible theoretical mistakes regarding capitalism:

If we are speaking of capitalism as a specific mode of production, then it follows that we cannot date the dawn of this system from the first signs of the appearance of large-scale trading and of a merchant class, and we cannot speak of a special period of "Merchant Capitalism," as many have done. We must look for the opening of the capitalist period only when changes in the mode of production occur, in the sense of a direct subordination of the producer to a capitalist. (1963: 17)

The warning is important for several reasons. First, it precludes the designation of rich rural dwellers (referred to as *kulaks*) as capitalists if they just hire labor, given the fact that the hired labor has the option to do other things, including *not* working for the kulak. The implication of this for Africa will be discussed further below. Second, as has already been pointed out, a trading or merchant class does not define capitalism. Markets and exchange processes have to be rooted in a particular system of appropriation for capitalism to exist. Finally, historically the capitalist system was accompanied by rapid technical changes and efficiency in production. While this is not a necessary condition of capitalism, it provided a stimulus for further accumulation (Kay, 1975: 96–98).

A common error associated with the designation of many African societies as capitalist derives from the existence of an exchange process in the rural areas, involving commodities produced internally in the rural economy and those produced outside the rural economy. Commodities produced in the rural economy include food and other means of subsistence determined by environmental conditions. Commodities produced outside the rural economy include clothes, bicycles, etc.—commodities that the rural economy is not technologically competent to produce. The medium of exchange of course is money, and money has been said to constitute capitalist penetration. The error of this application can be corrected by examining Marx's statement on the subject:

In so far as money itself plays a part here, it is only to the extent that it is itself an extremely powerful agent of dissolution which intervenes in the process, and hence contributes to the creation of the *plucked*, objective-less, free-*laborers*, it is certainly not by *creating* the objective conditions of such laborers' existence, but rather by accelerating their separation from them, i.e. by accelerating their loss of property. (1964: 110) (Author's emphasis.)

The statement by Marx helps to underscore our argument regarding the nature of, and what constitutes, capitalism. Given the clarity with which Marx defined capitalism, it is surprising that dependency theory has not taken a serious retreat from designating all African societies as capitalist (see, for example, Onimode, 1982). A mode of production must be defined by the *production* process, not the *exchange* process. In the following section, we attempt to outline the nature of the production process in Africa to further elaborate on the concept of capitalism and whether the system of production in Africa is capitalist. We are convinced that the best way to determine whether Africa is capitalist is to examine what the majority of the workers do in the production process.

A principal test as to whether a society is capitalist or not can be conducted by examining Marx's theoretical-historical examination of capitalism against socioeconomic reality as it exists in Africa today. In *Pre-Capitalist Economic Formations*, Marx stated that

one of the prerequisites of wage labor and one of the historic conditions for capital is free labor and the exchange of free labor against money, in order to reproduce money and convert it into values, in order to be consumed by money, not as use value for enjoyment, but as use value for money. Another prerequisite is the separation of free labor from the objective conditions of its realization—from the means and material of labor. This means above all that the worker must be separated from the land, which functions as his natural laboratory. This means the dissolution both of free petty landownership and of communal landed property, based on oriental commune. (1964: 67)

It should be pointed out that the definition of capitalism, using Marxian formulation, closely resembles some elements of capitalism as defined in the Weberian sense. Max Weber is probably best known for his work *The Protestant Ethic and The Spirit of Capitalism,* in which he identified specific attitudinal and motivational factors as central to the development of capitalism.

Recently, however, scholars have begun to point out that perhaps Weber's other two books, *General Economic History* and *Economy and Society,* stand out as better representatives of Weber's conceptualization of capitalism (Callaghy, 1988 n. 4). These scholars have pointed out that, in the last two works, Weber's conceptualization of capitalism was much broader in scope and predominantly institutional in its characterization of capitalism, as opposed to the narrow formulations contained in *The Protestant Ethic.* For our purposes we will regard the last two works as being more significant, thus being in agreement with scholars such as Callaghy (1984; 1988).[1]

In his broadest usage of the term, Max Weber defined capitalism as "the provision of human needs by enterprise, which is to say, by private businesses seeking profit. It is exchange carried out for positive gain, rather than forced contributions or traditionally fixed gifts or trades (1981: 275–76)." Since economic systems and historical epochs take a long time to evolve, Weber recognized and acknowledged the existence of early forms of capitalism. However, he was very strict in his conceptualization of capitalism. Weber categorically stated that an economy can only be considered capitalist "only as the provision for wants is capitalistically organized to such a predominant degree that if we imagine this form of organization taken away the whole economic system must collapse" (1981: 276). Of further significance, like Marx, Weber stressed that modern capitalism does not necessarily develop from extensive trade or accumulation—early modern Spain being a significant historical example. It is on this point regarding trade and accumulation that world-system/dependency theory significantly differs from Marxian/Weberian formulations. External trade in both Marxian and Weberian formulations is regarded as a contributing factor but not a *necessary* one, as trade merely reinforced social and institutional structures already existing in Europe prior to the nineteenth century. For example, Weber notes that

accumulation of wealth brought about through colonial trade has been of little significance for the development of modern capitalism.... It is true that the colonial trade made possible the accumulation of wealth to an enormous extent, but this did not further the specifically accidental form of the organization of labor, since colonial trade itself rested on the principle of exploitation and not that of securing an income through market operations. (1981: 300)

Indeed if one were to maintain that trade formed the basis for European capitalist accumulation, as dependency theory does, this would constitute a denial of independent (internal) development for European societies—a point that can be sustained neither theoretically nor historically. It is a theoretical denial of the original and natural autonomy of societies.

Weber listed six basic elements that characterized the evolution of modern capitalism:

1. Private appropriation by entrepreneurs of all the means of production, separation of the workers from the means of production
2. Formally free labor, but compelled to sell its labor
3. Rational technology based on calculation and knowledge, especially mechanization
4. Market exchange not burdened by irrational restraints
5. Calculable law in both adjudication and state administration
6. A rational monetary system and the general commercialization of economic life. (Collins, 1980: 928)

The fifth element in Weber's formulation can be attributed to the historical influence on Weber of the evolution of the German state in the nineteenth century given the active intervention of the state in promotion of capitalist development in Germany. The issue of law and adjudication was recognized by Marx but was never given the Weberian emphasis.

Thus it can be said that, although Marx and Weber had some differences in their approach, the main elements in their characterization of capitalism were essentially similar in a given broad conceptualization.[2]

As a final example, we take the issue of accumulation to compare the two approaches. We have already shown Weber's conceptualization of capital accumulation, which is rooted in the internal transformation of a mode to reflect certain characteristics. Weber's conceptualization, in our opinion, can be compared to the following statement by Marx:

The *original formation of capital* does not, as is often supposed, proceed by the *accumulation* of food, tool, raw materials or in short, of the *objective* conditions of labor detached from the soil and already fused with human labor. Not by means of capital creating the objective conditions of labor. Its original *formation* occurs simply because the historical process of the dissolution of an old mode of production, allows value, existing in the form of *monetary wealth* to buy the objective conditions of labor on the one hand, to exchange the *living* labor of the now free workers for money on the other. (1964: 110) (Author's emphasis)

We are convinced that, ultimately, a better way of analyzing modern capitalism and its historical evolution (and ultimately its application to African development) may depend on the synthesis between the Weberian institutional theory of capitalism and the Marxian social theory of capitalism. This approach, which others may consider too eclectic, may provide an avenue for escaping theoretical rigidities—either Weberian or Marxist—which may hamper genuine efforts at better understanding of capitalist development in Africa and elsewhere in the Third World.[3]

CHARACTERIZING MODES OF PRODUCTION IN AFRICA: ISSUES OF THEORY AND METHOD

In the past decade, literature on Africa's development has centered on the discussion regarding African participation in the international capitalist system and, ultimately, the failure of Africa to eradicate underdevelopment. This failure has largely been attributed to the unequal and exploitative nature of the international capitalist system in which Africa, along with other Third World countries, is but a junior partner. The predominance of the dependency paradigm in African intellectual circles has ensured that the international dimension of Africa's underdevelopment has continued to receive disproportionate attention compared to the internal evolution of modes of production in Africa itself. There are a few writers however, who have attempted to redress this imbalance by beginning to reexamine the concept of development and African society in general from the standpoint of the interaction between the externally generated capitalist systems of production and Africa's internally determined systems of production and their attendant social relations and institutions. By the very nature of their own internal logic, both the external and internal systems are inherently contradictory.

In the African context, one of the few authors to attempt a genuine exploration of the internal characteristics of African modes of production, and their interaction with international capitalism, is Claude Ake (1976).[4] In analyzing modes of production in Africa, Ake suggested that there is a juxtaposition of three modes of production.

The Primitive Community Mode: The basic means of production in this mode is land. The land is generally owned collectively by the lineage or clan or tribe, but its use is permitted to members of those primary groups, subject to certain conditions which vary from place to place. Labor is usually organized on the basis of the family or kinship, and the exchange of commodities is infrequent.

The Simple Commodity Mode of Production: This mode is based on private property, and depends on the personal labor of small-scale producers, who may be peasants, tradesmen, or artisans. Ake argues that "the wide prevalence of this mode can be gauged from the fact that in most African countries the proportion of wage-earners in manufacturing is usually less than 30 percent of all those engaged in production" (1976: 2). In this mode, simple commodity production meets and merges with the lower forms of capitalism, although Ake notes the problematic that "it is not clear that (simple commodity production) is yielding ground to capitalism, although it seems hardly economically viable in many cases" (ibid.).

The Capitalist Mode of Production: In characterizing this mode, Ake makes important qualifications which are significant to note: "The capitalism of African economies is unique, and may be described as 'derivative' in the sense that it developed as an effect of the quest by Western capitalists for market, raw materials, and profits; certainly much of the capital, the technology, and even the entrepreneurial skills still come from abroad. *It is a form of capitalism grafted on the societies in which the forces of production are still very rudimentary.* Although capitalism is rapidly penetrating African economies it has still a long way to go if we assess its importance by the extent to which the national economies are based on wage labor" (ibid.). (Emphasis added.)

Obviously, Ake's characterization of Africa's modes of production is very schematic, and it is at a very high level of abstraction. There are numerous variations in each of the modes presented not only within one country or geographical area, but also across the entire sub-Saharan Africa region. The most important point in Ake's work however, is the emphasis on the very strong presence of precapitalist modes of production in Africa—and indeed his suggestion that due to the prevalence of simple commodity production, Africa may not qualify to be called capitalist. It is this point which has become of major interest to those scholars who are attempting to understand seriously Africa's contemporary political economy in light of the current crisis in political and economic development.

One such scholar is Goran Hyden. His two books, *Beyond Ujamaa in Tanzania: Underdevelopment and as Uncaptured Peasantry* (1980) and *No Shortcuts to Progress: African Development Management in Perspective* (1983), have in recent years stirred much discussion and controversy regarding the nature of African society and its relationship to the outside world. While advocating an Africanist perspective in viewing development issues, he offers a scathing critique of both modernization and dependency theories. His most serious critique however, is reserved for world-systems/dependency theory:

To view Third World countries as mere extensions or satellites of modern societies is unsatisfactory. Leaders of these countries may be committed to one or other modern ideology. Their development orientation may be capitalist or socialist. Their economies, on the other hand, are still largely pre-modern. They have to operate on a material base which does not easily lend itself to capitalist or socialist policy solutions. (1980: 3)

Hyden then proceeds to state how he perceives Africa's failure to develop:

The problems of underdevelopment do not stem from excessive penetration by world capitalism. Rather they stem from the inability of capitalism to produce the same dynamic transformation of the material base as it once did in Europe and America. Capitalism fails to break down the precapitalist barriers that still exist in Third World countries. In fact, in many cases, it prolongs their life. (1980: 3–4)

The linchpin of Hyden's thesis on the persistence of precapitalist modes of production in Africa is peasant society and its attendant institutions. In fact, Hyden perceives peasant society as essentially reactionary in view of its outlook toward life in general, and its behavior in the production process in particular. Like Ake, Hyden notes that a peasant community may be involved in commodity production—but this is usually not its total culture. He argues that the economic structures that give precapitalist social formations longevity are still at work, thus assuring their survival in the contemporary period. One may argue that Hyden's thesis is largely a synthesis of Marxian and Weberian concepts of capitalism—especially his emphasis on an African "uncaptured" peasantry by other classes. The "capturing" or destruction of the peasantry by classes representing higher forms of sociotechnological reproduction has historically been the beginning of the end of a "natural economy." Thus Hyden notes that

Africa is the only continent where the peasants have not yet been captured by other social classes. By being owners of their own means of production, the many smallholder peasants in Africa have enjoyed a degree of independence from other social classes large enough to make them influence the course of events on the continent. (1980: 9)

Given Hyden's conviction that capitalism provides the best chance for Africa to develop, it then follows that he considers the capturing of the peasantry by the state as essential, in view of the absence of an independent national bourgeoisie in African countries. His position on the African state is problematic however, given the record of its performance since independence. We will deal with the issue of the state in Africa in the next chapter. Suffice it to say here that while Hyden's discomfort with a predominant peasantry makes sense, his perceived solution via state action is unduly optimistic given the uncapitalistic behavior of African states in general.

Hyden (1980: 13–19) and others (see, for example, Klein, 1980: 11; Forrest, 1982) have delineated the basic characteristics of a "peasant mode of production" in the following terms.

Domestic orientation. The peasant mode is characterized by a rudimentary division of labor, small production units, minimal product specialization, and little exchange between various units of production. Because of the last characteristic, there is little functional interdependence between the various units. As a result, "there is a long-term planning perspective within the peasant household, but it relates less to productive rather than to socially reproductive needs ... the needs of man rather than those associated with the development of the means of production take precedence ... [peasants] operate according to the law of subsistence rather than the law of value. [Because of other social obligations,] the cost of reproduction is high and it leaves the peasant with limited interest in adopting practices that may raise agricultural productivity" (Hyden, 1980: 14).

Resource-based agriculture. Given the low level of technology, peasant agriculture is based on human labor using simple hand tools (the hoe), shifting cultivation to allow regeneration of land, organic knowledge as opposed to science-based agriculture, etc. As a result, production is limited by the confines derived from low technology.

Peasant culture (or "economy of affection"). Peasant culture is based on the concept of reciprocity, where affective ties are based on common descent, common residence, and so forth. Peasant action is always limited by the very confines of his horizon and, as Hyden notes, "peasants are not likely to engage in class action unless their chances of reproducing their own mode of production are in danger" (1980: 19).

All the above characteristics of peasant society in Africa—which, incidentally, are similar to the ones analyzed by Ake—do reinforce one fundamental point. Given the characterization of capitalism in both the Marxian and Weberian sense—generalized wage labor; money capital with which means of production may be purchased and wages paid; the existence of means of production which may be purchased, that is, commodity production; and finally the existence of a complex of commodity markets and their institutional support—then it is extremely difficult, if not erroneous, to characterize African society as predominantly capitalist, as world-system/dependency theory contends. Teodor Shanin (1973), in an authoritative study of peasant societies, distinguished the modus operandi of the peasant economy from that of a capitalist enterprise in the following terms:

Firstly, the personal supervision of a [peasant] enterprise makes strict control and planning less necessary, while the owner's limited education would make their execution difficult. Some stumbling blocks are . . . inherent in the very character of peasant economy. A major part of the production is consumed while labour is utilized directly. The pricing of both of these is therefore to a considerable degree arbitrary. . . . The consumption, rather than accumulation, aims of family farms find expression in the fact that use-value repeatedly takes precedence over exchange-value in the peasant's consideration. The often-noticed tendency to reduce risks by "unprofitable" diversification of crops [for example] illuminates the rationale for such planning in peasant economies. (Shanin, 1973: 70)

Thus Weber's rationality in capitalist planning is effectively undermined by the parameters of peasant society itself. Since modern governments in Africa require some basic planning for economic development, the society which supposedly stands to benefit from that planning becomes a hindrance toward fulfilling that objective. This observation obviously has serious implications for the future of capitalist (or socialist) development on the continent, a point recognized by the World Bank in its analysis as to why agricultural production has declined in Africa in the past two decades:

The dominance of subsistence production presented special obstacles to agricultural development. Farmers have to be induced to produce for the market, adopt new crops, and undertake new risks. Established farming systems, which have evolved over centuries and were well adapted to the local environment, had to be revamped if production was to increase. (World Bank, 1981: 12)

Peasant studies of other Third World societies—especially in Asia and Latin America—have shown serious social stratification in peasant societies based on the nature of ownership of the basic means of production (land) and the organization of labor (Wolf, 1966, 1969; Midgal, 1974; Popkin, 1979; Scott, 1976). Serious social and political conflicts have been generated as a result of the inequitable distribution of the means of production. Revolutions, such as the one in Nicaragua under the Sandinistas, are but a product of these conflicts. It has also been shown that the nature of villages in Africa and their organizations is fundamentally different from those of either Asia or Latin America in the sense that African villages are essentially "open," with little social stratification and internal control, while those of Asia and Latin America are "corporated" villages which are dominated and controlled by powerful landholders who, for the most part, do not live in the same villages (Popkin, 1979; Scott, 1976). Most African societies, however, differ from their counterparts in Asia and Latin America in that they lack a well-defined landowner class and thus lack the antagonistic socioeconomic relations that sometimes result in peasant-landowner conflict. Indeed, as Martin Klein (1980: 13) has noted, in most of Africa there was free land for the taking and in many areas there still is. African land is often poor, but there is a lot of it. Even in the rich areas, land was still available in the 1960s. This was a key factor inhibiting the development of landownership, hence the lack of serious local social conflict based on the distribution and ownership of the major means of production—land.[5]

This external ownership of the means of production has serious implications for the organization of labor and the application of technology. In the African case, open villages have a sense of autonomous existence, with land ownership being essentially communal under some form of traditional arrangement. The village socialization process ensures, in a minimal sense, availability of subsistence for either kith and kin, or other village dwellers—thus minimizing potential for conflict. Historically, the existence of such communal land arrangements and other avenues of subsistence has undermined capitalism's potential to systematically destroy this "natural" economy, given the direct access to land. This suggests that there is a basic internal blockage to capitalist development within the African peasant mode of production. As Emmanuel Terray reminds us:

The advent of capitalist production is conditional upon the divorce of the laborer from the means of production on the one hand, and the existence of the free laborer on the other. What were characteristic of pre-capitalist modes of production, on the contrary, were non-economic bonds between producers, means of production, and sometimes also non-producers. These bonds were not only the political or ideological representation of the relations of production, but also entered into them as constituent elements. (1972: 148–149)

Elsewhere, Terray points out that in precapitalist socioeconomic formation, the unity between labor and its material conditions is mediated by the laborers' membership in a commune, and the individual's access to the means of production is through membership in this commune, a point we have already emphasized.

The issue of the separation of laborers from ownership of the means of production thus determines one of the basic elements of capitalist production—the others being the expansion of capital and the existence of the market to facilitate capitalistically produced commodities, including labor. It has been argued that in the African circumstance, one may begin to understand the difference in the development of capitalism between South Africa and countries that are equally or comparatively resource-rich, such as Nigeria, Zambia, or Zaire. Frederick Cooper, for example, has argued that

primitive accumulation is not the mere amassing of productive resources, it is the exclusion from access to the means of production of an entire class. It implies not merely the acquisition of titles to land, but the effective denial of access: it thus requires both the systematic exercise of force and its legitimation, hence it requires the exercise of state power. Accumulation is thus a process that one class must do to another and one that will be resisted. It is an historical phenomenon.

He further suggests:

By focusing on accumulation in Africa, one might understand the limits of responses to market expansion from the early nineteenth century onward as much as its extent. *Through consideration of how a relatively small group of whites in South Africa gained control of land and the subsequent transformation of the collection of rent into the control of labor, one might begin to distinguish the course of capitalist development in South Africa from Nigeria or Zambia. It is necessary not just to stress the exclusionary nature of primitive accumulation but also to examine the dynamics, implications, and limitations of other forms of accumulation.* (1981: 18) (Emphasis added.)

We wish to suggest that the failure of capitalism to develop in Africa can therefore be partly explained by its inability to effectively deny peasants access to the means of production and subsistence. As Cooper has further suggested, it would seem that African peasants are not dependent enough.

If a dominant class could not control land and labor, the pressures of the market and the interventions of the state circled around the peasant farm without entering it directly. A household that grew its own food might respond vigorously to market incentives (for example) and be hurt grievously by depression, but still had a significant ability to hold the market at arm's length. Markets *per se* do not lock in peasants. (1981: 34)

The same point is made by Hyden when he points out that compared to his/her Asian or Latin American counterpart, the African peasant is socially and economically more independent of outside forces. As a result, African peasants are also less integrated in the cash economy than peasants elsewhere. This does not mean, however, that there are no capitalist farmers in Africa. But the majority of peasant producers still make a living without much dependence on inputs from other sectors.

Our discussion so far has suggested that there is a very strong element of an African peasant or "natural" economy which pervades the continent's production landscape. Studies have suggested that the continuance of this system of production is based on the inability of capital to effectively penetrate this natural economy and to break its cycle of reproduction. The question therefore becomes, "Why hasn't capitalism been able to perform and accomplish this historic mission?"—especially when there is ample evidence of the existence of simple commodity production in the peasant mode of production. Perhaps it is best to answer the question by making a distinction between simple commodity production and capitalist commodity production. In this regard, we find Henry Bernstein's work most helpful:

Simple commodity production is distinguished from capitalist commodity production by its logic of subsistence (meeting the needs of simple reproduction), as opposed to the logic of the appropriation and realization of surplus = value and the accumulation of capital on the other hand, the simple commodity producer is not a proletarian as (a) he/she retains some control over the organization of production; (b) household production, while occupying a definite place in the social division of labor *internal* to the production process (relative to that of capitalist production enterprises) and therefore, cannot produce the 'collective worker' in Marx's sense. The spatial concentration of peasants, when this occurs, is not equivalent to the *social* concentration of workers in capitalist production. (1977: 63)

Bernstein's work thus brings us full circle. Given what we have determined as the basic characteristics of capitalist production, the dominance of simple commodity production, which forms Ake's second characterization of African systems of production, suggests that capitalist production in Africa still has a long way to go. Indeed, part of the problem of underdevelopment in Africa may be explained as the failure of capitalist production to take root. This is not to deny, however, that any forms of capitalist production exist in Africa. The theoretical task is to try to understand the specific processes of accumulation which either enhance or block economic change, and to analyze specific circumstances of the interaction between local systems of production and externally generated capitalist production. This study joins numerous others that have suggested the articulation of modes of production approach to the study of African socioeconomic systems. (For a summary of this approach, see Seddon, 1978; Livingstone, 1982; Wolpe, 1980.)

THE ARTICULATION OF MODES OF PRODUCTION IN AFRICA

We take *articulation* at its simplest usage to refer to "the relationship between the reproduction of the capitalist economy on the one hand and the reproduction of productive units organized according to precapitalist relations and forces of production on the other" (Wolpe, 1980: 41). In the African sense, this typically refers to an externally generated capitalism—predominantly in the modern/formal sector—coming into contact with various forms of precapitalist production, predominantly in the rural and informal sector. In a typical African country, the rural/informal sector accounts for over 80 percent of national employment and other economic activity.

Although this study has adopted articulation of modes of production approach to understand the nature of African socioeconomic systems, we recognize objections to its use. For example, William Roseberry (1978: 3–18) seriously doubts its utility, given the fact that he views peasant societies as adjuncts to wider systems; therefore, the most appropriate approach would be to study the wider systems as rather than how the two systems converge:

If peasants exist within larger societies, let us begin with those societies, examine the social, political, and economic processes of development (or underdevelopment) which are at work in them, and then analyze rural regions in terms of those larger processes. The problem of "articulation" disappears because we are no longer talking about two discrete units which somehow are related but about a total society. (Roseberry, 1978: 3)

We suggest that Roseberry's methodology denies autonomy to peasant societies or any other precapitalist economic systems, in spite of overwhelming evidence of that autonomy as demonstrated by Hyden and others. Roseberry's approach may be valid at a very high level of abstraction, but it is essentially irrelevant to the concrete world of micro-level understanding of precapitalist society—which has implications for development planning. Our approach and understanding of articulation partly derives its impetus from what Maurice Dobb advised several decades ago. He correctly pointed out that socioeconomic systems and their transitions have to be examined as a process with changing structures which incorporate old and new elements:

We must not let it be implied that the frontiers between systems are to be drawn across a page of history or a sharp dividing line . . . systems are never in reality to be found in their pure form, and in any period of history elements characteristic both of preceding and of succeeding periods are to be found, sometimes mingled in extraordinary complexity. (Dobb, 1963: 11)

Our study contends that African society reflects a system of production which is "mingled in extraordinary complexity," one which combines elements of both capitalist and precapitalist modes. Their articulation thus becomes the point of departure for our discussion. We make an a priori assumption that once the logic of capitalism is interrupted by a system (or systems) which operate with a different logic, its dynamism becomes substantially compromised and thus the very essence of the system becomes significantly altered. In the African case, evidence of this compromise abounds. Callaghy's (1984) analysis of Zaire and Schatz's (1977) study of Nigeria, for example, both show how capitalism in those two countries has failed to transform the economic system due to the persistence of precapitalist behavior inimical to capitalist "rationality." Such behavior includes corruption and unexpanded reproduction based on capital investment. While condemning capitalism in general, Guy Gran's (1979) book on Zaire also shows how the statist and peasant ideology characterizing Zaire's political economy has contributed to the corruption that has recently become Zaire's legend. Goran Hyden's statement is based on this general understanding of the interaction between capitalist and precapitalist forms of production.

There is good reason ... to start from the assumption that in the contemporary development context in Africa, there are two contending modes of production which influence economic structures as well as social formations. . . . Maybe because there is no evidence of any well-known pre-capitalist modes . . . there has been a tendency to analyze the situation as if there were no other than the capitalist mode of production. Writers have referred to pre-capitalist formations but have not acknowledged that they operate according to a social logic of their own, that is, they are derived from a mode of production other than capitalism. (1980: 19–20)

In theoretical terms, we are thus confronted with the issue of which mode of production predominates in Africa, and how one determines this. Frederick Cooper (1981: 14) aptly summarized the specific problem in the analysis of African socioeconomic systems: the issue is not the classic transition of feudalism to capitalism but its opposite: how does capitalism become dominant in Africa without replicating itself in each instance? But Cooper's question is loaded with assumptions that need to be clarified. Foremost among them is the question of capitalist dominance in Africa; it is here that Goran Hyden's theoretical contribution is of greatest value. Hyden takes to task the dependency argument (in Gutkind and Wallerstein, 1985, for example)—that transformation of the precapitalist formations have stalled because the international capitalist system wants to keep the indigenous societies in Africa as sources of primitive accumulation, and not as societies that can independently sustain expanded reproduction for their own benefit (the so-called preservation/destruction thesis). Instead, he argues that capital does not *by design* seek the impoverishment of Africa. Capital, in order to expand, must replace inefficient precapitalist forms of production with more efficient ones (Hyden, 1980: 22). Hyden points to internal barriers to capitalist forms within the peasant society; he suggests that an examination of internal socioeconomic and cultural structures is the best way to study capitalist development (or underdevelopment) in Africa. He concludes that

the ingredients of the explanation to internal barriers to capital's expansion lie in the sphere of production. The persistence of pre-capitalist relations of production retard productivity growth in the production of wage goods—the means of subsistence. This retardation sooner or later creates a problem to capital because capitalism can only expand and reproduce itself if it continuously finds ways of cheapening the production of these means of subsistence. (Hyden, 1980: 22)

One such internal barrier to capital's expansion is Africa's very low socioeconomic base, as shown in chapters 1 and 2 of this study. The absorptive capacity of Africa's industry, in terms of both labor and raw materials is severely limited by, among other things, the nature of technology introduced on the continent since independence (Rweyamamu, 1973). In England, the enclosure system drove the peasantry away from the land, but the expanding factories were able to absorb the "excess" labor. In Africa, even if an enclosure system were to develop, there is no manufacturing sector to absorb newly migrated peasants who have hardly any skills with which to cope in the urban areas (Hunt, 1984; Bienen and Diejomaoh, 1981). Thus the expansionary character of capital is severely compromised regardless of the existence of abundant labor—which theoretically should cheapen the labor cost of production.

The inability of the excess labor to find employment in urban areas has further economic implications that undermine capital's expansionary nature. Since no effective demand exists among these migrants, they end up for the most part becoming dependent on the state for their survival (in terms of urban food subsidies, transport, etc.). In countries such as Zaire, Zambia, or Tanzania, industry capacity utilization has constantly remained below 40 percent. This can partly be explained by ineffective demand, which is also a function of a disarticulated industrial sector.

All this suggests something critical to the understanding of capitalism in Africa, and hence articulation of modes of production. There do not exist in Africa institutions that are supportive of the capitalist system in the Weberian sense. Neither are Marxian capitalist social relations expressed in the sphere of production. Those who suggest that the existence of the *market* presupposes capitalist relations of production err in their equation of a mode of production with commodity exchange. Indeed, markets have historically existed in modes of production prior to capitalism. But, as Teodor Shanin has pointed out, in peasant society the market system is not generalized; there is marginal exchange at the marketplaces, as opposed to the universal system of production for exchange governed by more or less free interplay of price, supply, and demand. Thus in peasant society

market places are typically related to conditions in which a major part of the goods never reaches the market but is consumed within the family units. In this sense markets form a typical component of the peasant system of economic organization, providing a place where primary producers sell part of their production to obtain cash and to supplement home produce by outside supplies of immediate needs. (Shanin, 1973: 74)

This suggests that peasant society, like other societies, operates a market system. But its market system does not purely or exclusively depend (or feed on) production, which is internal to the system itself. Thus the relationship between peasant society and capitalism is substantially at the commercial exchange level. The exchange level—especially in commodities that are produced in systems with a different production logic—does not itself constitute an independent and clearly defined mode of production. The relationship between peasant markets and extra-nonpeasant society is thus mediated through a complex maze of exchange processes which is determined by local circumstance and the nature and strength of the extra peasant economy. As Teodor Shanin notes:

In contemporary peasant societies the local markets are ... linked with regional and national ones into a two—or three tier system in which the central markets draw rural produce from the local one and supply these with industrial goods. It is through the development and contradictions of this structure that the peasant market gradually becomes a part of the market system of economy. (1973: 74)

Articulation defines the "development and contradictions of this structure." The contradictions between the logic of peasant subsistence and capitalist production—in the African situation, the latter seems to be the preserve of the state—provide the avenue for articulation. While acknowledging this contradiction, we find difficulty in accepting Bernstein's supposition that the only way to look at peasant household production is that such production is brought about through the pressure of the state—which, in our opinion, diminishes a legitimate role of the internal operation of the peasant economy itself. Bernstein states that

peasants have to be located in their relations with capital and the state, in other words, within *capitalist relations of production* mediated through forms of household production which are the site of a struggle for effective possession and control between the producers and capital/state. (1977: 73)

However, his subsequent qualification—that there is a limit to peasant subjugations and real subsumption of household labor by capital, to the extent that the producers are not fully expropriated nor dependent for their reproduction on the sale of labor-power through the wage-form—brings us full circle to our original determination of what constitutes capitalism. Thus his posing of peasants as "wage-labor" equivalent has little theoretical value. Bernstein's dismissal of articulation thesis is thus also rejected (Bernstein, 1979: 422).

CONCLUSION: PEASANT SOCIETY, CAPITALISM, AND ECONOMIC DEVELOPMENT

We have argued in this chapter that in Africa, the development of capitalism has encountered numerous barriers some of which have their origin and substance in the character of peasant society. Unlike moral economists and romantic local scholars of peasant societies, our study perceives peasant society as essentially self-limiting, backward, and operating in a framework and logic that limits the expansion of productive forces. Without the expansion of productive forces, serious development is unlikely in Africa in the immediate future; thus the day-to-day existence of peasants—already difficult and tenuous—will become even more so. It is with the realization and appreciation of the difficulty with which peasants satisfy their everyday needs that this study categorically concurs with Samuel Popkin's condemnation of those who romanticize the village. Thus, in opposition to moral economists, Popkin argues that

a way of life that may have existed for lack of alternatives is extolled as a virtue. Peasants who had little or nothing to eat are assumed to have had a rich spiritual life. Some who may have stayed with their fathers only in order to survive are credited with filial piety. What may have been the absence of incentives to change becomes a resistance to innovation and a defense of traditional ways. The rich who hid their wealth are perceived as having shown great modesty, and hostility among villages is converted to village solidarity. Somehow what might only have been the necessities or oppressions of one era come to be interpreted as traditional values during the next. (1979: 3)

Thus, unlike moral economists, our study recognizes internal contradictions within peasant societies that work to retain existing oppressive and exploitative social relations and also to contribute to the fending off of capitalism's onslaught. Sidney Mintz, for example, recognized the problem of analyzing peasant society as if such society was morally superior—something which clearly was (and still is) a fallacy.

Part of the difficulty (in looking at peasants as helpless victims) is that in observing how external groups may profit by controlling the peasantry, one may overlook how members of different sectors of the peasantry profit—and, often, remain culturally conservative—by controlling each other. (Mintz 1973: 94)

In the African case, Claude Meillassoux's work in agricultural self-sustaining societies and Bogumil Jewsiewicki's work in Equatorial Central Africa clearly demonstrate this point, especially in the evolution of a "lineage mode of production" based on kinship relations. (See contributions in Crummey and Stewart, 1981; Seddon, 1978.)

Our study also argues that the low level of socioeconomic development—reflected in the low base of technology—has in the past few years contributed to the seriousness of the economic crisis in Africa. In the case of Tanzania, for example, Michaela von Freyhold has shown that:

The agricultural crisis which began to affect one part of the country after another [in the 1970s] was due to the rigidity of the agricultural systems, a rigidity which made it impossible for the peasants to respond adequately to environmental changes, population pressures or changes in the prices they received for the products. *What made these agricultural systems so rigid was that they had little scope for the development of the means of production and for the development of the division of labor inside the country.* (1979:4) (Emphasis added.)

Although the emphasis on the development of technology as the basis for economic development has been variously criticized as an ideology of developmentalism, with an essentially negative connotation emanating from the era of modernization theory (Shivji, 1985: 1–2), one cannot deny technology's centrality in the transformation of the productive structure of a country.

In terms of modes of production in Africa, we cannot help but conclude that the issue—both theoretical and practical—is that of imperfect integration between capitalist and precapitalist modes of production. By now it is clear that Africa did not replicate the historical experience of European capitalist development. In Europe, capitalist relations of production and institutions emerged out of the internal contradictions of feudalism, accompanied by generalized commodity production, a phenomenon clearly lacking in Africa. Indeed, Goran Hyden has cynically stated that in Africa, the problem of underdevelopment is due less to capitalist exploitation than to multinational corporations exploiting African resources. Or, as Frederick Cooper put it, "The laments of international organizations and development economists about the intractable backwardness of Africa is not a conspiratorial attempt to conceal the pillage of Africa, but a reflection of the fact . . . that Africa is an underexploited continent" (1981: 52). Whatever the case may be, the resilience of peasant society clearly has affected the evolution of capitalism in Africa. Consequently, other institutions in society, especially the State, have to be analyzed in relation to what happens in this imperfectly integrated material base.

NOTES

1. I am greatly indebted to Tom Callaghy for the ideas developed in this section. In the past few years I have been influenced by his synthesis of Marxian and Weberian

notions of capitalism and their application to Africa. (See Callaghy, 1984; 1988.) I, however, remain ultimately responsible for the positions developed here.

2. Some scholars have noted the significance of the similarity and difference in Weber's and Marx's approach to capitalism. One such scholar of note is Tom Bottomore in his recent book: *Theories of Modern Capitalism* (London: Allen and Unwin, 1985). In his book, Tom Bottomore notes that

the relation of Weber's conception of capitalism to Marx's theory is undoubtedly complex, but the principal affinities and divergencies should not be apparent. In defining capitalism Weber recognizes the importance of those elements which Marx had emphasized, namely, private ownership of the means of production, the creation of a working class dependent for its existence and reproduction on the sale of its labor power, and the continuous transformation of the process of production through technology. . . . Equally, Weber's emphasis upon rational law and administration, and the modern European state, as essential conditions for capitalist development is not incompatible with Marx's theory in which "political centralization," involving the creation of one nation, one code of laws, etc. is treated as a necessary concomitant of the bourgeoisie's rise to power. Here, as in the case of the "capitalist spirit," the extent of the divergence between Marx and Weber has to be judged in terms of the degree of autonomy and causal significance assigned to the various elements; and the circumstances which Weber identified as favorable to the rise of Western capitalism can be accommodated without difficulty, I think, in the framework of a Marxist theory which treats major historical changes as the outcome of interrelations and interactions among several elements in a total social structure. (1985:31) (See also Dobb, 1963.)

3. It is on this point that I differ with Tom Callaghy, who thinks that the Marxian social theory of capitalism can be adequately incorporated into the Weberian formulae without too much adjustment. (See Callaghy, 1988) Our study found much inspiration in John Lonsdale's review article, "State and Social Process in Africa," regarding the usefulness of incorporating Marxian and Weberian formulations in the quest for better understanding of historical and social processes in Africa. As Lonsdale emphasizes in his review:

No matter how straightforwardly one may wish one's history to be asked its questions, it must nevertheless be true that greater understanding can only come by moving to and fro—like migrant workers, intellectual *navetanes*—between the theory which suggests hypotheses and the facts uncovered by hypothesis, which must interrogate the theory. If a hypothesis is tried and found wanting, there ought then to be severe limits to the extent by which it can acceptably be made more abstract or more complex so as to accommodate the prickly particularities of the data; the simplest alternative hypothesis ought to be preferred. If the simpler hypothesis implies a different grand theory to that employed (however "silently") elsewhere in one's explanation, it may well mean not that one's explanation is fundamentally flawed but, rather, that *human actions are not reducible to any single theory of causation. There seems to me no good reason why one should not employ the approaches of both Marx and Weber, particularly at different levels of explanation.* (Lonsdale, 1981:140) (Emphasis added.)

See also Norbert Wiley, ed., *The Marx-Weber Debate* (Newbury Park, Calif.: Sage, 1986).

4. Claude Ake's subsequent work, however, has had a strong dependency flavor. See, for example, his two books, *Revolutionary Pressures in Africa* (1978) and *A Political Economy of Africa* (1981). In a later work, however, he reverts back to a mode of production approach that is, in our judgment, better than dependency. Thus, Ake states that, in much of Africa,

pre-capitalist relations of production prevail, though in various stages of decay; in so far as the atomized man (and hence the legal subject proper) is yet to emerge, people are only nominally in civil society. In the circumstances the social formation cannot institutionalize individualism, competition, freedom, equality or even proprietorship as its operative norms. (1985: 4)

5. The exception to this general statement is of course those countries that were occupied by European settlers: Algeria, Kenya, Zimbabwe, South Africa, Mozambique, Angola, and Guinea Bissau.

5

The State in Africa

It is necessary to rethink the general concept of the state and the peculiar character of the state in contemporary Africa. This rethinking might go along the lines of thinking of the state as a modality of class domination ideally engendered by the capitalist mode of production. What is unique to this modality is that the system of mechanisms of class domination is autonomized by the mediation of commodity. In the contemporary African socio-economic formation this autonomization exists only in the most rudimentary form, if at all. When we explore the significance of this state of affairs we see that it sheds light on the interplay of social forces, political struggles and the possibilities of the development of productive forces.

—Claude Ake, "The State in Contemporary Africa"

INTRODUCTION

This chapter explores in more detail Claude Ake's characterization of the state in contemporary Africa. It also builds upon the discussion in the last chapter which sought to establish the essential uncapitalistic (if not anticapitalistic) nature of African economies. Because our approach to the study of Africa is materialist in conception, it is inescapable that the treatment of the state in contemporary Africa must be rooted in the material basis of society. However, the state, once in existence, can develop interests of its own. The state in various instances has historically exhibited autonomy relative to various classes—the Bonapartist state being a prime example. Our general contention, therefore, is that what the state does in Africa will ultimately depend on its interaction with the material base which in the final analysis must sustain it. This approach does not ignore other significant sources of sustenance for the state in contemporary Africa. The case of Zaire immediately comes to mind. According to Thomas Callaghy:

Zaire was born in the international arena, and it has remained there. International assistance has been a continuous and pervasive factor supporting the emergence, consolidation, and survival of the Mobutu regime in Zaire. Such support was crucial to Mobutu's control of the armed forces from the earliest days, . . . crucial to the emergence and consolidation of an absolutist state with its political aristocracy, and crucial to its ability to survive a severe debt crisis and two external invasions in 1977 and 1978. A word of caution is necessary however, for although external assistance has been essential it has not been all determining. The Mobutu regime *would not* exist today without external support, past and present, but its ruler and his political aristocracy have successfully fought off important challenges to their relative autonomy. (1983: 61)

This study would not go as far as to say the Mobutu regime *would not* exist today without external support, because other possibilities exist. For example, it is quite possible that with deliberate benign neglect by the authorities in Kinshasa, substantial areas of Zaire could revert to a "natural" state, that is, a disintegrated political economy, and in turn would not be able to pressure the government for either political or economic goods. Admittedly, this scenario carries negative connotations regarding Zairian development. However, one cannot rule out the possibility of its actualization. The deteriorated state of affairs in Equatorial Guinea in recent years should serve as a reminder to all of us regarding that possibility.

Studies of the state in contemporary Africa in the last decade or so made the state famous for its omnipotence and pervasiveness in the political and economic lives of the population. Studies of the mid- to late 1970s owed their inspiration to the *relative autonomy* thesis initially used by Hamza Alavi (1972) in his study of the state in Pakistan and Bangladesh. The thesis formed the basis for analyzing the postcolonial state in Kenya (Leys, 1975; Swainson, 1980), Tanzania (Saul, 1974), and others. The relative autonomy thesis sought to establish that the neocolonial state was a combination of a capitalist/colonial state which had been imposed on African societies during colonialism. Its bureaucracy and coercive apparatus, as it were, had been foreign in origin. Because of this external imposition, the colonial state was necessarily overdeveloped. The succession to the colonial state was no better, since only the personnel changed, not the fundamental structures. This meant that the neocolonial state was essentially capitalist and, within a dependency framework, still externally dependent (Ziemann and Lanzendörfer, 1977).

We seek to demonstrate in this chapter that, while forms of external dependence by the African state exist, the underlying force that overwhelmingly influences state behavior and performance is the socioeconomic base that is only sporadically capitalistic in nature. The kind of state that subsequently obtains on the continent plays a negative role in the transformation of the productive forces. In other words, we seek to answer the question posed by Thomas Callaghy (1988) among others: Is the state in Africa a hindering or facilitating factor to economic development? Posed differently, the question would be, in light of the absence of serious socialistic alternatives on the continent, how capitalist is the African state?

THE STATE IN AFRICA: PROBLEMS OF METHODOLOGY

In current theorizing about the state in contemporary Africa, there is a general lack of a systematic treatment or one overriding approach. In a way, the lack or absence of *a* theory of the state in Africa is a positive development, given the dangers associated with generalizing theories, which purport to explain each and every phenomenon of the state. Marxian approaches to the state in Africa have often been guilty of this generalizing practice. The result of this theoretical practice is that the state in Africa has rarely been given an independent existence away from the economic base—regardless of evidence to the contrary. Our approach is based on one basic premise: societal attributes, of which the economy and polity are constituent parts (but not the only ones) should form the basis for analyzing the role of the state in society. Societal attributes in Africa are heavily conditioned by the *fact* of articulation of pre- and capitalist elements and underdevelopment. Because of the peculiar nature of underdevelopment in Africa, the way the state influences and affects the economy and society in general cannot lend itself to a single generalizing theory.

Thus, following the advice of Douglas C. Bennett and Kenneth E. Sharpe (1985), the approach that we find more appropriate to Africa is one which conceives of the state as an actor—not necessarily a simple or unified one, but at least one having identifiable behavior of its own that sets it apart from other actors with which it may cooperate or conflict. How the state copes with the pressures of economic decline and political pressure from various groups in society necessarily depends on the state's capacity to handle its own internal contradictions, and its ability to project a cohesiveness that will make it a formidable actor in the process of social struggles. Adopting such an approach to the study of the state in contemporary Africa also helps to redefine the conceptualization of development theory by moving away from simplistic dependency arguments. Timothy M. Shaw, for example, advises that

dependence needs to be reconceptualized as unequal relations between classes rather than countries; and *underdevelopment* needs to be reconceptualized so that uneven growth and distinctive class forms are recognized in the periphery. In short, African states are not robots that merely react to "external" inputs and instructions. Rather, ... structural linkages exist between social formations in the periphery and those in the center; incorporation [in the international system] consists of a continuous "transnational" relationship. (1982: 241)

Conceiving of the state as an actor means being able to explain why the state has the interests that it does. It also means being able to explain its particular characteristics within a framework of underdevelopment and "un-development" by examining issues such as classes and class alliances, state intervention in the economy, etc. In this way, one is able to capture the contradictory elements of the state in Africa, as Clive Thomas does.

It is clear that with the major classes underdeveloped, the state itself will also be an underdeveloped institution. In addition, in the non-capitalist society the state is dominated by the petty-bourgeois elements. These two circumstances contribute to giving the state the appearance of being "independent" and "autonomous" if not indeed a supra-class, institution. But because the state does not reflect the clear domination of one social class over all others, control of the state itself becomes remarkably susceptible to narrow shifts in alliances among the ruling petty-bourgeois elements. The coups and counter-coups which have prevailed in many of these countries reflect little more than shifts of power and position among the petty-bourgeois elements. (1978: 22)

The observation by Clive Thomas compares well with that of Claude Ake in the quotation at the beginning of this chapter. Both authors point to the difficulties associated with the relative autonomy thesis of the state. The question inevitably has always been, autonomous from whom? And to what extent? And, what are the limits of that autonomy?

Our study finds Richard Sandbrook's observations regarding the state in Africa a useful starting point to answer the questions raised above. Sandbrook's premise is that sociopolitical factors in Africa place severe limitations on economic development and on the state's ability to pursue an effective program to eliminate underdevelopment. To make his point, Sandbrook compares the existing circumstances in Africa with those of other regimes.

Elsewhere the state has played a central role in capitalist development, indirectly through the generation of a conducive framework of political order and rational law and administration, and directly through the provision of adequate infrastructure, subsidies to promising firms and sectors and even productive public investment in strategic industries. But African states are not, in any real sense, capitalist states. The peculiar conditions of postcolonial Africa impel an adaptation of colonial-inspired political structures and processes in a patrimonial . . . direction. The omnipresent danger in this adaptation is a degeneration of neopatrimonialism into an economically irrational form of "personal rule." This decay, manifested in political instability, systemic corruption and maladministration, introduces irrationalities into economic life, but nonetheless is shaped by a particular political logic. These political phenomena cannot, therefore, simply be dismissed as mismanagement or ineptitude. (1985: 13)

In other words, states in Africa compare poorly with capitalist interventionist states such as Bismarck's Germany in the nineteenth century, or the state in the Soviet Union after 1917. These earlier states had a particular socioeconomic environment which predicated their behavior (and ultimately success) on the economic transformation of their societies. Thus, Sandbrook correctly suggests that it is necessary to comprehend the sociopolitical constraint on capitalism in Africa through an analysis of the historical and social factors conditioning political adaptation, the logic of personal rule and the consequences of this for economic life. In other words, our treatment of Africa's socioeconomic base in the previous chapter is a necessary step to understanding the state in contemporary Africa. To put it differently, politicians and bureaucrats in Africa are not inherently corrupt or "tribalist." Their behavior is a response to a particular kind of a socioeconomic system in which they find themselves. That environment is not capitalist. We cannot expect a capitalist state to emerge in a society whose basic nature of political economy is essentially noncapitalist. Thus a capitalist logic found in such a society would be an abnormal trait, severely constrained by other societal attributes that are anticapitalist. Thus, in concurrence with Thomas Callaghy, the state in Africa is *not* capitalist. Given the reasoning that the state in Africa is not capitalist, theoretical concepts such as "the bureaucratic-bourgeoisie" begin to make less sense, for we cannot have a bourgeoisie without a bourgeois economy. If we allow ourselves to employ such concepts at all, they must be qualified and thoroughly elaborated as to their meaning and relevance.

The peculiarity of the African socioeconomic system has led to the theorizing that the state in Africa has *no* roots in society. Goran Hyden is a representative of this school. He bases his contention on the empirical generalization that African societies have a very weak economic base and that peasant societies cannot sustain elaborate state structures because they are materially incapable of doing so. The state, on the other hand, cannot impose its will on (or control) the peasants because of the state's alienation from the peasants' production cycle.

As the productive and reproductive needs of the peasants can be met without the support of other social classes, relations between those who rule and those who till the land are not firmly rooted in the production system as such. . . . [A]ppropriation by those in control of the state are made in the form of taxation and as such they are simple deductions from an already produced stock of values. *These are tributary rather than productive relations and they do imply a much more limited degree of social control. In this respect, African countries are societies without a state. The latter sits suspended in 'mid-air' over society and is not an integral mechanism of the day-to-day productive activities of society.* (Hyden, 1983: 7) (Emphasis added.)

Hyden's argument brings us full circle in relation to the 1970s propositions of dependency theory that the state in peripheral societies actively participates in the economy and *substantially controls it*. (See Gutkind and Wallerstein, 1985, for example.) Hyden's argument suggests the notion of the "soft" state, an ineffective state which struggles to impose its will on all sectors of society— unsuccessfully due to the limited practical and relevant resources at its disposal. The economic crisis which has engulfed the continent in recent years has not made things any easier for the state.

A major political consequence of the dominance of a precapitalist economy on the African continent is the resistance (active and passive) by peasants to operating in a framework of impersonal rules which the state may wish to impose on them. The reaction of the majority of peasants in Africa to the state's attempt to incorporate them into its organizational framework has been to operate outside the formal economy (Hyden, 1980; Kasfir, 1983; Callaghy, 1988). The continuing economic crisis, especially in the formal sector (which is controlled by the state) has further contributed to the alienation between the peasants and the state. The measurable decline in marketed cash crops in Africa (Shao, 1985) is evidence of the deliberate effort by peasants to escape the state's long but unwelcome arm. It should be noted, however, that peasants for the most part have not necessarily abandoned production; rather, they are concentrating on production of food crops and other commodities which have a higher exchange value in the informal sector, away from the state's watchful, if not greedy, eyes.

The issue of peasants' disengagement from and/or resistance to state encroachment in their lives raises several fundamental theoretical and practical issues regarding African states' viability as effective institutions capable of transforming societies they ostensibly rule. The issue of state authority over its citizenry is theoretically usually assumed under conditions of normalcy, where the legitimacy of the state is largely accepted or taken for granted. The continuing economic—and hence political—crisis in Africa, however, makes that assumption highly questionable. Robert H. Jackson and Carl G. Rosberg (1982: 1–24), for example, raise the question of actual (practical) authority of many African states within their respective territories. The two authors contend that many African states hardly qualify as authoritative centers of power if one were to adopt an empirical definition of the state based on its ability to control the population within its territory. Jackson and Rosberg further argue that what actually maintains African states as *states* is a juridical definition, which identifies them as the recognized territorial units of the international community. In this view, some states may be more relevant in the international arena than they are within their own territorial boundaries.

The case of Zaire again comes to mind, given the general deteriorated condition of the state, as several empirical studies have attempted to demonstrate (Callaghy, 1983; 1984; Young and Turner, 1985). Young and Turner have suggested that in Zaire, "the pathology of state decay is expressed by three processes: shrinkage in competency, credibility, and probity of the state" (1985: 399). The two authors warn, however, that in considering each of the three processes, "it should be borne in mind that the state is an exceedingly complex social formation, institutional matrix, and ideological domain. Decline is not a single process or an absolute condition; rather, it consists of corrosion which occurs unevenly in different portions of the state." Sudan and Mozambique are two other examples. In both countries, the ongoing civil wars have rendered large portions of the respective countries practically out of reach of the central authorities.

Juridical authority of the state in most African countries, however, remains unquestionable. This authoritative resilience in part can be explained by the state's monopoly of the coercive machinery in society, although this also is becoming increasingly questionable in countries experiencing civil wars: Sudan, Mozambique, Ethiopia, and Angola. The important theoretical and practical question here is to determine the relationships between the juridical authority of the state and the practical authority which in earlier times was legitimized via the provision of social services—roads, hospitals, schools, etc.—and the monopoly of coercive force. The social services equation is rapidly diminishing in most African countries due to the diminished capacity of the state to extract resources from society and because of general economic decline. The state in Africa is much less a welfare state than it was before. Perhaps the problem of state control over society—and its relative success or failure—can best be understood as a continuing state-society struggle: the state attempting to assert its control over the population while the population struggles to retain its autonomous existence. One positive aspect of this struggle is the evidence that civil society can successfully achieve this objective, as the documented case of Zaire demonstrates.

The most important response by civil society is withdrawal into a plethora of survival activities. The decay of the state has opened up new economic and social space, which is being rapidly organized into parallel markets. The vitality of these mechanisms demonstrates not only the creative energies of civil society, but also the possibility of survival. If one took only measurements from the public economy (real urban wages, for example), not only impoverishment but starvation would be indicated; but while the impoverishment of large segments of the populace is real, so also is their survival. (Young and Turner, 1985: 405)

Victor Azarya and Naomi Chazan (1987) have provided an interesting and useful account of civil society response to state decay and deteriorating economic conditions in Ghana and Guinea. Azarya and Chazan point out that, as in Zaire, the essential weapon with which the populace in both Ghana and Guinea have coped with state decay has been withdrawal or disengagement from the state.

The two authors point to four major mechanisms of disengagement from the state, which contain different combinations of social, economic, religious, political, and cultural elements. The first mechanism of disengagement is what they call *suffer-manage*. This strategy "encompasses an array of activities aimed at a reconciliation to a declining standard of living and learning to manage in these circumstances. . . . finding ways of coping with shortages." The second mechanism is what they call *escape*. "[T]hose opting for escape remove themselves not only from the state but from the country as a whole" (1987: 118). They either go to more affluent African countries or, if they are well educated, they seek jobs in Europe and North America. The third mechanism is the evolution of *parallel systems* to those of the state. As Azarya and Chazan state, "Parallel systems are alternative outlets for needs that remain unfulfilled by official channels and they reduce dependence on these channels.

Typical examples include blackmarkets, smuggling, corruption and the use of alternative justice methods." A fourth form of disengagement is what Azarya and Chazan call *self-enclosure*.

This kind of withdrawal entails a reduced use of the state channels but, unlike the formation of parallel systems, it does not involve a deviance from its regulations. . . . Examples of self-enclosure include moving back from export to subsistence crops, from urban to rural habitation, renouncing public service or any position of high visibility that would increase one's exposure to state pressure. Self-enclosure may also involve a retreat to traditional forms or to narrower bases of solidarity (regional, ethnic, kinship). (1987: 126–27)

It would seem that in many African countries, this last option of self-enclosure has been the most popular.

The state-society struggles demonstrated in the studies cited above point to an underlying basic problem in analyzing African political economy. As the economic fortunes of the continent remain uncertain, the state's ability to control civil society becomes increasingly a questionable proposition. The state, however, has continued to have a monopoly control of the coercive apparatus. Moreover, the administrative apparatus of the state continues to be a force to be reckoned with even in remote regions of the continent. This uneasy balance needs further explanation. (See also Azarya, 1988: 3–21.)

THE STATE IN AFRICA: THE CORPORATIST FACTOR

For Africanists, corporatism has not been a popular concept, with a few notable exceptions, of course (Shaw, 1982; Callaghy, 1984; Nyang'oro, 1986–87). A recent volume of interesting and insightful essays helps to redress the balance (Nyang'oro and Shaw, 1989), but much remains to be done. The concept of corporatism is important for the study of state-society relations in Africa because it deals with the state's attempt to grapple with two problems simultaneously: managing the economy and controlling the population. In the past few years, this dual task has been made more difficult and more pressing as the African economy has continued to contract. As we pointed out at the beginning of this chapter, a better understanding of the state under these conditions requires conceiving of the state as an actor—not necessarily a simple or unified one, but at least as one having identifiable behavior. It is this dual contradiction which helps to underscore the peculiarity of the state in Africa.

Corporatist practice in Africa is predominantly statist, that is, it reflects the attempt by the state to control and structure interest representation in society. This differs from societal corporatism (the predominant form of European corporatism), which entails cooperation among varying interests in placing demands to the state. State corporatism in Africa thus closely resembles that of Latin America. In a popular work on corporatism in Latin America, Alfred Stepan points out that corporatism refers to a particular set of policies and institutional arrangements for structuring interest representation. Where such arrangements predominate, the state often charters or even creates interest groups, attempts to regulate their number, and gives them the appearance of a quasi-representational monopoly along with special prerogatives. (1978: 46)

Contributors to the Nyang'oro and Shaw volume have shown how corporatist practice by the state in various African countries has been effected with varying degrees of success and failure. As a general observation, however, it can fairly be said that corporatism in Africa has substantially undermined democratic practice via the state's practice of controlling interest articulation. For our purpose, however, of more concern is the original basis for state corporatist behavior in postindependent Africa, which was closely tied to the evolution of political economy in general. Following Alfred Stepan's theorization of corporatism in Latin America, Timothy Shaw has suggested that Africa is poised to move away from *inclusionary* to *exclusionary* forms of corporatism, precisely because of the exhaustion of the particular kind of development strategy—Import Substitution Industrialization (ISI)—adopted at independence:

[I]nclusionary corporatism . . . is more likely in the earlier stages of import substitution industrialization, where modern elites and urban working classes perceive significant room for populist multiclass coalitions. Exclusionary corporatism, on the other hand, is more likely to be attempted if, after the import-substitution phase, the pattern of industrial development begins to stagnate, the political and economic struggle intensifies, and politics is increasingly perceived in zero sum terms. (Shaw, 1982: 256)

Guillermo A. O'Donnell's 1979 study of South American politics pointed to this trend. Authoritarianism as a corporatist mode in Latin America followed the exhaustion of ISI in the late 1950s and early 1960s. As demands for greater political participation and economic benefits increased, states in Latin America opted for an easy solution to the problem: clamping down on popular classes and instituting repressive policies—but within a corporative framework under the state's tutelage. Our study suggests that the similarity of the situation between Latin America and Africa is only valid to an extent. While ISI was inherently limited in its capacity to transform Latin American society, it went a long way toward restructuring class relations and the economy and firmly placing Latin America in an elaborate international division of labor. Africa, on the other hand, adopted ISI at a much later date and remained marginal in the international division of labor. The current crisis in African political economy has exposed that marginality. While the working class in Latin America could not be ignored by the state, since their alienation from land was substantially complete, the same cannot be said of African workers. The ease with which parallel economies exist in Africa, and the traditional/kinship ties to land, even for urban dwellers, have cushioned the populace from the worst effects of the economic contraction, but with one severe consequence to the state: the state is less able to pursue its corporatist objectives effectively; while it may aspire to total hegemonic control, fewer resources and the relative autonomy of the majority of the population make the objective a far more formidable task.

Therein lies the paradox of African corporatism and state-society relations in general. The state in contemporary Africa is caught in contradictions between social, political, and economic conditions within its territory and conditions arising from its peculiar relation to international capital. Due to the incompleteness of the capitalization process, the state's relation to both sides of the contradictory process remains uncertain, giving credence to Goran Hyden's characterization of the state as being "suspended in mid-air." This contradictory nature of the state in Africa is well-captured by contributors to an important volume on the state in Africa edited by Henry Bernstein and Bonnie K. Campbell (1984).

In a summary of the contributions, Bernstein and Campbell point to the general observation that the state is a site of continual struggle between different social forces and interests, one effect of which is "the *fracturing* of the state, and indeed of particular state institutions, which themselves enter into conjunctural alliances and oppositions." The complexity that results "is not reducible to a 'last instance' hegemony of national or transnational capital because in the current historical moment . . . the question of that hegemony is precisely one of the central issues which are at stake" (1984: 10–11). In his contribution to the volume, Björn Beckman points to this crisis of hegemony in the Nigerian case. While his contention—that the Nigerian state is busily promoting capitalist development in close cooperation with foreign capital as well as a growing class of Nigerian capitalists (p. 76)—is highly arguable and needs qualification, his other statement regarding the dilemma cum contradictory role in capital accumulation is worth acknowledging:

While the Nigerian state serves as an organ both for the penetration of international capital and for the emancipation of the domestic bourgeoisie, it cannot be reduced to either. Nor is it possible to comprehend the significance of either of the two aspects, without examining such activities of the Nigerian state for which the distinction foreign/domestic is not relevant. *The primary role of the Nigerian state is to establish, maintain, protect, and expand the conditions of capitalist accumulation in general, without which neither foreign nor Nigerian capital can prosper.* (1984: 101)

Björn Beckman's contribution captures the "active participant" nature of the state in Nigeria and points to the contradictions involved in such a process. In the case of Tanzania, the essay by Peter Gibbon and Michael Neocosmos in the Bernstein/Campbell volume points to the negative results of the state's active involvement, which begins with the creation of a *state bourgeoisie*. Following Issa Shivji's arguments in *Class Struggles in Tanzania* (1976), Gibbon and Neocosmos (1985) point out that the basis of the state (or bureaucratic) bourgeoisie is the creation and centralization of state property as the means of collective (class) appropriation and accumulation, free from any popular control—through the single political party. The distinctive feature of this type of ruling class and the mode of its formation is that the economic instance is subordinated to the political and administrative instance, leading to bureaucratic irrationalism; thus

the anarchy and disorder of the state economic sector, as well as its prevalent corruption and ineffectiveness, result from the tension within the state bourgeoisie between maintaining its collective means of appropriation and the tendency to private appropriation and accumulation by individual members of the class. (Bernstein and Campbell, 1985: 16)

What we notice in the practice of the state in Tanzania is the contradiction associated with a state that is not thoroughly capitalized. The behavior of the Tanzanian state is behavior associated with precapitalist socioformations, which further raises the question as to how capitalist Africa is:

Forms (and uses) of appropriation by the bureaucratic bourgeoisie do not represent *accumulation* in the capitalist sense (expanded reproduction of capital and the development of the productive forces), but *predatory exaction of a pre-capitalist type* ("predation") whereby goods and money are centralized in the control of the ruling class and redistributed to establish and expand groups of followers. In this way, the bureaucratic bourgeoisie inherits the practices of the ruling class of the pre-colonial mode of production—the landed and military aristocracy. (Bernstein and Campbell, 1985: 17)

Accordingly, the expansion of the state economy is primarily determined by the politics of clientelism rather than by any economic imperative of profit or developing production and productivity. It leads to what some scholars have called patrimonial capitalism (Callaghy, 1988; Young and Turner, 1985). Under patrimonial capitalism, the state becomes the easiest avenue of extraction and access to personal power. Unfortunately, as Callaghy notes, such a structure of opportunity has rarely been conducive to the development of modern capitalism—direct extraction is too easy, productive investment too difficult. The state in Africa lacks Weberian rationality.

But why pursue a corporatist strategy under conditions of economic contraction? Certainly even in Nigeria where the 1970s economic expansion was fueled by oil revenues, the state's attempt to control both the economy and the popular classes showed little success. Richard A. Joseph (1983: 22) theorizes that central to the deepening crisis in Nigeria is the ambivalent nature of state power, inherited from the colonial era and expanded considerably since independence in ways which have deepened this ambivalence. Central to this ambivalence is the range of contradictory features in both the structure of state power and the uses to which it has been put—issues which are also central to Björn Beckman's thesis. We would further argue that corporatist tendencies not only in Nigeria but across the African continent are desperate attempts by the state to simultaneously impose its authority on, and seek legitimacy from, the popular classes who have sought to keep the state at an arm's length because of its residual basis in colonialism and its inability to be truly capitalist. In other words, the popular classes see the state both as an unreliable oppressor (inefficient capitalist) and as an unpredictable "godfather" whose generosities (social services) cannot be taken for granted. Goran Hyden's assessment of the state in Africa, with which we largely agree, gives little hope for the state as a basis for economic development in Africa.

The post-independence, or post-colonial, state is at present unable to be progressive. Whether this is so because of corruption and inefficiency stemming from patronage politics or paralysis resulting from red tape and overregulation, the effect is to incapacitate those institutions that have the ultimate responsibility for promoting and managing national development. In this significant respect there is very little difference between African countries. The trend for the state to lose its role as instrument of development is evident throughout sub-Saharan Africa. Instead of becoming more effective, the post-colonial state is in danger of becoming good for little except provision of boundless employment. In fact, in many African countries serious doubts must be raised about the ability of the state to ensure economic expansion and development unless some drastic changes are allowed in the present structures of development management. (1983: xii)

The inability of the state in contemporary Africa to effect economic development, however, has not deterred it from officially propagating "progressive" or "nationalistic" policies as the preferred strategy of development. In Nigeria, for example, the state over the last decade has instituted measures aimed at indigenizing economic production via the Nigerian Enterprises Promotion Decrees. The decrees were aimed at making production in Nigeria more *Nigerian*, rather than controlled by transnational companies and other forms of international capital. But as was the case with Tanzania's nationalization measures via the Arusha Declaration in 1967, and President Mobutu's Zairianization measures in 1973, Nigeria's indigenization decrees have been a dismal failure, mostly because of a disjointed and unarticulated political economy and generalized corruption following the indigenizing decrees. (See Joseph, 1983, 1988.) The formal sector is still largely controlled by international capital while the informal sector still operates largely independent of state control. The indigenization decrees were never equipped to effect a fundamental transformation in the social relations of production. Claude Ake summarizes the problem of Nigerian indigenization as follows:

[G]iven its objective character, the Nigerian bourgeoisie can only effect very limited change in the distribution of control of the economy between it and foreign capital. In the final analysis, the localization of control must presuppose overcoming the structural features in the Nigerian economy which constitute it as a weak, exploited dependence.... [T]his change—of revolutionary magnitude—cannot be effected in a manner

compatible with the maintenance of the present international division of labor, impe-
rialist subordination and existing property relations. The pursuit of indigenization in
Nigeria is typical of the self-defeating manner in which development is pursued in Africa—through policies which presuppose the very structural features which underlie
underdevelopment. (Ake, 1985: 199–200)

Ake's reading of the overwhelming influence of international capital on the
formal sector is right on the mark. However, he ignores the residual cultural
and social traits of precapitalist behavior that pervade Africa's production
landscape—many of which were pointed out in the previous chapter. As a result, the external *dependency* angle is overplayed. From a corporatist view-
point, one may argue that indigenization as a policy was an attempt by the
state in Nigeria to attract support from wealthy Nigerians who could afford
to buy a few shares in foreign companies to give those companies a Nigerian
look. At the same time, the state would gain the distinction of being nation-
alist, and further its legitimacy claim. The failure of the indigenization process
thus should be viewed as resulting from several interrelated factors, including
failure of the local wealthy Nigerians to buy out successfully foreign companies. This failure emanates from a weak socioeconomic base; the strength of
international capital's activities; and the absence of an effective institutional
machinery within the state to effect the decrees emanating from the general
weakness and "messiness" of the state, given its inability to fully control both
the formal and informal sectors of the economy.

The Nigerian case is not unique—indeed, it is universal in contemporary
Africa. But we need to put more emphasis on the internal structural weakness
of the local economies (and classes) in order to come to terms with why the
state in Africa, in its present constitution, cannot play a developmental role.
The seemingly authoritarian tendencies of the state in Africa can also be attributed to its frustration at not being able to have its way with either international capital or its own population.

CONCLUSION AND REFLECTIONS

This chapter has been concerned with the nature of state and the state's role
in capitalist economic development in Africa—society relations in general.
The general conclusion is that the state is very weak in the sense that it is still
steeped in precapitalist behavior that undermines capitalist rationality. We
think that Thomas M. Callaghy is right on the mark when he answers the
question regarding capitalism in Africa.

[H]ow capitalist is Africa? I think the appropriate answer is "not very." Certainly there
is not much modern capitalism as Weber defined it: the calculability nexus is very
weak; state arbitrariness, instability, corruption, and inefficiency are very high; patrimonial, not bureaucratic administration and adjudication are the norm; the person-
alization of power and authority structures, political and nonpolitical is pervasive; en-

trepreneurs, both domestic and foreign, do not control all the means of production, especially in the rural areas as important restrictions on the commodification of these factors remain; . . . technologies remain rudimentary and not easily transferable; important restrictions on a free labor market continue to exist; markets are not well developed as economic, political and social impediments continue to exist, and in many cases formal markets are actually shrinking while *magendo* economies grow into much of the gap; noncapitalist modes of production remain very important; only partial incorporation into the world economy is the norm; national financial banking, and monetary systems are quite unsophisticated; and transportation and communications infrastructure, already weak, is disintegrating in many areas of the continent. (1988: 77–78)

Many of the studies cited in this chapter and in the previous chapter support Callaghy's conclusion. One thing, though, needs to be repeated: the descriptions and statistics cited all relate to human beings in the final analysis. The desperate nature of the statistics thus reflects the desperate nature of the human condition in Africa. The decline of the state on the continent is symptomatic of the decline of the human condition.

The state has attempted to retain both its authority and legitimacy in society. The problem, however, has been that to a great extent the state has failed to achieve both goals. Most states on the continent today are centralizing, but distinctly limited, authoritarian patrimonial-bureaucratic states. As Callaghy notes, "They have low levels of development and penetration and limited coercive and implementation capabilities. Politics is highly personalized, and a ruling class is emerging with the gap between the rulers and the ruled increasing" (1988: 83). The state has attempted to resolve this contradiction through corporatist practice and promulgation of "progressive" ideologies, such as nationalization and even socialism. Clive Y. Thomas shows how the "trick" is sometimes employed:

[T]he identification of the ideals of socialism, peace, equality, and freedom with dictatorial practices seems to raise no particular difficulty, for "dictatorship of the proletariat" becomes the cover for one party—and even one-man—rule, while political democracy is dismissed as a "bourgeois illusion" that the masses in a "socialist" country do not need! (1984: xiv)

Thus, some of the most oppressive states on the continent (Sékou Touré's Guinea and Mengistu's Ethiopia) have always had the most "progressive" rhetoric.

The African state's failure to effect economic development is perhaps more evident in the industrial and manufacturing sector. Most of sub-Saharan Africa's industrial capacity is operating at less than 30 percent of installed capacity. The state is heavily involved in the industrial sector. Given the exorbitant costs of establishing industries, the state has been the only realistic institution to undertake the task of industrialization. The state's uncapitalistic nature has in part contributed to the deterioration in the industrial sector's productivity; thus, the failure of the industrial sector is also a failure of the state. This conclusion suggests that if economic change were to occur on the continent, it would be unrealistic to maintain that the state in its present constitution would have any meaningful role to play. There is no doubt that economic contraction on the continent has bred some of the severe political crises. The need to overcome the current crisis in Africa's political economies cannot be overemphasized. The concluding chapter in this study discusses some possible alternatives available to them.

Alternative Futures in Africa

Industrial civilization is the outcome of the convergence of two processes of cultural creativity: the bourgeois and scientific revolutions. I see the bourgeois revolution as the imposition of instrumental rationality or the organization of production, and the scientific revolution as the predominance of that view of nature as a system endowed with a rational structure which, in Galileo's phrase, is "written in the language of mathematics."
—Celso Furtado, *Accumulation and Development: The Logic of Industrial Civilization*

It is not enough to set tasks; we must also solve the problem of the methods for carrying them out. If our task is to cross a river, we cannot cross it without a bridge or a boat.... Unless the problem of method is solved, talk about the task is useless.
—Mao Tse-tung, "Be Concerned with the Well-Being of the Masses, Pay Attention to Methods of Work"

INTRODUCTION: GRAPPLING WITH ISSUES OF DEVELOPMENT

Many studies of the current crisis in Africa's political economy have been brilliant in the description of its major elements. Both scholarly studies and official documents have outlined the crisis as having economic, political, social, ecological, and other dimensions. Indeed, a substantial portion of this study has attempted to summarize the major findings of other studies regarding the African crisis. It is fair, however, to point out that despite their brilliance in describing the African condition, many of the studies have fallen short in their *prescriptive* analysis. Official documents such as the World Bank's *Accelerated Development in Sub-Saharan Africa* (1981) have suggested government policy changes, especially in agriculture, as a basis for reviving African economies. The OAU's Lagos Plan of Action (LPA) (1982) proposed substantial external finance to supplement broad (but unspecified) local initiatives to improve the economy. Critique of the World Bank's program has been well-documented, as our analysis indicated in chapter 2. The LPA's major weakness is its lack of concrete proposals to solve Africa's crisis and, indeed, its failure to admit explicitly the need for a serious and dramatic change in the policies pursued by African governments internally.

It has been common to brand the World Bank's program as essentially conservative, given its free market orientation and its assault on governmental intervention in the economy. Our study proposes that the LPA should also be viewed as essentially a conservative document, given African governments' reluctance to accept responsibility for economic mismanagement and tendency to single out external variables as central to the crisis. In chapter 2, we argued that development policy involves a very strong element of choice. African governments since independence have *chosen* a particular kind of development path and they should fully accept the responsibility and consequences of that choice. Indeed, we suggest that the reluctance of African governments to accept full responsibility for failure is one of the more fundamental problems facing the continent. John Ravenhill has summarized the major problems with the LPA as follows:

The LPA is vulnerable to four principal lines of criticism: a failure to specify practical policy measures that might make a realistic contribution towards the attainment of its long-term objectives; a failure to consider the implications of a self-reliant strategy—particularly the question of how such a strategy would be financed; and absence, analogous to that in the Bank's *Agenda* of any consideration of the political obstacles to implementation; and, most importantly, an unjustified faith in the ECA's long-proclaimed objective of establishing an African Common Market as a *deus ex machina* for Africa's economic woes. (1986: 86–87)

African governments' pervasive involvement in the economy, especially the formal sector, is a well-documented phenomenon. Indeed, given the general lack of capital on the continent, the state has proven to be the logical instrument for capital accumulation given its predominant position in the political economy. However, the states' failure to achieve the objective of sustained capital accumulation suggests that there is something wrong somewhere—within the state itself. If a transformation is to be undertaken and changes effected, it is only logical that the starting point should be the state itself. This chapter, therefore, emphasizes the need to transform the state and analyzes the state's relationship with the economy and society in general. The imperative for economic transformation is discussed against a projected ideal of what a self-sustaining economy in Africa should entail, in the first instance. Whether Africa can really afford to maintain its current links with the international economy is discussed with an emphasis on a political imperative of African unity, which in turn is related to the economic imperative of an effective market. Thus the element of *choice* looms even larger.

The two quotations at the beginning of this chapter serve two interrelated purposes. Celso Furtado's quotation betrays our conception of what *ultimately* should obtain in Africa, an industrial society based on scientific rationality. Mao Tse-tung's quotation serves as a guide in the investigation process. We have to know what we are investigating before we can determine the methods of investigation. This in turn will help us in determining what is fundamental to our problem and, conversely, what is not. We believe that a study of Africa's economic problems requires such a method.

There are several issues that need to be raised regarding economic development in Africa today—issues that suggest the uniqueness of the African situation. In most African countries, the current discourse on economic development does not evolve around questions of what *rates* of development are required in either agriculture or industry to achieve a certain positive developmental objective—rather, what measures must be undertaken in order to rehabilitate the economy to pre-1975 or pre-1980 levels. Thus questions of long-term versus short-term planning for economic development are essentially irrelevant for the time being—unless it can be established that rehabilitation of economies can be achieved in the first place. As Lloyd Timberlake has remarked in quoting the World Bank:

Africa's plight is unique. The rest of the world is moving "forward" by most of the normally accepted indications of progress. Africa is moving backwards. Features of modern society to which many Africans have been exposed are withering: trucks no longer run because there are no spare parts and roads have become impassable; aeroplanes no longer land at night in some places because there is no electricity to light the runway. (Timberlake, 1986: 7) (Emphasis added.)

For Africa, therefore, the issue of rehabilitation—not long-term (or even medium-term) development—is the most pressing issue. *Rehabilitation* as a conceptual issue in the discourse of African development, however, has to be clarified.

In many documents, both official and unofficial, rehabilitation is simply discussed as the goal of attaining production at the pre-decline level. In other words, in agriculture for example, efforts are concentrated toward increased cash crop yields to be sold on the world market to get the scarce foreign exchange, which would in turn help to rehabilitate the industrial sector through the importation of industrial raw materials. The World Bank's *Accelerated Development in Sub-Saharan Africa* adopts such a position when it states that

the agriculture-based and export-oriented development strategy suggested for the 1980s is an essential beginning to a process of long-term transformation, a prelude to industrialization. It is not a permanent course for any country, but one that in Africa generates resources more quickly than any alternative and benefits more people. . . . A strategy focused on agriculture and exports is thus open-ended, a necessary beginning. (1981: 6–7)

But that is the last thing Africa needs today. Africa does not need a rehabilitation of an export-oriented economy because part of the problem as we demonstrated in chapter 2, has been the unreliability of the international commodity markets because of cyclical changes in primary commodity prices. Coffee producing countries in Africa, for example, cannot do rational planning when their income from coffee sales depend on a frost freeze in Brazil and a willingness of consumers in the developed countries to consume more of their product. In any case, there is always a limit on how many cups of coffee a person can consume, regardless of his or her ability to pay for it.

A similar story can be told regarding another commodity: copper. In a recent report, the United Nations pointed to the uncertainties in the copper market, which closely resembles the situation in other primary products. The report shows that in the early 1980s, a major increase in copper production in Chile led to a tremendous shock in world copper prices. In 1983–1984, the world price of copper, already down from the 1980 index of $100.00, decreased further from $73.00 to $63.00 (UNCTAD, 1985). Thus, neither Zambia nor Zaire, both major copper producers in Africa, could find any relief, despite increased production.

Lloyd Timberlake's study, already cited, makes an important connection between cash crop production in the Sudan and the catastrophic results of the recent and continuing drought. According to Timberlake, the tragedy is not only in the production of cash crops, but more seriously, in the "environmental bankruptcy" caused by cash crop farming:

To describe Africa's crisis as "environmental" may sound odd. . . . What have environmental concerns to do with the fact that in 1985 the entire Hadendawa people of northeastern Sudan faced extinction due to starvation and dispersal? The Sudanese government, with the help of [foreign aid], has put vast sugar and cotton plantations on its best land along the Nile. It has ignored rapidly falling yields from smallholder farming in the 1970s. It seems not to have noticed that the land—the "environment"—upon which eight out of every [ten] Sudanese depend for their livelihoods is slowly perishing due to over-use and misuse. It invested little in dryland regions where people like the Hadendawa live. So when drought came, these pastoralists and peasants had no irrigated settlements in which to take temporary refuge, no government agencies to buy their livestock, no sources of drought-resistant sorghum seeds ready for planting when the rains resumed. *But neither have the government's investment in cash crops produced money to pay the nation's way through the drought.* The result is starvation and debt: Sudan's external debt in 1985 was estimated at $9 billion. President Nimeiri, overthrown in April 1985, has paid a personal price for leading Sudan to environmental bankruptcy. (1986: 9–10) (Emphasis added.)

Sudan's tragedy, however, continues. The new government of General Suwar al Dahab has not demonstrated that it has learned its lesson. There has been no radical shift away from Nimeiri's policies. Rather, it is more of the same as the country continues to suffer the twin plight of civil war and economic decline.

The same logic of rehabilitation applies to industry. The concern of many African countries has been to rehabilitate industrial production to at least 50 percent of installed capacity as opposed to the current 10 to 30 percent in the majority of the countries. Many studies of the 1970s showed the limits of the particular kind of industrialization that had taken place in Africa. (See, for example, Rweyemamu, 1973, 1980; Swainson, 1980; Nyang'oro, 1983.) These studies suggested that the industrialization in Africa had started on the wrong foot, given its highly dependent nature and the general inappropriateness of the technology employed. By the mid-1970s it could be concluded that dependent industrialization in Africa had not enabled the economy to generate self-sustaining development or to create an economic system that displayed a reasonable symmetry between the structure of production and the structure of consumption. The little industrialization that had taken place appeared to have involved merely an adoption of more sophisticated patterns of consumption without the corresponding process of capital accumulation and technical progress (Thomas, 1974). Talk of rehabilitation of that structure of industry in Africa is, therefore, a dead end because it is concerned with rehabilitation of an already discredited kind of industrialization.

Thus both agricultural and industrial development must be addressed from a totally different angle. Export production in agriculture will not do because of the uncertainty of the world market. Dependent industrialization will not do because of the inherent problems associated with imported technology and the limits of the market for industrial goods given the lack of effective demand. The fact that there is inherent inequality in the social structure does not help the situation. Furthermore, most urban and rural dwellers cannot afford the industrial goods locally produced due to, among other things, the uncertainties in the labor market. The question then becomes, what next? We think the answer could lie in the nature of the *state*.

THE PROBLEM OF THE STATE

One thing that can be said about the state in African countries is that it is overexposed internationally and underexposed nationally. Thus there is much to be said about Robert H. Jackson and Carl G. Rosberg's (1982) claim that many states in Africa make more sense as territorial entities in the international system than as effective instruments of governance internally. In terms of economic policy, this international overexposure helps to explain why states in Africa are fully wedded to the continuance of export crop production and import substitution industrialization (ISI), despite the historical demonstration of the fallacies involved in such a strategy. The state in Africa is materially rooted in the international system; therefore, it cannot afford to break the link.

Africa, through its famous spokesmen, such as Julius K. Nyerere of Tanzania and others, speaks of the need for a NIEO. The general argument has been that a New International Economic Order (NIEO) would help alleviate rapid price fluctuation in commodity prices, improve the aid regime, support Third World industrialization, etc. In spite of the obvious difficulty in achieving this objective, African countries have based their international economic policy on the promises of an NIEO. There is only one conclusion that can be discerned from such thought and practice: the alternative of directing efforts of economic development internally bears consequences that many (if not all) African states are unprepared or unwilling to entertain. The alternative efforts would require African states to acknowledge misplaced development priorities, essential incompetence, and ultimately, the question of legitimacy.

The World Bank's insistence on policy reform in agriculture and a move toward privatization of the economy as a basis for economic development also fall short of addressing the real issues confronting African states. Failure of policy in both agriculture and industry is a *consequence* of a more fundamental sociopolitical structure, not the *cause*. It is the fundamental sociopolitical structure upon which the state rests that has to be examined. There can be no serious change unless that sociopolitical structure is radically changed. We propose that the appropriate way to examine this issue is to conceptually disaggregate the complex set of interrelationships between the state and international capital and between the state and civil society.

We have already noted the close economic link that exists between the formal sector of African economies and international capital. Indeed, we argued in chapter 2 that economic development in Africa historically has been perceived as a process of successfully participating in the international economy through Africa's ability to sell its raw materials and buy industrial goods from the international market. The disappointing results of this strategy notwithstanding, African countries have steadfastly campaigned to remain a part of this system. Arguably, the state in Africa, in its quest for capital accumulation and to achieve certain objectives—including its aspirations to become a welfare state—has found the international system to be a more reliable and willing partner. But that reliability has come at a great cost. As returns from this international transaction have declined, the state has found itself facing a financial crisis. While the consequences of reduced returns from the international sphere are obvious, internally the state can no longer with any degree of certainty impose more taxes on cash crop growers because of the latter's demonstrated ability to escape the state's bureaucratic control of the production process (Hyden, 1980, 1983; Azarya and Chazan, 1987; Nzongola-Ntalaja, 1986; Kasfir, 1983). Thus, the state finds itself in a double bind.

As the state is increasingly unable to impose its will in the production sphere in the countryside, the issue of state authority and legitimacy begins to loom large in the equation of state-society relations. Thus, Goran Hyden's notion of the state being "suspended in mid-air" becomes a serious proposition. We would wish to add, however, that the state in reality cannot be "suspended in mid-air," because of the necessity for materially grounding state existence. The precarious nature of state existence in African countries can be explained by the precarious nature of its relationship to international capital and to its own civil society (Rothchild and Chazan, 1988). Without being unduly pessimistic, we need to recognize that African societies at all levels have very low margins of survival, given their technological backwardness. The consequences of the mid- to late 1980s drought serves as a prime example of this marginal existence and a cruel reminder of how quickly life in Africa can change from being "normal" to desperate. Of course African societies have shown remarkable resilience given the tortuous history of the continent—from slave trade to the present—the resilience, however, has to be juxtaposed to what is possible, given the scientific and technological knowledge available in the world today. African states are institutions reflecting a confused and desperate situation which needs radical reordering.

At the political level, there is a desperate need for the present leadership in many African countries to simply leave. This applies equally to the military and civilian leadership. The general absence of democratic practice in most African countries has stifled political initiative on the part of those who have been shut out of the political processes because of their non-proximity to power—or the possibility thereof. Although the most pressing problems in Africa today are economic in nature, governments on the continent are more concerned about their political survival. As a result, a disproportionate amount of national resources is spent on buying military hardware to protect the governments from their own populations. In recent years, Uganda, Zaire, Ethiopia, and the Sudan have exemplified this practice (Nyang'oro, 1987). Naomi Chazan has described this phenomenon in the case of Ghana as one of "managing political recession" (1983). The state for the most part is preoccupied with its own survival.

The nonrepresentative and nondemocratic nature of African governments betrays one fundamental political reality in Africa. The national question, historically a prerequisite for national development and economic transformation (e.g., Germany under Bismarck, 1870) has not been resolved in most African countries. It is doubtful, for example, whether the Sudan or Ethiopia can have national development plans when over 50 percent of the population in both countries do not psychologically or politically perceive themselves as part of their respective states. As a result, these states have become major purchasers of military equipment at the expense of economic development, in order to retain the colonially determined nation-state. It is not a coincidence that while the 1982–1985 drought was devastating the Ethiopian countryside, the state was purchasing $1 billion worth of arms a year and building the largest army in sub-Saharan Africa (Stockholm International Peace Research Institute (SIPRI), 1985).

The civil war of 1966–1970 in Nigeria exposed the fragility of that state. The end of the civil war and the subsequent "democratization" attempt through civilian rule ended abruptly on December 31, 1984, when the military returned to reinstate "order" to an obviously chaotic political situation. The underlying cause of the political crisis in Nigeria since independence has been the nonresolution of the national question. Unless the national question is resolved, Nigeria can expect to be under military rule for a long time to come. Examples of the national question and its nonresolution can be repeated for almost every African country—with variations accounted for by local circumstances.

Our study suggests that the current leadership in Africa for the most part does not perceive political problems in *national* terms, but rather in *particularistic* and *parochial* terms. There must evolve in Africa a corps of leaders who are dedicated to change and a genuinely progressive and developmental ideology, who must deliberately work to eradicate the particularistic and parochial mentality so ingrained in the present leadership. The new leadership should have an interest in such a proposition. As the old leadership clings to a particularistic ideology, its political practice will inevitably alienate the interests of the new, progressive leaders by diminishing political and economic rewards available to sustain particularism. With increased demands from the general population for further political and economic participation, the new leadership can build a powerful political base that would eventually undermine the old order. Furthermore, as the economic crisis continues and as the international material base of the state continues to erode, the present leadership will have to make attempts to appeal to the already alienated populations. However, the record of the present state's relationship with its population since independence would suggest that that base of support is no longer there. (See contributions in Nyang'oro and Shaw, 1988.) In short, given the dynamics of change in Africa's political economy, transformation at the political level calls for a change in leadership—with the current crisis in political economy providing the opportunity for such a change.

At the economic level, Africa's legacy of underdevelopment predicates the central agency for accumulation: the state. The absence of a clearly defined national bourgeoisie in Africa makes it necessary that the state should take a leading role in effecting economic development. However, the post-independence history of African states' intervention in the economy has been a disaster. This fact has been extensively documented (World Bank, 1981; Young, 1982; Ravenhill, 1986; Hyden, 1983). The reasons for the disaster are many and varied. The synthesis that we discern from studies of the state and its intervention in the economy is that the African state rather than being a developmental state is largely a regulatory state. Even in those states that have been actively interventionist through economic rationalization (e.g., Tanzania and

Zambia), the bureaucracy has failed to make independent eco omic rational decisions to warrant their intervention. Thus, while state intervention in the economy in Africa is desirable (indeed necessary) in principle, the nature of intervention and the results have been catastrophic.

For example, in countries such as Tanzania, wholesale state intervention in the economy has left little room for individual initiative. Since 1967, the state in Tanzania has systematically infringed upon the autonomy of individual producers through the villagization process, cash-crop marketing boards, etc. Throughout the process, the individual producers have seen both their autonomy and return from sales of cash crops progressively dwindle. The result has been the now familiar "exit option" (Hyden, 1980). The growth of a parallel economy and its dynamism vis-a-vis the formal (government-controlled) economy has shown that some of the economic problems facing Tanzania (and indeed many other African countries) can be resolved by the state simply getting out of the economic lives of individual producers. Even for states which perceive themselves as socialist, collective ownership is not necessarily the answer to economic (under)development:

A socialist state cannot force unwilling peasants to adopt an economic structure of collective ownership based on principles which were developed in the context of industry. They would be unlikely to agree unless this form of production provided them with considerable material advantages by the wholesale adoption of modern techniques— and not only mechanization. (Dumont with Mazoyer, 1973: 42)

Dumont and Mazoyer further suggest that economic reform cannot be fully realized unless producers have more initiative and responsibility and the public greater critical awareness. But for this to happen, greater cultural, and therefore greater political, freedom is required.

But therein lies Africa's dilemma. The state in Africa, rather than provide greater cultural and political freedom, has systematically worked to curtail both. The crucial interplay between economic reform/development and cultural/political freedom has been undermined by the state's ineffectual attempt at the former and systematic denial of the latter. The result has been the *underdevelopment* of both, manifested in the economic crisis and political authoritarianism. Once again, it can be said that the rapid growth of the parallel economy has resulted from this essentially negative behavior by the state.

It should be pointed out that many of the pitfalls associated with state intervention in the economy are not peculiar to Africa. Corruption, bureaucratism, etc., can be found in advanced industrial countries as well. The difference between Africa and the industrialized countries is that the impact of corruption or bureaucratism will be greater in Africa because of the lower material base. It is for this reason that the African state should be less *regulatory* and more *developmental*. Perhaps the example of modern Japan can be applied to Africa for purposes of comparison and reflection. Chalmers Johnson's study of modern Japan provides us with a good example:

Looked at historically, modern Japan began in 1868 to be plan rational and developmental. After about a decade and a half of experimentation with direct state operation of economic enterprises, it discovered the most obvious pitfalls of plan rationality: corruption, bureaucratism, and ineffective monopolies. Japan was and remained plan rational, but it had no ideological commitment to state ownership of the economy. Its main criterion was the rational one of effectiveness in meeting the goals of development. Thus Meiji Japan began to shift away from state entrepreneurship to collaboration with privately owned enterprises, favoring those enterprises that were capable of rapidly adopting new technologies and that were committed to the national goals of development and military strength. (1982: 23)

We will not deal with the issue of building military strength here because we feel that the development of military capabilities in many African countries has been for internal repression rather than national defense. Most of the military hardware, moreover, has been imported, not internally produced; thus technological development in the civilian sector as a result of military technological innovations is inapplicable to Africa.

What is important to us in the above quotation is the way the Japanese state collaborated with privately owned enterprises to achieve and effect economic development. Elsewhere, Chalmers Johnson shows how the state in Japan encouraged particular kinds of research and gave bonuses and contracts to companies that undertook research in state-preferred projects. In the African case, rather than encourage this kind of private participation, the state has created monopolies that are top heavy with bureaucrats and thoroughly inefficient. Innovative research in such a bureaucratic environment is all but nonexistent. Again, for all practical purposes, the state should act as a facilitator for private production and research, not as a bureaucratic monopoly. For this to happen, however, the state as presently constituted must be reordered. Bureaucrats and politicians currently in government have developed objective interests in the existing conditions. It would be unrealistic to expect them to simply give up these objective interests.

Transforming the state in Africa from a regulatory role to a developmental one requires the systematic transformation of the current bureaucracy from simply an administrative bureaucracy to one that is technical. How is this to be achieved? The current economic crisis in Africa has provided an opportunity for bureaucratic transformation that otherwise would not be possible under normal circumstances. States in Africa are hard-pressed to solve political and economic problems far beyond their current technical means. Pressure from international agencies which provide foreign aid, and the internal need for reform as political and economic demands increase, can combine to effect change in the way the bureaucracy responds to political and economic reform. Ideally, the occupation of the state bureaucracy by a corps of personnel that is technically competent would begin to systematically undermine a system that is particularistic and parochial. The undermining of such a system on both technical and political grounds would be a significant first step.

THE IMPERATIVE OF INDUSTRIALIZATION

In the final analysis, modern civilization is based on industrialization. While the economic crisis in Africa has been discussed mostly in terms of agricultural decline—since approximately 90 percent of the population is rural and agricultural—the underdevelopment of Africa is primarily a consequence of its nonindustrialization, its failure to harness nature to the advantage of its population. The process of industrialization is also historically and conceptually tied to the development of capitalism as a social system. That is why our discussion of capitalism as a socioeconomic system and its manifestation in Africa (in chapter 4) is so important. We recognize that no two historical experiences are exactly similar. But, as we pointed out above in the case of Japan, there are elements of other experiences that can be used as historical lessons (or reference points) to help us determine the viability of industrial development in Africa. Thus, without becoming historical determinists, we accept Alexander Gerschenkron's reasoning:

We cannot approach historical reality except through a search of regularities and deviations from regularities, by conceiving events and consequences of events in terms of our mind, patterns, or models. There is an infinite variety of possible models, each one of them subject to change or rejection. And yet, as long as we think in terms of a given model, we are all determinists in the sense that we pose a certain interrelation, or sequence, of events and phenomena which is "inevitable." (1962: 31–32)

According to Gerschenkron, for industrialization to occur, certain major obstacles must be removed and certain things propitious to it must be created. The following discussion will be devoted to an explanation of some of the obstacles that must be removed for industrialization to take place in Africa. The discussion is predicated on our earlier discussion on the necessity for the transformation of the state. It is also predicated on the discussion in chapter 1 of the status of industrial development in Africa. In chapter 1, we saw that, according to current projections, the ECA estimates that if the present industrial trends persist, Africa will remain unindustrialized even by the year 2008. (ECA, 1983: 35)

Perhaps the first step toward industrialization is implicit in the development pattern of social relations in Africa. Our strong reservation in designating Africa as essentially a capitalist society was based on the overwhelming predominance of a social system that has allowed rural producers a more or less unrestricted access to the major means of production: land. Historically, no society has been able to industrialize with this kind of social relations. Indeed,

Gerschenkron, among others, has pointed to this fact in characterizing "backward" countries.

The overriding factor to consider is that industrial labor, in the sense of a stable, reliable, and disciplined group that has cut the umbilical cord connecting it with the land and has become suitable for utilization in factories, is not abundant but extremely scarce in a backward country. (1962: 9)

We recognize that historically the alienation of labor was accompanied by terrible suffering on the part of the working class in the now industrialized countries. However, present-day Africa has the benefit of history to help it minimize the potential sufferings and disruptions that would inevitably result from a process of alienation. For example, labor laws could be instituted to protect workers from the negative aspects of capitalist industrialization. The enforcement of such laws would be possible given the close relationship the state would have with industry itself.

Alienation of labor would have to be accompanied by a legal system assuring the rights of the individual and satisfactory protection of property. In our opinion, the lack of such a legal system of protection has made investment in property too risky an enterprise for would-be individual entrepreneurs. The more or less universal principle of nonindividual/private land ownership in African countries, for example, has made long-term investment in agriculture impossible. For agricultural production to increase, some mechanization process will have to be introduced. However, without a well-defined land tenure system, it would be too much to expect that individuals would risk investing in mechanization when land belongs to the *clan* or the *state*. Evidence has shown that whenever there is some form of secure freehold land tenure system, investment in mechanized agriculture is more common and more developed. (Leys, 1975: esp. chapter 3) Social relations in the agricultural sector, given the appropriate circumstances, would closely follow relations in the industrial sector. The critical point here is that as mechanization in both agriculture and industrialization proceed, the state should ensure that a safety net exists to protect a substantial number of people who inevitably would be dislocated by the process. It is in this regard that the state's welfare role assumes an added importance. Besides the provision of services such as roads, railways, postal service, etc., a minimum purchasing power must be guaranteed, unlike in recent industrialization cases such as Mexico and other Latin American countries. One of the main reasons why development of Latin American industry is at a standstill is the lack of customers with money to spend (Dumont with Mazoyer, 1973: 71).

State participation or intervention in the economy in the Third World has had a mixed bag of results. In Brazil and Mexico, it has resulted in a tremendous acceleration in industrialization (Evans, 1979; Gereffi, 1983). However, as our discussion in chapter 3 suggested, the kind of industrialization achieved in Mexico, Brazil, and other Newly Industrializing Countries (NICs) is essentially a *dependent* industrialization. Dependent industrialization was possible for these NICs because these countries experienced ISI at an earlier stage and had developed characteristics which were conducive to the expansion of ISI to include products such as automobiles, sophisticated machinery, airplanes, chemicals, etc. Those conditions no longer exist in the world economy today. Africa, therefore, cannot look at Latin America or South Asia as examples for emulation. Rather, Africa must now begin to raise the issue of what kind of technology it will import from abroad. Obviously, the kind of technology to be imported cannot be similar to the one that has characterized Africa's attempt at industrialization. (See contributions in Fransman, 1982.) Neither can it delude itself with "comparative advantage." Thus several issues must be raised in order to place Africa's industrialization in the appropriate context.

First, if we accept the general proposition that industry is the main lever of African development, then the social relations that will support the process of industrialization must be closely scrutinized. Our general discussion of these social relations in Africa in previous chapters suggested that these social relations lack the capitalist dynamic that made industrialization such a transforming force in countries such as England. For capitalist industrialization to take place, the state must support the emergence of indigenous capitalists who will behave as capitalists; that is, these indigenous capitalists *must* show a propensity to *expand* and *accumulate* capital. "Capitalists" in Africa have usually invested in real estate or in other service industries (e.g., hotels, restaurants, lorries, etc.)—industries that are not expansionary in the capitalist sense. The building of a mere fifteen houses in a city, for example, does not necessarily improve the technological base of a society. Thus, social relations must be transformed, and capitalists should behave in a capitalist manner.

Second, because of minimal social differentiation, the kind of technology that should be allowed must reflect the capacity of the population to absorb it. The classic underutilization problem in African industry partly stems from the inability of the local population to utilize successfully imported technology. The consequence is that factories always operate at less that 50 percent of capacity. The underutilization problem applies equally to more differentiated economies such as Nigeria and the Ivory Coast and to less differentiated economies such as Tanzania and Uganda. The state, however, must take a leading role in determining and designating the appropriate technology. The present state(s) is less capable of making this determination of appropriate technology because of their historical connection to ISI. For example, it would be unrealistic for the present state in Tanzania to alter fundamentally its industrialization strategy when it already has "white elephant" projects, such as the automated bakery in Dar es Salaam and the fertilizer factory in Tanga. The state is too closely attached to these projects to allow changes to occur (Coulson, 1979). Indeed, rather than abandoning and dismantling these factories, the state is busy struggling to rehabilitate them.

Critics of "appropriate" technology have suggested that technology tailor-made to meet the needs of developing countries may in the long run be harmful to the industrial development potential of these countries. Arghiri Emmanuel (1982), for example, has suggested that "appropriate" technology is not a technology specially designed for these countries, but an *impoverished* technology. He argues that adoption of "appropriate" technology does increase the technological distance between the developed and underdeveloped countries. Further, what is important is the amount of goods produced, not the number of jobs created to produce these goods. Emmanuel's argument is based on two assumptions: first, it is the amount of goods produced that establishes the level of social welfare, as well as economic and political independence; and second, most modern and capital-intensive technologies are more productive than the old "appropriate" technologies, which are labor intensive. Thus, looking at it globally, the transfer of this most modern technology accelerates development in the most industrialized countries and cuts short the development path taken by the Third World.

What Emmanuel's position ignores is that industrialization in the Third World is now not simply an issue of theoretical proposition but rather one that has a historical record to stand on. African countries in particular attempted to follow Emmanuel's suggestions as they began their industrialization process soon after independence. The result has been the capacity underutilization phenomenon, and the inability of local technological skills to sustain capital-intensive industries. The level of social differentiation simply is not there to carry out Emmanuel's vision of Third World industrialization. Neither is there effective demand nor foreign exchange to buy the necessary industrial raw materials from abroad. Indeed, Clive Thomas has pointed to the difficulties of undertaking industrialization based on Emmanuel's suggested path.

Extensive reliance on the import of technology does not mean *free access* to the marketplace of technology. If technology is basically a monopoly of the capitalist center, it follows from the dictates of the profit motive that its distribution from the capitalist center must inevitably follow certain market norms. Among these are the need to balance the distribution of technology (i.e. the gains from its use) in order to be assured that the monopoly is maintained, not in a static sense, but dynamically, through concentrating on the really strategic areas of technological leadership as they emerge. (1974: 64)

In other words, technological change under such a system will be a response to the needs of capital, not the needs of the Third World. It cannot be assumed that somehow technological advance will always affect production in the periphery. For technological advance to affect production in the periphery, there must be a symmetry between production and consumption.

Third, given the miserable performance of state bureaucracies in the industrial sector, there is an absolute necessity that a technological bureaucracy capable of determining the utility of imported technology be established. This techno-bureaucracy *must* have a statutory independence (or autonomy) to al-low it to make economically rational decisions—insulated, so to speak, from parochial political pressure. It is conceivable that, had this kind of techno-bureaucracy existed in Ghana, the Volta Dam project may not have been un-dertaken, or the building of the fertilizer factory in Tanzania. Its many faults not withstanding, it could be argued that the technical bureaucracy in Brazil has performed remarkably well—and indeed Brazil's industrialization success is partly attributable to the existence of this technical bureaucracy (Evans, 1979).

The state's role in industrialization, therefore, cannot be viewed entirely negatively as, say, dependency theory would, or as the free marketers would have us believe. The state could be a progressive force of immense proportions in terms of industrialization. And, to emphasize an important point, discus-sion of Africa's industrialization at this stage of (under)development does not require a stark choice between either capitalism or socialism as Thomas Kanza, among others, suggests:

African countries are increasingly finding themselves faced with an absolute choice: should they adopt the traditional capitalist method, which means in effect, dependence on foreign capital and subordination of their own development to the special interests of monopoly capitalism? Or should they, on the contrary, take a socialist road and plan their development rationally in the general interest of Africa and its people? (1978: 70–71)

Manfred Bienefeld, in response to arguments such as Kanza's, provides a se-rious reflective position regarding the role of the state in Third World devel-opment, especially in industrialization.

The dependency debate's unacceptable tendency to reject all cases of state intervention within a non-socialist framework as necessarily incapable of generating any significant short- or long-term benefits for the working people involved [has] a political rationale, and an analytic foundation, and the unwarranted crudeness of such a conclusion should not be allowed to obscure its substantial grain of truth. (1981: 87)

But the state, in order to be "progressive" and to serve the short- and long-term interests of the working people, must see the limits of a development strategy that places a premium on open-ended participation in the interna-tional economy. Continued incorporation within the world system has led to neither growth nor redistribution for the majority of Africa's peoples. What is even more significant is the fact that of the NICs, none of these states has pur-sued a laissez-faire strategy based entirely on the so-called market forces. The role of the state has been strategic and decisive in promoting particular kinds of industries. African states, on the other hand, have opened themselves up to the importation of all kinds of useless or inappropriate technologies and to the exporting of primary goods to the extent that they essentially do not control their economies. This must be reversed.

Finally, it should be pointed out that development (and implicitly industrialization) is, in the final analysis, a *political* problem. Political variables necessarily impinge upon economic decisions; and, indeed, there is a very strong element of choice in whatever developmental decision is undertaken. In the specific case of industrialization, there are several politico-economic variables that come into play—variables that cannot be ignored. In Africa, these variables include market size and the potential for continental political unity. Dependency theory, to its credit, has conclusively shown the limits of ISI industrialization and the market limits for imported goods. Given the already existing industrial capacity in Africa, however, optimal use of that capacity is only conceivable under conditions of a wider market. Political differences between countries, however, have prevented rational planning in industrial production to the extent that duplication of industries in neighboring countries is the norm. Political unity—as opposed to regional economic organizations such as the East African Community (EAC) or the Economic Community of West African States (ECOWAS)—is our preferred solution because of the historical experience of failures in attempts at regional economic organizations. Perhaps their basic shortcoming is that they are usually established

without the explicit aim of transforming the production structures, ... such arrangements will merely expand the permissive area of exchange (i.e. enlarge the market for neocolonial penetration) and increase the opportunities for a further deepening of the underdevelopment process—without even the compensating possibilities of developing a large national industrial structure or a capitalist class. (Thomas, 1974: 68)

But political unity as such would be meaningless unless it is accompanied by the other transformations we have already discussed: change in the character of the state, social relations of production, choice of technology, mechanized agriculture, etc.

TOWARD AN ALTERNATIVE FUTURE

The discussion in this chapter—indeed, the entire study—has suggested that in order for Africa to escape the worst effects of underdevelopment, a radical transformation in the way development has been conducted must be undertaken. With its tremendous underdevelopment, Africa is still highly dependent on the international economic system. This dependency, however, has brought few benefits to the continent. A new development strategy in Africa, therefore, must restructure Africa's relationship with the international economy—inevitably moving toward less association. Without such a move, Africa will face further economic decline and a continuing crisis of political economy: political/ethnic/cultural crises reinforced by the crisis of the economy.

Societies will remain fragmented, and separatist movements—already prevalent on the continent (Zaire, Ethiopia, Sudan, etc.)—will gain momentum. Political crises will inevitably reinforce the African states' already authoritative disposition as they become increasingly unable to govern.

An alternative future calls for the state to restructure itself and to allow political and economic initiatives by individuals to be the guiding principles of governance. This is not to suggest, however, that the state completely abandon its welfare role in society or its role as a principal facilitator for capital accumulation in society—given Africa's history of underdevelopment. Rather, it is a suggestion that the state should recognize its own limits and adopt a development strategy that will maximize the realization of Africa's potential.

Bibliography

Adams, F. Gerard, and Jere R. Behrman. *Commodity Exports and Economic Development*. Lexington: Lexington Books, 1982.

Adedeji, Adebayo. "Development and Economic Growth in Africa to the Year 2000: Alternative Projections and Policies." In *Alternative Futures for Africa*. Edited by Timothy M. Shaw. Boulder: Westview, 1982: 281.

Africa Confidential, London, Various Issues 1984–1986.

Africa Report, New York, Various Issues 1984–1986.

Ake, Claude. "Explanatory Notes on the Political Economy of Africa." *Journal of Modern African Studies* 14, 1 (1976).

———. *Revolutionary Pressures in Africa*. London: Zed, 1978.

———. *A Political Economy of Africa*. London: Longman, 1981.

———. ed. *Political Economy of Nigeria*. London: Longman, 1985.

Alavi, Hamza. "The State in Post-Colonial Societies: Pakistan and Bangladesh." *New Left Review* 74 (July–August 1972).

Allison, C., and R. H. Green, eds. "Accelerated Development in Sub-Saharan Africa: What Agenda for Action?" *Institute for Development Studies Bulletin* 14, 1/2 (1983).

Almond, Gabriel, and Sidney Verba. *The Civic Culture: Political Attitudes and Democracy in Five Nations*. Princeton: Princeton University Press, 1963.

———, and James S. Coleman, eds. *The Politics of the Developing Areas*. Princeton: Princeton University Press, 1960.

Amin, Samir. *Accumulation on a World Scale*. 2 Vols. New York: Monthly Review, 1974.

———. *Imperialism and Unequal Development*. New York: Monthly Review, 1977.

Apter, David E. *The Gold Coast in Transition*. Princeton: Princeton University Press, 1955.

———. *The Political Kingdom in Uganda: A Study in Bureaucratic Nationalism*. Princeton: Princeton University Press, 1961.

———. *The Politics of Modernization*. Chicago: University of Chicago Press, 1965.

Aronwitz, Stanley. "Introduction." *In* Paulette Pierce. *Noncapitalist Development*. Totowa, N.J.: Rowman & Allanheld, 1984, viii–ix.

Azarya, Victor. "Reordering State-Society Relations: Incorporation and Disengagement." In *The Precarious Balance: State and Society in Africa*. Edited by Donald Rothchild and Naomi Chazan. Boulder: Westview, 1988.

———, and Naomi Chazan. "Disengagement from the State in Africa: Reflections on the Experience of Ghana and Guinea." *Comparative Studies in Society and History* 29, 1 (1987).

Babu, A. M. *African Socialism or Socialist Africa?* Dar es Salaam: Tanzania Publishing House, 1981.

Baer, W. "Import Substitution and Industrialization in Latin America." *Latin America Research Review* 7 (1972).

Balabkins, Nicholas. *Indigenization and Economic Development: The Nigerian Experience.* London: Jai Press, 1982.

Barnet, Richard, and Ronald E. Muller. *Global Reach: The Power of the Multinational Corporations.* New York: Simon & Schuster, 1974.

Beckman, Björn. "Neo-Colonialism and the State in Nigeria." In *Contradictions of Accumulation in Africa: Studies in Economy and State.* Edited by Henry Bernstein and Bonnie K. Campbell. Beverly Hills: Sage, 1984.

Bennett, Douglas C., and Kenneth E. Sharpe. *Transnational Corporations Versus the State: The Political Economy of the Mexican Auto Industry.* Princeton: Princeton University Press, 1985.

Bernstein, Henry. "Notes on Capital and Peasantry." *Review of African Political Economy* 10 (September–December 1977).

———. "African Peasantries: A Theoretical Framework." *Journal of Peasant Studies* 6, 4 (1979).

———, and Bonnie K. Campbell, eds. *Contradictions of Accumulation in Africa: Studies in Economy and State.* Beverly Hills: Sage, 1985.

Bienefeld, M. "Dependency and the Newly Industrializing Countries (NICs): Towards a Reappraisal." In *Dependency Theory: A Critical Reassessment.* Edited by Dudley Seers. London: Frances Pinter, 1981.

Bienen, Henry, and V. P. Diejomaoh, eds. *Inequality and Development in Nigeria.* New York: Holmes & Meir, 1981.

Binder, Leonard, et al. *Crises and Sequences in Political Development.* Princeton: Princeton University Press, 1971.

Black, C. E. *The Dynamics of Modernization.* New York: Harper & Row, 1966.

Blömstrom, Magnus, and Björn Hettne. *Development Theory in Transition.* London: Zed, 1984.

Bottomore, Tom. *Theories of Modern Capitalism.* London: George Allen & Unwin, 1985.

Bratton, Michael. "Patterns of Development and Underdevelopment." *International Studies Quarterly* 26, 3 (1982).

Brenner, Robert. "The Origins of Capitalist Development: A Critique of Neo-Smithian Marxism." *New Left Review* 104 (1977).

Brett, E. A. *Colonialism and Underdevelopment in East Africa.* London: Heinemann, 1972.

———. *International Money and Capitalist Crisis: The Anatomy of Global Disintegration.* London: Heinemann, 1983.

Brietzke, Paul, ed. "The World Bank's Accelerated Development in Sub-Saharan Africa: A Symposium." *African Studies Review* 27, 4 (1984).

Brown, Lester R., and Edward C. Wolf. *Reversing Africa's Decline.* Washington, D.C.: Worldwatch Institute, 1985.

Browne, Robert S., and Robert J. Cummings. *The Lagos Plan of Action vs. The Berg Report: Contemporary Issues in African Economic Development.* Lawrenceville, Va: Brunswick Publ., 1984.

Callaghy, Thomas M. "External Actors and the Relative Autonomy of the Political Aristocracy in Zaire." *Journal of Commonwealth and Comparative Politics* 21, 3 (1983).

———. *The State-Society Struggle: Zaire in Comparative Perspective.* New York: Columbia University Press, 1984.

———. "The State and the Development of Capitalism in Africa: Some Theoretical and Historical Reflections." In *The Precarious Balance: State and Society in Africa.* Edited by Donald Rothchild and Naomi Chazan. Boulder: Westview, 1988.

Campbell, Bonnie K. "The Fiscal Crisis of the State: The Case of the Ivory Coast." In *Contradictions of Accumulation in Africa: Studies in Economy and State.* Edited by Henry Bernstein and Bonnie K. Campbell. Beverly Hills: Sage, 1984.

Cardoso, F. H. "Dependent Capitalist Development in Latin America." *New Left Review* 74 (July–August 1972).

Chazan, Naomi. *An Anatomy of Ghanian Politics: Managing Political Recession, 1969–1982.* Boulder: Westview, 1983.

Chilcote, Ronald H. *Theories of Development and Underdevelopment.* Boulder: Westview, 1984.

———, and Joel S. Edelstein, eds. *Latin America: The Struggle with Dependency and Beyond.* New York: Wiley & Sons, 1974.

Coleman, James S., and Carl G. Rosberg, eds. *Political Parties and National Integration in Tropical Africa.* Berkeley: University of California Press, 1966.

Collins, Randall. "Weber's Last Theory of Capitalism: A Systemization." *American Sociological Review* 45 (December 1980).

Cooper, Frederick. "Africa and the World Economy." *African Studies Review* 24, 2/3 (1981).

Coulson, Andrew, ed. *African Socialism in Practice: The Tanzanian Experience.* Nottingham, England: Spokesman Books, 1979.

Crummey, Donald, and C. C. Stewart, eds. *Modes of Production in Africa: The Precolonial Era.* Beverly Hills: Sage, 1981.

Cunha, Antonio-Gabriel M. "Africa and the IMF: Toward a New Deal." *Africa Report* (May–June 1985).

Curry, Robert L., Jr. "Zambia's Economic Crisis: A Challenge to Budgetary Politics." *Journal of African Studies* 6, 4 (1979a).

———. "Africa's External Debt Situation." *Journal of Modern African Studies* 17, 1 (1979b).

Dell, Sidney. *On Being Grandmotherly: The Evolution of IMF Conditionality.* Princeton: International Finance Section, Department of Economics, Princeton University, 1981.

Dobb, Maurice. *Studies in the Development of Capitalism.* Rev. ed. New York: International Publ., 1963.

Doob, Leonard. *Becoming More Civilized: A Psychological Exploration.* New Haven: Yale Univ. Press, 1960.

Dos Santos, T. "The Structure of Dependence." *American Economic Review* 60 (May 1970).

Dumont, René, with Marcel Mazoyer. *Socialisms and Development.* London: Andre Deutsch, 1973.

Duvall, R., et al. "A Formal Model of 'Dependencia Theory': Structure and Measurement." In *From National Development to Global Community.* Edited by Richard L. Merritt and Bruce M. Russett. London: George Allen & Unwin, 1981.

Economic Commission for Africa. *ECA and Africa's Development 1983-2008: A Preliminary Perspective Study.* Addis Ababa: United Nations Publs., 1983.

Economic Commission for Latin America and the Caribbean. *External Debt in Latin America: Adjustment Policies and Renegotiation.* Boulder: Lynne Rienner, 1985.

Emerson, Rupert. *Africa and United States Policy.* Englewood Cliffs, N.J.: Prentice-Hall, 1967.

Emmanuel, Arghiri. *Appropriate or Underdeveloped Technology?* New York: Wiley & Sons, 1982.

Europa Publications Ltd. *Africa South of the Sahara 1980–81.* London: Europa Publications, 1981.

Evans, Peter. *Dependent Development: The Alliance of Multinational State and Local Capital in Brazil.* Princeton: Princeton University Press, 1979.

Fernandez, R. A., and J. F. Ocampo. "The Latin American Revolution: A Theory of Imperialism, Not Dependency." *Latin American Perspectives* 1 (Spring 1974).

Flint, J. E. "Economic Change in West Africa in the Nineteenth Century." In *History of West Africa.* Vol. 2. Edited by J. F. A. Ajayi and M. Crowder. London: Longman, 1974.

Forrest, Joshua B. "Defining African Peasants." *Peasant Studies* 9, 4 (1982).

Frank, Andre Gunder. *Capitalism and Underdevelopment in Latin America.* New York: Monthly Review, 1967.

———. *Latin American: Underdevelopment or Revolution?* New York: Monthly Review, 1969.

———. *Lumpenbourgeoisie: Lumpendevelopment.* New York: Monthly Review, 1972.

———. "Dependence is Dead, Long Live Dependence and the Class Struggle." *Latin American Perspectives* 1 (Spring 1974).

———. *Dependent Accumulation and Underdevelopment.* London: Macmillan, 1978.

Fransman, Martin, ed. *Industry and Accumulation in Africa.* London: Heinemann, 1982.

Freyhold, Michaela von. *Ujamaa Villages in Tanzania: Analysis of a Social Experiment.* New York: Monthly Review, 1979.

Furtado, Celso. *Accumulation and Development: The Logic of Industrial Civilization.* Oxford: Martin Robertson, 1983. English ed.

Fyfe, C. "Reform in West Africa: The Abolition of Slave Trade." In *History of West Africa.* Vol. 2. Edited by J. F. A. Ajayi and M. Crowder. London: Longman, 1974.

Gereffi, Gary. *The Pharmaceutical Industry and Dependency in the Third World.* Princeton: Princeton University Press, 1983.

Gerschenkron, Alexander. *Economic Backwardness in Historical Perspective.* Cambridge, Mass.: Belknap Press, 1962.

Gordon, David F., ed. "Special Double Issue on the Berg Report." *Rural Africana* 19, 20 (1984).

Gould, David J. "Local Administration in Zaire and Underdevelopment." *Journal of Modern African Studies* 15, 3 (1977).

Gran, Guy, ed. *Zaire: The Political Economy of Underdevelopment*. New York: Praeger, 1979.

Green, Reginald H. "Political-Economic Adjustment and IMF Conditionality: Tanzania, 1974–81." In *IMF Conditionality*. Edited by John Williamson. Cambridge: MIT Press, 1983.

———. "From Deepening Economic Malaise Towards Renewed Development: An Overview." *Journal of Development Planning* 15 (1985): 9.

Grieco, Joseph M. *Between Dependency and Autonomy: India's Experience with the Computer Industry*. Berkeley: University of California Press, 1984.

Gutkind, Peter C., and Immanuel Wallerstein, eds. *Political Economy of Contemporary Africa*. 2nd ed. Beverly Hills: Sage, 1985.

Henry, P. "The United Nations and the Problem of African Development." In *Africa and World Order*. Edited by N. J. Padleford and Rupert Emerson. New York: Praeger, 1962.

Hunt, Diana. *The Impending Crisis in Kenya: The Case of Land Reform*. Aldershot: Gower Publ., 1984.

Huntington, Samuel P. *Political Order in Changing Societies*. New Haven: Yale University Press, 1968.

———, and Jorge I. Dominguez. "Political Development." In Handbook of Political Science. Vol. 3. Edited by F. I. Greenstein and Nelson Polsby. Reading, Mass.: Addison Wesley Publ., 1975.

Hyden, Goran. *Beyond Ujamaa in Tanzania: Underdevelopment and an Uncaptured Peasantry*. Berkeley: University of California Press, 1980.

———. *No Shortcuts to Progress: African Development Management in Perspective*. Berkeley: University of California Press, 1983.

International Monetary Fund. *World Economic Outlook*. Washington D.C.: n.p., 1982.

Jackson, Robert H., and Carl G. Rosberg. "Why Africa's Weak States Persist: The Empirical and Juridical in Statehood." *World Politics* 27 (October 1982).

Johnson, Chalmers. *MITI and the Japanese Miracle*. Stanford: Stanford University Press, 1982.

Joseph, Richard A. "Class, State, and Prebendal Politics in Nigeria." *Journal of Commonwealth and Comparative Politics* 21, 3 (1983).

———. *Democracy and Prebendal Politics in Nigeria: The Rise and Fall of the Second Republic*. New York: Cambridge University Press, 1988.

Kanza, Thomas. *Evolution and Revolution in Africa*. Cambridge, Mass.: Schenkman, 1978.

Kaplinsky, Raphael, ed. *Third World Industrialization in the 1980s: Open Economies in a Closing World*. London: Frank Cass, 1984.

Kasfir, Nelson. "State, Magendo, and Class Formation in Uganda." *Journal of Commonwealth and Comparative Politics* 21, 3 (1983).

Kay, Geoffrey. *The Political Economy of Colonialism in Ghana*. London: Cambridge University Press, 1972.

———. *Development and Underdevelopment: A Marxist Analysis*. New York: St. Martin's, 1975.

Kilby, Peter. *Industrialization in an Open Economy: Nigeria 1945–1966*. London: Cambridge University Press, 1969.

Kindleberger, Charles. *The Terms of Trade*. New York: Harper & Row, 1956.

————. *Foreign Trade and the National Economy.* New Haven: Yale University Press, 1962.

Kleeimeier, Lizz L. "Empirical Tests of Dependency Theory: A Second Critique of Methodology." *Journal of Modern African Studies* 16, 4 (1978).

Klein, Martin A., ed. *Peasants in Africa.* Beverly Hills: Sage, 1980.

Kuhn, Thomas S. *The Structure of Scientific Revolutions.* Chicago: University of Chicago Press, 1970. Second ed., enlarged.

Langdon, Steven N. *Multinational Corporations in the Political Economy of Kenya.* New York: St. Martin's, 1981.

Lerner, Daniel. *The Passing of Traditional Society: Modernizing the Middle East.* Glencoe, Ill.: Free Press, 1958.

Lewis, W. Arthur. "Industrialization of the British West Indies." *Caribbean Economic Review* 2, 1 (1950).

Leys, Colin. *Underdevelopment in Kenya: The Political Economy of Neo-Colonialism 1964–1971.* Berkeley: University of California Press, 1975.

————. "Underdevelopment and Dependency: Critical Notes." *Journal of Contemporary Asia* 7, 1 (1977).

Lipset, Seymour M. "Some Social Requisites of Democracy." *American Political Science Review* 21, 4 (1961).

List, Frederick. *National System of Political Economy.* Trans. by G. A. Matile. Philadelphia: Lippincott, 1856.

Livingstone, Ian, ed. *Approaches to Development Studies: Essays in Honour of Athole Mackintosh.* Hampshire: Gower, 1982.

Lonsdale, John, "States and Social Processes in Africa: A Historical Survey." *African Studies Review* 24, 2/3 (1981).

Luke, David F., and Timothy M. Shaw. *Continental Crisis: The Lagos Plan of Action and Africa's Future.* Lanham, Md: University Press of America, 1984.

Mamdani, Mahmood. *The Myth of Population Control: Family, Caste and Class in an Indian Village.* New York: Monthly Review, 1972.

Mao Tse-tung, "Be Concerned with the Well-being of the Masses, Pay Attention to Methods of Work." *Selected Works.* Vol. 1. Peking: Foreign Languages Press, 1970.

Marcussen, Henrik Secher, and J. E. Torp. *Internationalization of Capital: Prospects for the Third World, A Re-examination of Dependency Theory.* London: Zed, 1982.

Marx, Karl. *Pre-Capitalist Economic Formations.* New York: International Publ., 1964. Intro. by Eric J. Hobsbawm.

Matlon, Peter. "Structure of Production and Rural Incomes in Northern Nigeria." In *The Political Economy of Income Distribution in Nigeria.* Edited by Henry Bienen and V. P. Diejomaoh. New York: Holmes & Meir, 1981.

Meek, Ronald L. *Marx and Engels on the Population Bomb.* 2d ed. Berkeley: Ramparts Press, 1971.

Meir, Gerald M. *International Trade and Development.* New York: Harper & Row, 1963.

Merhav, M. *Technological Dependence, Monopoly and Growth.* New York: Pergamon, 1969.

Midgal, Joel S. *Peasants, Politics and Revolution: Pressures Toward Political and Social Change in the Third World.* Princeton: Princeton University Press, 1974.

Mintz, Sidney W. "A Note on the Definition of Peasantries." *Journal of Peasant Studies* 1, 1 (1973).

Morrison, Thomas K. "The Political Economy of Export Instability in Developing Countries: The Case of Ghana." *Journal of African Studies* 6, 3 (1979).

Nowzad, Bahram. *The IMF and Its Critics.* Princeton: International Finance Section, Department of Economics, Princeton University, 1982.

Nyang'oro, Julius E. *Development and Dependency: A Theoretical Critique and an African Case Study.* Ph.D. Diss., Miami University, 1983.

———. "On the Concept of 'Corporatism' and the African State." *Studies in Comparative International Development* 21, 4 (1986–87).

———. "Political Choices and the African Development Experience." *African Political Science Review* 1, 1 (May 1986).

———, and Timothy M. Shaw, eds. *Corporatism in Africa: Comparative Analysis and Practice.* Boulder: Westview, 1989.

Nyerere, Julius K. Speech at the Royal Commonwealth Society. London, March 20, 1985a.

———. Speech at the City of London Lunch, Mansion House, Guildhall. London, March 19, 1985b.

Nzongola-Ntalaja, ed. *The Crisis in Zaire: Myths and Realities.* Trenton, N.J.: Africa World Press, 1986.

O'Donnell, Guillermo A. *Modernization and Bureaucratic—Authoritarianism: Studies in South American Politics.* Berkeley: Institute of International Studies, University of California, 1979.

Onimode, Bade. *Imperialism and Underdevelopment in Nigeria: The Dialectics of Mass Poverty.* London: Zed, 1982.

Organski, A. F. K. *The Stages of Political Development.* New York: Knopf, 1967.

Organization of African Unity. *Lagos Plan of Action for the Economic Development of Africa, 1980–2000.* 2nd rev. ed. Geneva: International Institute for Labour Studies, 1982.

Paul, James C. N., ed, "The World Bank's Accelerated Development in Sub-Saharan Africa: A Symposium." *African Studies Review* 27, 4 (1984).

Peemas, J. Ph. "The Social and Economic Development of Zaire Since Independence: An Historical Outline." *African Affairs* 74, 295 (1975).

Popkin, Samuel L. *The Rational Peasant: The Political Economy of Rural Society in Vietnam.* Berkeley: University of California Press, 1979.

Preston, P. W. *New Trends in Development Theory: Essays in Development and Social Theory.* London: Routledge & Kegan Paul, 1985.

Price, Robert M. "Neo-Colonialism and Ghana's Economic Decline: A Critical Assessment." *Canadian Journal of African Studies* 18, 1 (1984).

Przeworski, Adam, and Henry Teune. *The Logic of Comparative Social Inquiry.* New York: Wiley & Sons, 1970.

Pye, Lucian. *Aspects of Political Development: An Analytical Study.* Boston: Little, Brown, 1966.

Raj, K. N. "The Causes and Consequences of World Recession." *World Development* 12, 3 (1984).

Ravenhill, John. *Collective Clientelism: The Lome Conventions and North-South Relations.* New York: Columbia University Press, 1985.

————. "Collective Self-Reliance or Collective Self-Delusion: Is the Lagos Plan a Viable Alternative?" In *Africa in Economic Crisis*. Edited by John Ravenhill. New York: Columbia University Press, 1986.

Ricardo, David. *Principles of Political Economy and Taxation*. London: Pelican, 1971.

Rodney, Walter. *How Europe Underdeveloped Africa*. Dar es Salaam: Tanzania Publ. House, 1972.

Rosberry, William. "Peasants as Proletarians." *Critique of Anthropology* 3, 11 (1978).

Rostow, W. W. *The Stages of Economic Growth: A Non-Communist Manifesto*. Cambridge: Cambridge University Press, 1960.

Rothchild, Donald, and Naomi Chazan, eds. *The Precarious Balance: State and Society in Africa*. Boulder: Westview, 1988.

Rothstein, Robert L. *The Weak in the World of the Strong: The Developing Countries in the International System*. New York: Columbia University Press, 1977.

————. *Global Bargaining: UNCTAD and the Quest for a New International Economic Order*. Princeton: Princeton University Press, 1979.

Ruggie, John Gerard, ed. *The Antinomies of Interdependence*. New York: Columbia University Press, 1983.

Russett, Bruce M., and Harvey Starr. *World Politics: The Menu for Choice*. San Francisco: Freeman, 1981.

Rwegasira, Delphin G. "Exchange Rates and the Management of the External Sector in Sub-Saharan Africa." *Journal of Modern African Studies* 22, 3 (1984).

Rweyemamu, Justinian. *Underdevelopment and Industrialization in Tanzania: A Study of Perverse Capitalist Industrial Development*. Nairobi: Oxford University Press, 1973.

————, ed. *Industrialization and Income Distribution in Africa*. Dakar, Senegal: Codesria, 1980.

Sandbrook, Richard, with Judith Barker. *The Politics of Africa's Economic Stagnation*. Cambridge: Cambridge University Press, 1985.

Saul, John S. "The State in Post-Colonial Societies: Tanzania." *Socialist Register* (1974).

Schatz, Sayre P. *Nigerian Capitalism*. Berkeley: University of California Press, 1977.

Scott, James C. *The Moral Economy of the Peasant: Rebellion and Subsistence in Southeast Asia*. New Haven: Yale University Press, 1976.

Seddon, David, ed. *Relations of Production: Marxist Approaches to Economic Anthropology*. London: Frank Cass, 1978.

Sender, John, and Sheila Smith. *The Development of Capitalism in Africa*. London: Metheun, 1986.

Schmitz, Hurbert. "Industrialization Strategies in Less Developed Countries: Some Lessons of Historical Experience." In *Third World Industrialization in the 1980s: Open Economies in a Closing World*. Edited by Raphael Kaplinsky. London: Frank Cass, 1984.

Shanin, Teodor. "The Nature of the Peasant Economy: A Generalization." *Journal of Peasant Studies* 1, 1 (1973).

Shao, John. "Politics and the Food Production Crisis in Tanzania." ISSUE XIV. Los Angeles, 1985.

Shaw, Timothy M. "Beyond Neo-Colonialism: Varieties of Corporatism in Africa." *Journal of Modern African Studies* 20, 2 (1982).

————. *Towards a Political Economy for Africa: The Dialectics of Dependence.* New York: St. Martin's, 1985: 13.

————, and Olajide Aluko, eds. *Africa Projected: From Recession to Renaissance by the Year 2000?* New York: St. Martin's, 1985.

Shivji, Issa. *Class Struggles in Tanzania.* Dar es Salaam: Tanzania Publ. House, 1976.

————, ed. *The State and the Working People in Tanzania.* Dakar, Senegal: Codesria, 1985.

Sideri, S. *Trade and Power.* Rotterdam: n.p., 1970.

Sills, David L., ed. *International Encyclopedia of the Social Sciences.* Vol. 12. New York: Macmillan, 1968.

Smith, Adam. *The Wealth of Nations.* Edited by Andrew Skinner. Harmondsworth: Penguin, 1981.

Smith, Tony. "The Underdevelopment of Developed Literature: The Case of Dependency Theory." *World Politics* 31, 2 (1979).

Spengler, Joseph P. "The Economics of Population Growth." In *The Population Crisis and the Use of World Resources.* Edited by Stuart Mudd. Bloomington: Indiana University Press, 1964.

Spero, Joan. *The Politics of International Economic Relations.* 2d ed. New York: St. Martin's, 1981.

Staley, Eugene. *The Future of Underdeveloped Countries: Political Implications of Economic Development.* Rev. ed. New York: Harper & Row, 1961.

Stepan, Alfred. *The State and Society: Peru in Comparative Perspective.* Princeton: Princeton University Press, 1978.

Stewart, Frances. *Technology and Underdevelopment.* London: Macmillan, 1977.

Stockholm International Peace Research Institute (SIPRI), *World Armaments and Disarmament.* Philadelphia: Taylor & Francis, 1985.

Swainson, Nicola. *The Development of Corporate Capitalism in Kenya 1918–77.* Berkeley: University of California Press, 1980.

Terray, Emmanuel. *Marxism and "Primitive" Societies: Two Studies.* New York: Monthly Review, 1972.

Thomas, Clive Y. *Dependence and Transformation: The Economics of Transition to Socialism.* New York: Monthly Review, 1974.

————. "Class Struggle, Social Development and the Theory of the Non-Capitalist Path." In *Problems of Socialist Orientation in Africa.* Edited by Mai Palmberg. Uppsala: Scandinavian Institute of African Studies, 1978.

————. *The Rise of the Authoritarian State in Peripheral Societies.* New York: Monthly Review, 1984.

Thomas, D. Babatunde. *Capital Accumulation and Technological Transfer.* New York: Praeger, 1975.

Timberlake, Lloyd. *Africa in Crisis: The Causes, the Cures of Environmental Bankruptcy.* Philadelphia: Earthscan, 1986.

Turok, Ben, ed. *Development in Zambia: A Reader.* London: Zed, 1979.

UNCTAD. "Trade and Development Report." New York: UN Publ., 1985.

Unger, Sanford J. *Africa: The People and Politics of an Emerging Continent.* New York: Simon & Schuster, 1985.

United Nations. *World Economic Survey: Current Trends and Policies in the World Economy.* New York: UN Publ., 1984.

United Nations. *World Economic Survey: Current Trends and Policies in the World Economy.* New York: UN Publ., 1985.

United Nations Center on Transnational Corporations. *Transnational Coporations in World Development: Third Survey.* New York: United Nations Publ., 1983.

United Republic of Tanzania. *Background to the Budget 1966–67.* Dar es Salaam: Government Printer, 1966.

Wall Street Journal. Various Issues, July 15–July 31, 1985.

Wallerstein, Immanuel. *The Modern World System.* Vol. 1. New York: Academic Press, 1974.

———. *The Modern World System.* Vol. 2. New York: Academic Press, 1980.

———. "The Three Stages of African Involvement in the World Economy." In *Political Economy of Contemporary Africa.* 2d ed. Edited by Peter C. Gutkind and I. Wallerstein. Beverly Hills: Sage, 1985.

Warren, Bill. "Imperialism and Capitalist Industrialization." *New Left Review* 81 (September–October 1973).

———. *Imperialism: The Pioneer of Capitalism.* London: New Left Books, 1980.

Watts, Michael. *Silent Violence: Food Famine and Peasantry in Northern Nigeria.* Berkeley: University of California Press, 1983.

Weber, Max. *The Protestant Ethic and the Spirit of Capitalism.* New York: Scribner's, 1930.

———. *Economy and Society.* Berkeley: University of California Press, 1978.

———. *General Economic History.* New Brunswick, N.J.: Transaction Books, 1981.

West Africa. London, Various Issues, 1984–86

Wiley, Norbert, ed. *The Marx-Weber Debate.* Newbury Park, Calif.: Sage, 1986.

Wionczek, Miguel S., et al. *Politics and Economics of External Debt Crisis: The Latin American Experience.* Boulder: Westview, 1985.

Woldring, Klass, et al. *Beyond Political Independence: Zambia's Development Predicament in the 1980s.* Berlin: Mouton Publ., 1984.

Wolf, Eric R. *Peasants.* Englewood Cliffs, N.J.: Prentice-Hall, 1966.

———. *Peasant Wars of the Twentieth Century.* New York: Harper & Row, 1969.

Wolpe, Harold, ed. *The Articulation of Modes of Production.* London: Routledge & Kegan Paul, 1980.

World Bank. *Accelerated Development in Sub-Saharan Africa: An Agenda for Action.* Washington D.C.; 1981.

———. *Sub-Saharan Africa: Progress Report on Development Prospects and Programs.* Washington D.C.; 1983.

———. *Ghana: Policies and Program for Adjustment.* Washington D.C.; 1984a.

———. *Toward Sustained Development in Sub-Saharan Africa: A Joint Program of Action.* Washington D.C.; 1984b.

———. *World Debt Tables: External Debt of Developing Countries,* 1984-85 ed. Washington D.C.; 1985a.

———. *World Development Report.* New York: Oxford University Press, 1985b.

Young, Crawford. *Ideology and Development in Africa.* New Haven: Yale University Press, 1982.

———, and Thomas Turner. *The Rise and Decline of the Zairian State.* Madison: University of Wisconsin Press, 1985.

Ziemann, W., and M. Lanzendörfer. "The State in Peripheral Societies." *Socialist Register* (1977).

Zolberg, Aristede R. *Creating Political Order: The Party States of West Africa.* Chicago: Rand McNally, 1966.

Index

About The Author

JULIUS E. NYANG'ORO is Visiting Assistant Professor of African Studies at the University of North Carolina at Chapel Hill. His articles have appeared in journals such as *African Political Science Review, Studies in Comparative International Development,* and *TransAfrica Forum.*